Atonement
Lutheran Theology:
Franz Pieper

Franz Pieper

Foreword
Jack D. Kilcrease

Biographical Introductions
Theodore Graebner
W. H. T. Dau

Translators
Susanne Russell
John Theodore Mueller
SynopticTranslate™

Synoptic Text Information Services, Inc.
Sidney, Montana

Synoptic Text

Synoptic Text Information Services, Inc.
303 3rd Street SE, Sidney, MT 59270

ISBN: 979-8-9910853-0-4

Contents

Foreword

Jack D. Kilcrease

In the translations contained in this volume, Francis Pieper achieves two distinct goals. First, Pieper successfully critiques alternative contemporary rivals to his theological positions. In this endeavor, Pieper gives special attention to nineteenth century German Liberal Protestantism. Secondly, Pieper outlines an appropriate confessional Lutheran account of the doctrine of atonement. Not unlike John of Damascus compiled and synthesized the great insights of Greek Patristic theology in his work *The Orthodox Faith*, Pieper takes the best insights of the Lutheran theologians of the sixteenth and seventeenth centuries in his treatment of the atonement. In the translations in this volume, Pieper is able to achieve these goals with impressive agility.

Pieper's treatment of atonement must be seen in its appropriate historical context in order to understand what he seeks to achieve theologically. Francis Pieper, as well as the other Lutherans connected with the Synodical Conference grew out of the Neo-Lutheran movement in Germany during the nineteenth century. Napoleon's dissolution of the Holy Roman Empire after his defeat of the Austrian Emperor and the Czar at the Battle of Austerlitz had a number of unintended consequences for Lutheranism. The Augsburg Confession had been part of the legal code of the Holy Roman Empire. Local churches could not function as a publicly established Church if one did not adhere to the Augsburg Confession, the Council of Trent, or (after 1648) the three Confessions of Reformed Unity, at least on paper. As a result, even with the rise of Enlightenment Rationalism and Pietism, Churches were held back from abandoning the fundamental articles of the Christian faith by legal sanction of the Empire. Likewise, secular rulers such as the Hohenzollern who were Reformed, but ruled over the thoroughly Lutheran Kingdom of Prussia, were legally restrained from herding Lutherans and Reformed into a single Church.

The end of the Holy Roman Empire and its legal code removed these barriers to attacks on confessional Lutheranism. The result was the rise of both Unionism and theological Liberalism. In Prussia in particular, the first step toward a unified Germany was a unified Protestant Church that melded together both Lutheran and Reformed confessions. Although a Lutheran free Church eventually gained toleration, in the meantime many faithful Lutheran pastors were jailed or immigrated to the US or Australia. Still other Lutherans who did not leave Germany took note of the fate of the Prussian Lutherans and organized resistance to maintain their individual churches.

Going hand in hand with the rise of Unionism was Liberalism. In some significant ways, Liberalism was a kind of synthesis between the Rationalism of the German Enlightenment (*Aufklärung*) and Pietism, both of which dominated the theological culture of eighteenth-century Germany. From the *Aufklärung*, Liberalism took over the belief from philosophical Foundationalism (Descartes, Leibniz, Wolfe) that all humans had an awareness of foundational truths which could falsify or confirm any position presented to human reason. This included the claims of Christianity, which might or might not be true based on whether they could be squared with the canons of human reason as discerned by Rationalist Foundationalism. From Pietism, Liberalism took the view that religion was based on human interior experience of the divine centered in Jesus. Whereas Pietists did hold to the biblical/creedal tradition of the Church and understood who Jesus Christ was in an orthodox manner, Liberalism would substitute alternative concepts of who Christ was drawn from both anti-supernaturalist re-narrations of the origins of the biblical texts and inferences drawn from religious experience.

The founder of the movement of Liberalism, Friedrich Schleiermacher, was a product of Pietism and the philosophy of Immanuel Kant, the philosophical fulfillment of German Rationalism. Schleiermacher's father was a Reformed Pietist military chaplain who had him educated by the Moravian Brethren, a group begun by the Lutheran Pietist and friend of John Wesley, Count Zinzendorf. Later Schleiermacher graduated from the University of Halle, the epicenter of Lutheran Pietism in the late seventeenth and eighteenth centuries. After having read the German Rationalists and concluded that the main doctrines of orthodox Christianity could not be sustained, Schleiermacher nevertheless felt that his religious experience (centering on a deep love and experience of God through Jesus) had not changed and therefore he could remain a Christian. Subsequently, he worked simultaneously as a fulltime pastor and professor of theology, his career culminating in his appointment to the University of Berlin and his production of the first Liberal Protestant systematic theology, *The Christian Faith.*

Schleiermacher's approach to the person and work of Christ in *The Christian Faith* explains why he and other more orthodox theological opponents of Pieper, (the most notable being Johannes von Hofmann) cannot accept the historic Lutheran doctrine of penal substitution. Following Immanuel Kant, Schleiermacher operates on the assumption that the human mind is bound within itself and can only make statements about how things have an impact on it. In theology, Schleiermacher held that we can speak of the impact of the universal and foundational experience of God as one of absolute dependence. The Christian variation on this was that this experience occurred through Jesus. Christians gained such an experience of the divine and a perpetual increase in it by way of faith in Jesus. From this fact Schleiermacher claimed that it may be inferred that although Jesus was not God in a traditional sense of the term, he was a man who had possessed a perfect and uninterrupted experience of God, and therefore the subsequent Christian Church could encounter God in him. This allowed Schleiermacher operating within the boundaries of post-Kantian epistemology and metaphysics to claim that he was in some tenuous sense upholding the doctrine of the Incarnation.

As noted above, Johannes von Hofmann stands out as another major figure opposed by Pieper. Since Hofmann was also a member of the Neo-Lutheran movement, and therefore Pieper saw his theology, which masqueraded as being confessional and orthodox, as being even more insidious than that of Schleiermacher, which was more blatantly heterodox. In resisting Liberalism and Unionism, Neo-Lutherans essentially broke into two factions. The first faction became the seed of North American confessional Lutheranism as it coalesced into the denominations of the old Synodical Conference. This approach to Lutheran theology might be called "Repristinating" theology, since it saw value in the Lutheran Confessions, and the Lutheran theologians of the sixteenth and seventeenth centuries as they stood, with no need to further develop their theology in new directions. Another group of Neo-Lutherans, mostly centering at the University of Erlangen, claimed loyalty to the Lutheran Confessions (a *quia* subscription to Confessions was required at Erlangen until 1969), while at the same time attempting to synthesize confessional Lutheranism with Romanticism, German Idealism, and the new historical research methods coming out of what where called "Romantic Research Universities" like the University of Berlin.

Hofmann was part of this latter group of Lutherans and became a professor of theology at the University of Erlangen in the mid-nineteenth century. He grew up in a Lutheran Pietist household, but was also a student of Schleiermacher, Ranke, and Schelling at the University of Berlin. Like Schleiermacher, Hofmann agreed that theological reflection began with the corporate religious experience of the Church, although he more directly connected this experience to the events of salvation history (*heilsgeschichte*). For Hofmann, the theologian analyzes his religious experience, and as a result comes to the conclusion that his individual experience would not be possible unless the events that are described as happening the Bible did in fact actually occur. In his dogmatics, Pieper therefore describes Hofmann as engaging in "*Ich-Theologie*" (ego theology). Hofmann claimed that the salvation history that the Bible witnessed to possessed two stages corresponding to the law and the gospel. Following Schelling and Hegel, Hofmann held that God evolved in history through his ever-developing relationship with his people. In his evolutionary scheme, the Old Testament was an era of divine law and wrath. In becoming incarnate in Jesus, God in a sense evolved into becoming a God of grace and love. Satan and sinful humanity sought to kill him and succeeded, but Jesus forgave and overcame their wickedness through the resurrection. The Christian community as one of love and peace now lives out the new ethos of the gospel. As can be observed, Hofmann does not so much see law and gospel as commandment and promise, but rather the contrast between wrath and inflexible legalism and a new ethos of love.

As should be clear from these brief descriptions of Pieper's opponents, the main opposition to the traditional Lutheran concept of substitutionary atonement rested in theologies of experience in rejection of what Robert Preus called "biblical realism." In other words, instead of talking about God as an objectively existing entity, whose qualities, as well as commandments and promises, were genuinely revealed in an epistemically realistic fashion (this not excluding the use of analogy and metaphor), Schleiermacher and Hofmann relied on internal experience and inference drawn from human experience to formulate their conception of God and his will. The logical consequence of the theology of experience is that redemption ceases to be about balancing the scales of divine justice and mercy as expressed in the two divine words of law and gospel, but rather replacing one experience with another. In the case of Schleiermacher, this is a sense of estrangement from the divine to one of unity with the divine. In Hofmann, it was a matter of replacing the experience of legal demand with one of love.

As Pieper correctly recognizes, the understanding of redemption present in these theologies of experience are diametrically opposed to that of Luther and the Lutheran Confessions. Hofmann's position is even more ironic, since he claimed the mantel of being a genuine Lutheran and one who had recovered the *Christus Victor* model present in Luther. The emphasis on experience over the objective reality of the Word of God is tantamount to what Luther referred to as "Enthusiasm" in his Genesis commentary and the Lutheran symbolic writing the Smaldkald Articles. Enthusiasm literally means "God-within-ism." It teaches that our interior experiences or reason is what counts in terms of discerning the truth of reality and not God's objective and external address.

The merit of Pieper's theology of atonement as it is represented by the two dogmatic pieces in this volume, is that it does not rely on unprovable theories about religious consciousness, or rationalistic speculations about what it would be fitting for God or Christ to do in order to reconcile humanity to himself. Indeed, in offering rebuttals to the objections to penal substitution, Pieper is quick to point out over and over again, that although humans may not like how God has structured his law, or his redemptive work, God's will and revealed Word are the ultimate standard of truth to which the human mind must bow.

Hence, every statement that Pieper makes throughout his dogmatic treatment is directly tied to the Word of God, or its exposition in the Lutheran confessional writings. Much like Johann Gerhard, Pieper structures his dogmatic treatment over the biblical designation of Christ as possessing an office of prophet, priest, and king. Pieper recognizes the importance of all three offices as a fulfillment of the types of the Old Testament.

Nevertheless, Pieper singles out the office of priest as possessing special significance for the work of Christ. Such a significance stems from his belief that Christ's redemption is centered in his work on the cross, offering himself up for the sins of humanity after having lived a perfect life in our place. Following the scheme first developed by Flacius, though drawing on Luther's Galatians commentary, Pieper affirms that through the active obedience of Christ to the law (something Lutheran Scholasticism called "active righteousness") and his acceptance of the imputation of the sins of humanity on the cross (what Lutheran Scholasticism called "passive righteousness"), Christ fulfilled the law.

Pieper's emphasis on Christ's priestly work feeds into his belief that justification through faith is the central doctrine of Christianity. That is to say, Christ's objective atonement for all sins leads into what post-eighteenth-century Lutheran theology came to call "objective" and "subjective" justification. Regarding "objective justification" or what Walther called the "Easter Absolution," Paul tells us that Christ not only died for our sins, but "rose for our justification" (Rom. 4:25). Most Protestant accounts of justification treat faith not as a receptive organ, but as a means of making the potential forgiveness wrought by the atonement an actual forgiveness by appropriating it by faith. For Lutherans, God pronounces the whole world justified in Christ prior to any appropriation by faith (Rom. 5:18). Faith does not make the promise of the gospel real, but rather appropriates it subjectively. In the same way, the response of a family to the pronouncement: "dinner is served!" does not make a meal any more or less cooked and on the table.

Ultimately, the reality of justification and the unconditionality of grace is the reason why Pieper is so insistent on the doctrine of penal substitution. As our author notes, many Liberal theologians argue that the traditional doctrine of atonement makes God into a moral monster who needs blood to forgive. Nevertheless, denials that God needs Christ to fulfill the law ultimately come down to a claim that humans must fulfill the law instead. If humanity is alienated from God in one way or another, then someone must bridge that gap by performing a work that will overcome the barrier. As much as Liberal theologians talk about the gracious character of God, they invariably place the burden on humanity to bridge this gap by positing that Christ has done something that will provoke a kind of response in us, i.e., cause us to comply with the law. The only understanding of the work of Christ that allows God to fully and graciously bridge that gap himself apart from our actions is belief in penal substitution.

Jack D. Kilcrease

Publisher's Preface

It is worthwhile to read the two biographical introductions to Franz Pieper in this volume.[1] These are written is a style no longer vogue in our day, but they deliver a blessing.

Graebner's sketch introduces a man humble toward all and in every circumstance. Wait until you see how he reacted to his welcome and reception as professor at Concordia Seminary. Graebner acquired that vignette from notes by Pieper's wife, Minnie. Graebner reveals a man of generous hospitality. He pulls back the curtain on a man of humor.

> Sometimes hearty bursts of laughter would rise from his classroom. Dr. Pieper's humor played about the most solemn subjects, though ever reverently. The knowing smile and the humorous twinkle of his eye would accompany such remarks made in lighter vein, and the effect, so artlessly achieved, was never wanting.

Dau highlights the object of Pieper's work. His aim was not just to "be right." He gave himself into an industry of love toward students, colleagues, pastors, congregations, synod, and the as-yet unbelieving. His tireless work had an aim unlike that of too many theologians then and now. He shared the motivation of C. F. W. Walther: to make theology practical. He wanted to give people a faith they could live.

Besides theology, Pieper was a man of his family, colleagues, students, congregation, community, and adopted nation. He was pleased to be a naturalized citizen of the United States. He knew the issues under debate in Congress and the many sorrowful pains in world events. He

---

[1] In addition to the two sketches presented here, from his personal memories, Ludwig Fürbringer wrote a series of six *"Erinnerungen an De Franz Pieper"* (Memories of Franz Pieper) published in German in *Der Lutheraner.* Part 1, 87:13 (June 30, 1931); Part 2, 87:14 (July 14, 1931); Part 3, 87:18 (September 8, 1931); Part 4, 87:19 (September 22, 1931); Part 5, 87:21 (October 20, 1931); and Part 6, 87:23 (November 17, 1931).

was especially interested in the United States Navy and proudly wore a lapel emblem of a naval support organization.

When I learned from Graebner how Pieper worked as professor; consultant to the many pastors who wrote to him for help; speaker at pastor conferences, district conventions, and synodical conventions; editor and writer for theological journals; etc., etc.; and on top of that his many this-worldly interests, I could not help but think to myself, "I have hardly done anything." In the service of others, this man worked himself into poor health. After a temporary retreat given to him by the synod, he turned in another 20 years of vigorous industry.

And why?

To return what he had received from the Lord to you in a practical theology, a faith of which you can be assured, a faith that can be lived.

Do yourself a favor. In this volume hear Pieper's rendition of the most vital topic in the world: Christ's work of atonement, forgiveness, reconciliation, justification, and life everlasting – Christ for you. Feel his exuberance as he says: "Reconciled to God! These words express the greatest happiness that mortal man can know."

Dr. Francis Pieper: A Biographical Sketch[1]

Theodore Graebner

Outline

I. Childhood and Youth.

Francis (Franz) August Otto Pieper was born June 27, 1852, at Karwitz (Carwitz) in Pomerania (Pommern), a Prussian province fronting upon the Baltic Sea. Karwitz is a small town, situated in the eastern part of Pomerania, northeast of Berlin and about seven miles from the Baltic Sea. It lies within the township (*Kreis*) of Schlawe. Franz's parents were August Pieper and Bertha, *née* Lohf. August Pieper was the *Schulze*, or town mayor, of Karwitz.

After passing through the grammar school, young Francis attended the colleges (*Gymnasia*) at Koeslin and Kolberg. Koeslin, situated about twenty miles west of Karwitz, is the capital of a Pomeranian county bearing the same name. It had, and still has, a junior college, or *Gymnasium*. The city of Kolberg, in which a *Gymnasium* likewise exists, is another fifteen miles farther west and is a harbor city on the

---

[1] Theodore Graebner, *Dr. Francis Pieper: A Biographical Sketch* (St. Louis: Concordia Publishing House, 1931, no copyright claimed), sourced from Internet Archives, https://archive.org/details/Pieper_Biographical_Sketch_T_Graebner).

Baltic Sea. Young Pieper's final report from the Kolberg *Dom-Gymnasium* is still in existence. It records the entrance of "*Franz Pieper, geboren den 27. Juni 1852 zu Carwitz bei Schlawe, Sohn des Schulzen Pieper daselbst, evangelischen Bekenntnisses,*" at Easter, 1869, in *Secunda*; he was transferred to *Obersecunda* Christmas, 1869. His deportment was characterized as "always good," his attentiveness and diligence as "praiseworthy." He attended classes in Religion, German, Latin, French, Mathematics, History, Geography, Physics, and Turning. The Director, Dr. Schmieder, added the note: "We give him his dismissal with the best wishes for his future development and for his career." The document was signed June 18, 1870.

When Francis was born, Frederick William III was King of Prussia. There was no emperor of Germany at that time, since we are speaking of the year 1852, which was eighteen years before the labors of Bismarck rebuilt the German Empire, with William I as its Kaiser. The union of Lutheran and Reformed elements had been established in 1817, and the Evangelical Church was the state church of Prussia. Strongly Lutheran sections retained the Lutheran Catechism, and among these was Pomerania. However, the mixture of politics with religion had brought about general disorganization, and the political aspect of this union of Church and State was in every way harmful to the confession of soundly orthodox doctrine. Pomerania had the advantage of possessing a number of soundly Lutheran leaders who at least in their own parishes maintained the standards of their Church in such fundamental articles as the Person and Work of Jesus Christ, Justification, and the Second Advent of Christ.

In 1861, when the subject of this story was nine years of age, William I became King of Prussia. This ruler was a pious man and throughout his life made no secret of his sympathy with the Lutheran cause. It was William I who [in]1873 addressed Pope Pius IX in such terms as these: "The evangelical faith which I profess, as must be known to you, together with the majority of my subjects, does not permit me to accept into my relation to God any other mediator than our Lord Jesus Christ." When he put the Jesuit Order out of business in Germany, his comment was: "I believe that I have the commission from above to do this."

The decay of Protestantism which Germany witnessed while the boy Francis Pieper was growing up in his Pomeranian home was due, however, not so much to the political interference with the conduct of church affairs as to the evil influences which were spreading throughout Germany from the high seats of learning, especially from the theological faculties at the universities of Northern Germany.

Among them were the Modernists of their day, whose works Professor and later Dr. F. Pieper subjected to such trenchant criticism in his lectures, in his articles, and particularly in his *Christliche Dogmatik.* There was Herman Cremer of Greifswald, who contributed a dictionary of the New Testament Greek, recommended by Professor Walther to his students although the author was a rationalist. (Dr. Walther excused this recommendation with the somewhat caustic remark that we are permitted to make use of the works of rationalistic authors even as the Israelites were instructed to make use of the Canaanites as hewers of wood and carriers of water.) Then there was Hengstenberg of Berlin, who wrote many brilliant books in the field of Biblical exegesis, but finally went wrong in the doctrine of Justification, which in his opinion has degrees, or stages. Pastor Euen, a fellow countryman of Pieper, about the same time went so far as to question whether justification is really the fundamental teaching of Lutheranism. Accepting the Romanizing tendency of Loehe, he announced that the Sacraments were the center of Christianity, and that the ministry was a holy order continued in the Church through the right of ordination. As a result of these various rationalizing and Romanizing tendencies, Lutheranism lost most of its identity in Northern Germany, being ground as it were between the upper and the nether millstone. It was Adolf Zahn, one of the few conservative theologians of forty years ago, who wrote: "The Lutheran doctrine of Justification is no longer to be found in Germany. And no one seems to be frightened by this fact."

Men close to the founders of the Missouri Synod were at this time in their prime. In Erlangen labored J. C. K. von Hofmann, one of the greatest interpreters of Scripture, teacher of our own Dr. Stoeckhardt, whose peculiarities of exegetical method were derived from the lectures of von Hofmann. In Bavaria, Adolf Harless was president of the Church Council in Munich in the year of Francis Pieper's birth. Wm. Loehe was still busy with his grand missionary projects, which extended to the Saginaw Valley in Michigan and our Fort Wayne college. But he was even then showing signs of his Romanizing doctrine of the Church and the Ministry. Franz Delitzsch had achieved world-wide fame as master of Hebrew and interpreter of the Old Testament. Walther reckoned him still among his friends. Later this gifted interpreter became enmeshed in the net of higher criticism. In Rostock, Professor Philippi was teaching New Testament interpretation, a master to whose method also our own exegetes owe much.

Much mischief, on the other hand, was being prepared for the theologians of Luther's land and of our own by another Pomeranian, Albrecht Ritschl, who taught in the University of Goettingen and through his discussion of Christian doctrine, into which he mixed the speculation of Kant, brought untold confusion into theology. Much of the so-called Modernism in the American churches is due to Ritschl. He is considered the outstanding dogmatician of modern Protestantism. The Protestant world would do better to follow the lead of that other Pomeranian teacher of Christian doctrine, the subject of this biographical sketch. Adolf Zahn wrote in 1893 with reference to the work of Ritschl:

> The Church of the Reformation, at the close of the century, lay prostrate before her enemies and had lost definitely her influence upon national life.

And again:

> Rome may rejoice — the faculties are doing their best to kill the Reformation. Scripture is being profaned, the doctrine of Justification neglected, our youth poisoned,

while in a note on Dr. Walther and his influence in Germany the same keen-eyed observer said:

> The thoughts of the Missourians move forward with the good right of Luther. (Adolf Zahn, *Abriss einer Geschichte der evangelischen Kirche auf dem europaischen Festlande im neunzehnten Jahrhundert*, page 49.)

Such was the religious background of Francis Pieper's early years.

The first of the Piepers to leave their ancestral home and to come to America were the two elder sons, Julius and Reinhold. The former became a miller by profession, and Reinhold was for many years Professor of Homiletics at our theological seminary in Springfield, Ill. The mother, then widowed, came in the year 1870 with four children, Francis, Karl, August, and Anton, leaving the oldest child (Minnie) in Germany. The emigration permit of the Prussian government was issued to the mother and her children March 10 of that year. Of the four brothers who accompanied their mother only one is living today, August, born 1857, now Professor of Theology at Thiensville, Wis., and these many years a prolific writer and the leading theologian of the Wisconsin Synod. Karl's talents carried him into newspaper work; he died as an editor at Menominee, Wis. Anton died as pastor of the Wisconsin Synod. Mrs. Pieper, having settled with her four boys at Watertown, Wis., died in 1893 while visiting at her son's home in St. Louis.

In 1865 the Wisconsin Synod had established at Watertown a college to which was given the name Northwestern University. It is now called Northwestern College and is an institution of the highest scholastic rank. Francis Pieper entered this institution as a member of the junior-college class (*Unterprima*) in the year 1870 and graduated in 1872.

Unfortunately, important files of this institution were destroyed in the fire of 1894. Hence the record of the work done by young Pieper in his American college years has been lost. In the catalog of the year 1870-71 his name appears for the first time as a member of the Junior class, then again as a member of the Senior class, 1871-72. At the graduation exercises on July 2, 1872, Francis Pieper delivered a Latin oration on the theme: *Quid iis quae sunt propria Germanorum in hac terra sit retinendum, quid dimittendum?"* — "Which Characteristics of the German People should be Retained in This Country and Which should be Discarded?" Among his classmates was the later Prof. O. D. A. Hoyer, who taught theological branches at Luther College, New Ulm, in the nineties of the past century and later was professor and director at Watertown. Another classmate is still living, the Rev. M. H. Pankow of the Wisconsin Synod. He was guest of honor at the reception given to Dr. Pieper on the fiftieth anniversary of his labors at Concordia Seminary in 1928.

The years 1872 to 1875 were young Pieper's student years at Concordia Seminary, St. Louis. The Wisconsin Synod, of which he was a member, then had no theological seminary of its own.

II. The Ministry.

When Francis was a student at St. Louis, the president of the institution was Prof. Carl Ferdinand Wilhelm Walther. Prof. G. Schaller was instructing in Church History, and Prof. M. Guenther taught Homiletics and Symbolics. Another member of the faculty was Prof. F. A. Schmidt, who was engaged by the Norwegian Synod for its students and who left in 1876, later becoming one of the chief opponents on the issue of Predestination. Prof. A. Craemer, later president of our Seminary in Springfield, was instructing in the so-called Practical Department.

The class of which Francis was a member graduated in June 1875, and the diploma of "Franz A. O. Pieper," signed by Dr. Walther, is still in existence. It is a bond sheet (size, 8½ x 12) and reads as follows:

Zeugniss. Dass Herr Franz A. O. Pieper, gebuertig von Carwitz, Kreis Schlawe, Pommern, seit dem 1. September 1872 bis Ende Juni 1875 in dem hiesigen Concordia-Seminar der deutschen evangelisch-lutherischen Synode von

Missouri, Ohio u. a. St. dem Studium der Theologie mit grossem Fleisse obgelegen, sich dabei eines unstraeflichen Wandels befleissigt und in dem vorschriftsmaessig mit ihm angestellten oeffentlichen Examen pro Candidatura zu Uebernähme des heiligen Predigtamts als sehr wohl vorbereitet sich erwiesen habe: solches wird demselben unter Anwuenschung goettlichen Segens hierdurch nach Pflicht und Ge wissen bezeugt.

St. Louis, im Staate Missouri, den 1. Juli 1875.

Das Lehrercollegium:

C.F.W. Walther, praes.

The call extended to Francis Pieper upon his graduation from Concordia Seminary was issued by a small congregation at Centerville, Wis., now called Hika. This is a small town situated on Lake Michigan about midway between Sheboygan and Manitowoc. From the study window of the parsonage the young minister had a view of the lake.

The Centerville call was issued by a parish consisting of St. John's in Centerville and of St. Peter's, near that settlement. The call issued by St. John's Church was dated January 17, 1875. In addition to residence and fuel the congregation pledged itself to pay a salary of $400 annually. The call was signed by the church council: Win. Doersch, E. G. Fischer, K. Grimmer, and P. Heinz. The call to St. Petri Church of Town Centerville, Manitowoc County, Wis., was dated January 24, 1875, and was signed by the board of elders: Carl Toepel, C. G. Fritzsche, Julius Unger, and C. Lutze. This congregation pledged itself to pay an additional $100 in quarterly instalments.

During his labors at Centerville the young pastor became engaged to Miss Minnie Koehn, daughter of Frederick Koehn and Sidonia, *née* Seifert. Mr. Koehn had immigrated at the age of sixteen from Germany and had entered business life at Sheboygan, Wis. The marriage took place at Sheboygan, January 2, 1877, the ceremony being performed by the Rev. Carl Manthey-Zorn.

In November 1877, having served the Centerville charge for a year and four months, Rev. Pieper was called as successor to the Rev. G. A. Thiele to Manitowoc.

The call from the First German Evangelical Lutheran Church was accompanied by a letter signed by the secretary, August Mueller, and was dated October 15, 1876. It reads (in translation): —

> Reverend Pastor: I enclose the call from our congregation. As you observe, it announces that there is with us still the same feeling of attachment for you that you gained for yourself when we saw and heard you the first time. That you are the personality who is able to bring our congregation on its feet again is the only remark heard among our congregation members ever since you were here. Probably it will be hard for you to part from your congregation. However, according to reports the Centerville congregation is not so divided into factions as is ours, and also another pastor would be able to serve them successfully. On the other hand, we are wandering about like lost sheep and request you not to put off your decision as we are in trouble and have placed all our confidence, next to God, in you. Do not permit our hope and trust to be disappointed. May God, whose work it is, enlighten you that you may accept this call as His own and will soon send us a satisfying answer.

Pieper accepted the call and arrived with his mother at Manitowoc in the first part of November. He served this congregation until called to the professorship at St. Louis.

III. Call to the Seminary and Early Years of Professorship.

The Missouri Synod had established the method of electing professors for her colleges and seminaries through an electoral board. Nominations were made, not as at present, by the congregations, but by the electoral board itself, the list of candidates being printed in *Der Lutheraner* four weeks previous to the election in order that congregations might voice approval or disapproval. However, the right of electing professors through the Synod itself when meeting in convention had been reserved by an earlier resolution. In 1878, at the meeting of the Delegate Synod in St. Louis, this method was adopted.

Two new professors were to be elected for St. Louis. The need of an English professor was described as essential since Prof. F. A. Schmidt had been called by the Norwegian Synod to its new seminary at Madison, Wis., in 1876. During the past two years there had been no English instruction whatever. The minutes continue: "Also for systematic theology a professor should be engaged who during the lifetime of Prof. Dr. Walther should work himself into this office." Synod quickly became convinced that also this new professorship was an absolute necessity and that it should be erected without further delay. Candidates for the English professorship were Prof. M. Loy of Columbus, O., and Pastor R. Lange of Chicago, Ill. For the new chair of Dogmatics the following were proposed: Rev. C. Gross of Buffalo, N. Y., Rev. R. Lange of Chicago, and Rev. F. Pieper of Manitowoc, Wis.

When the name Pieper was proposed, a delegate received the floor and protested against calling Pastor Pieper to St. Louis. He urged that the climate in St. Louis would be ruinous to the health of Pastor Pieper. When Rev. Zorn arose and explained that this protest came from the father-in-law of Pastor Pieper, there was general merriment, and the nomination was carried by a large majority. The balloting followed, and Professor Loy and Pastor Pieper were declared elected by absolute majority, the former being voted a salary of $1,000 annually and Professor Pieper a salary of $800, in both cases with free residence.

It should be said that the call from the Delegate Synod came as a complete surprise to the recipient, the first news of it being contained in a telegram which Pastor C. Manthey-Zorn, who attended the convention as delegate from his congregation at Sheboygan, sent to Pastor Pieper.

Immediately after the election, Rev. Zorn addressed his friend ("*Mein lieber, teurer Pieper*") with a personal letter, giving some details about the election. It reads in part as follows: —

> Our telegram of yesterday you no doubt have received. It must have surprised you and crushed you, — if I know you rightly. But *God* has done it.

> At the request of Dr. Walther and others I will write you a little detail. On the morning of May 21 nominations for the German professorship, especially for Systematic Theology, were made: Stoeckhardt, Gross (Buffalo), R. Lange, F. Zucker, and Stellhorn. The forenoon was spent in discussing these candidates, while the students were excluded from the meeting. The discussion was continued in the afternoon, and ... your name was submitted by Link. This supplementary nomination was made unanimous. After the discussion, Gross, Lange, and yourself remained as candidates. After the election of Professor Loy for the English professorship (Loy, 151; Lange, 7) the German professorship was put to a vote. You received 115 votes, with the rest distributed among the other two.

> Loy's name and yours are now on their way to the printer to be announced in *Der Lutheraner*. If no one objects on account of false doctrine or scandalous life (other reasons do not count) against your nominations, you will receive your diplomas of vocation. Now be courageous and of good cheer and remain filled with humble amazement over God's ways (pardon me for addressing you thus). The Lord, our God, has done it, and our Delegate Synod looks to you with joyful confidence and prays that God may bless our young professor unto His own glory. Walther is happy to receive his pupil under his own special tutorship (*unter seine besondere Leitung*) and for his own special support. Practically all the old fathers and heads of Synod are happy about this election.

> You will tremble and plead your unworthiness. That is good. 'When I am 'weak, then I am strong.' Oh, that God may

keep you in this humble frame of mind! He it is who will work through you. And to resist His will, made evident in this call, — that you cannot do.

But I must return to the meeting. Let me request you to come to Sheboygan on Tuesday if possible. There is much to be told, especially about the Seminary, which is to be relocated and enlarged.

The Lord, our God, and our Lord Jesus Christ be with your spirit!

Faithfully yours,

C. M. Zorn."

The first notice of young Pastor Pieper's election to the professorship in St. Louis is found in the *Lutheraner* of June 1, 1878. A report on the convention of the Missouri Synod held in St. Louis during the previous month has this item: —

With reference to the Theological Seminary in St. Louis, it was resolved to postpone the erection of buildings which had become so necessary. However, it was resolved to fill the vacant position of an English professorship and to found another German professorship. For the former position, Prof. M. Loy of Columbus, O., and for the latter, Rev. F. Pieper of Manitowoc, Wis., was elected.

In the same issue, President Schwan requested the congregations of Synod to address to him within four weeks either their approval of these elections or their protests.

A few months later it was announced that Professor Loy had declined the call to the English professorship and according to the custom then in vogue the electoral board proposed a number of candidates in order to give opportunity for protest on the basis of false doctrine or an evil life. Of the four candidates submitted Rev. Rudolph Lange of Chicago was elected. His arrival in St. Louis November 30 was signalized with the ringing of bells at the Seminary. He held the English professorship until his death in 1892.

When the call to St. Louis reached the young Manitowoc pastor, he was at first disinclined to leave his parish. President Bading came up from Milwaukee and confirmed him in his resolution to stay with the Manitowoc congregation. His congregation thoroughly concurred with him, and the call was returned.

When the call came to Pastor Pieper the second time, he saw the finger of God in the synodical resolution and obtained a release from his congregation.

On August 27, 1878, Prof. C. F. W. Walther addressed the newly called colleague as follows: —

> Beloved friend and brother in the Lord: —
>
> Having just returned yesterday from a journey, I find among other [26] letters also yours of August 22. Let me reply in all haste as follows to your inquiry.
>
> Exegesis of Galatians has already been prepared by Professor Schaller for the next school-year. With your approval your arrangement of lectures will be as follows: —

Monday at	10 a.m.,	Review of Dogmatics with Senior Class.
	2 p.m.,	one of the synoptic gospels with Junior Class.
Tuesday at	3 p.m.,	exegesis of Psalms, Middle Class.
Wednesday at	8 a.m.,	Latin disputation with Junior Class.
	9 a.m.,	one of the synoptic gospels with Junior Class.

Thursday at	2 p.m.,	a synoptic gospel with Junior Class.
	3 p.m.,	Hermeneutics with Junor Class.
Friday at	2 p.m.,	Psalms.
	3 p.m.,	Hermeneutics.

Accordingly, you would have nine lectures a week and no more than two on any day. If you are satisfied with this assignment of work, kindly notify me. I am sorry that most of your lectures will be in the afternoon. It was not possible to arrange it otherwise.

If at all possible, do not come later than already announced in your letter in order that you can begin October 1.

Wishing that God will bless your going out and coming in within our midst and looking forward to your arrival, I am,

C. F. W. Walther.

P. S. Lic. Stoeckhardt has been called by our Holy Cross Church as successor to Brohm and has accepted. You will rejoice in this good news.

In the *Lutheraner* of October 15, 1878, the name of Professor Pieper, with the address Concordia Seminary, St. Louis, Mo., was recorded among the changes of addresses. The following month the installation of Rev. C. G. Stoeckhardt as pastor of Holy Cross Church was announced in the official organ.

Professor and Mrs. Pieper, with their baby daughter, Paula, arrived at the old Union Station on Twelfth Street in St. Louis, October 1. They were met at the depot with the college coach, a relic exhibited to curious thousands at the dedication of Concordia Seminary in 1926. This coach was built by the St. Louis joint congregation as a mark of love and respect for Professor Walther. It is now the property of the Concordia

Historical Institute. It was drawn by a great black horse, driven by two students, one being the brother of the young professor, August, then member of the Senior Class; the other, Henry Jungkuntz (now *P. em.* at Jefferson, Wis.).

The distance to the Seminary was about three miles. Quite some distance from the school, Mrs. Pieper noticed that the building flew a large United States flag and was decorated with many small flags. She pointed out to her husband the festive appearance of the building and asked him what it might signify, what kind of celebration might be on. To this day she remembers that her husband blushed and hung his head, too modest to answer, realizing as he did that the decorations were part of the reception tendered to him by the institution.

The Piepers stayed during the first four days with Professor Guenther, who with Professor Schaller lived in the double house on the corner of Winnebago Street and Texas Avenue, later occupied by Drs. Stoeckhardt and Graebner and in still later years by Professors Fuerbringer and Bente. The accommodations were ample, and the Guenthers were glad to prove their hospitality to the new colleague and his family. Immediately after their arrival Dr. Walther called and in his cordial manner bade them welcome to St. Louis and Concordia Seminary. He at once took the new professor to the students of the Seminary, who were gathered in the chapel for the reception. On the very next day Dr. Pieper began his lectures in dogmatics, — a labor continued from 1878 to the year of his death, 1931, being interrupted only twice by a nervous breakdown.

Dr. Walther already dwelt in his residence fronting Texas Avenue. This residence was removed when the addition to Concordia Seminary was built in 1907. It was a spacious building, but by no means of a palatial type, being very like the residences built by the fairly well-to-do in St. Louis at that time. The basement was damp, a failing which was not corrected as long as the house stood. At the time of Professor Pieper's arrival Dr. Walther explained that he was unable to offer him the hospitality of his home since he was expecting Pastor George

Stoeckhardt and family to arrive any day from Germany. Pastor Stoeckhardt had left Germany after some turbulent years of conflict with the state church. He arrived October 4. When they were made welcome in the Walther residence, the students of the Seminary gathered in the college yard adjoining the president's home and sang German airs. Mrs. Pieper, from whose lips these memoranda were jotted down, remembers with much amusement that of the songs selected for this serenade was *Deutschland, Deutschland ueber alles!* — a song hardly appropriate when it is considered that the Rev. Stoeckhardt had found the soil of Germany unsuited for those who wished to profess a consistent Lutheranism. He was under a four months' jail sentence, pronounced upon him for failure to live up to the regulations which the Saxon state had made for the conduct of the office of the Lutheran ministry! Needless to state, so eminent a preacher and theologian as Rev. Stoeckhardt was eagerly welcomed by the faculty of St. Louis. He was since 1878 pastor of Holy Cross Church and, while holding this pastorate, lectured on Old and New Testament Exegesis at Concordia Seminary. In 1887 he was elected professor. In 1903 Luther College, Decorah, Iowa (Norwegian), created him a Doctor of Divinity. He died January 9, 1913.

After their furniture and other household goods had arrived, the Piepers moved into the home provided for them. This was the so-called schoolhouse, a building which had been used by Holy Cross Congregation as a school for the parish until the "new school" was built at the corner of Ohio Avenue and Potomac Street (now the property of a *Turnverein*). The old school had four rooms of moderate size and a basement. It had been occupied for some time by Mr. Emmerich Kaehler, secretary to Dr. Walther and later in the editorial employ of *Die Abendschule.* Into this building the Piepers moved. The various apartments were arranged as study, living-room, bedroom, and kitchen. To the north of the building was a vacant lot, used as pasture for the college cow. In the basement were the quarters of as strange a tenant as any theological family has ever had. Her name was Lisette. She was an Indian half-breed, unmarried and about forty years of age, whom Professor Craemer had brought with him as a ward from the Indian Mission at which he had labored in Michigan. Lisette worked in the Seminary kitchen during the day and spent her evenings in her basement quarters. The Piepers would then hear her croon her weird half- savage Indian melodies, memories of the primeval forest of Michigan. Soon Lisette was moved to the Seminary.

The Piepers lived for three years in the schoolhouse, until the old buildings were wrecked in order to make way for the splendid new Seminary built in 1882. The salary of Professor Pieper had been fixed at $800, but was immediately raised to $1,000, since during the first years the Professor was placed under heavy expense by the purchase of necessary books. This act of the Seminary Board was approved by the Synod of 1881, which then raised the salary to $1,200. The Synod of 1881 also passed a resolution to build a residence for Professor Pieper "because his present residence is not only small and inconvenient, but damp and unwholesome." Also, it was necessary to raze the old school, since it occupied part of the ground on which the new Seminary was to be built.

At this time let us take a glance at the rest of the faculty and at the student-body of the Seminary.

There were enrolled 69 students of the Missouri Synod during the first year of Professor Pieper's labors at the Seminary. In the Senior Class 15 of our own students were enrolled, among these J. Bernthal, J. G. Goesswein, F. Pennekamp, and L. Wagner. In the Middle Class 16, the list containing the names W. Harms, Im. Mayer, F. Pfotenhauer, and F. Sievers. Among the 38 Juniors we note Fr. Bente, Fr. Brust, A. Detzer, H. Frincke, Th. Lamprecht, G. Mezger, Fr. Otte, and J. Schaller. Four students of the Wisconsin Synod attended, among these A. Pieper and J. Koehler. Among the 19 Norwegians we note A. R. Sagen, later a District president, P. Stroemme, who became a noted journalist, N. J. Bakke, pioneer in Colored Missions, and J. T. Ylvisaker. There was one Icelander, Thorvildsen. In the year 1879-80 the number of the students was 96, among them 2 from the Wisconsin and 9 from the Norwegian

Synod, 24 taking the final examination. In 1880-81 there were 93 students, of whom 7 were Norwegians, 33 taking the final examination.

The faculty at this time consisted of Dr. Walther, Professor Schaller, Professor Guenther, and Professor Lange. Prof. Gottlieb Schaller had served Eastern charges and since 1854 Trinity Church, St. Louis, and came to the Seminary in 1872. He taught chiefly Church History, was a fine preacher, mild-mannered in his dealings with the students, and highly gifted as a poet. He died in 1887, only a half year after the death of Dr. Walther. When Martin Guenther had come with the Stephan immigration, he studied in the log cabin in Altenburg and later graduated from St. Louis. He was pastor of congregations in Wisconsin and Michigan and served St. Matthew's in Chicago when he was called to St. Louis as professor of Symbolics, Homiletics, Catechetics, and kindred branches. Not a man of many words, he had a keenly critical mind and like all the other members of the faculty was an assiduous student of Luther's writings. Professor Lange had just been called, as related earlier in this chapter.

The relations between the members of the faculty were ideal. There was not only high mutual regard, but sincere friendship. This was evident to all who came into contact with their circle. Differing greatly in age and in previous experiences, also in gifts of mind and speech, these men were nevertheless held in high esteem by their students, who could learn from them in their classroom and outside of it what constitutes a soundly Lutheran theologian and a soundly Christian character.

The meetings of the faculty were held at the homes of the professors. Invariably cigars were served, and in his reminiscences told in later years to his younger colleagues, Dr. Pieper commented with a hearty laugh upon the wretched quality of the tobacco which went into the making of these cigars. No luncheon was provided. At the meetings the business of the institution was discussed, questions of discipline were introduced whenever necessary, and the manuscripts of articles written for the *Lutheraner* and *Lehre und Wehre* were read before they were sent to the printer.

Letters would be read from pastors far and near requesting a theological opinion on some problem of doctrine or life.

Other meetings of the faculty were of a more social character. The birthdays of the professors were celebrated in their respective homes, the families usually being invited. Dr. Walther's birthday was celebrated at the college in the dining hall. Later these celebrations took on the character of a German *kommers*, a gathering of faculty and students, enlivened with speech-making and music. There would be original poems in German, English, and Latin, and usually some student would be found who possessed the necessary temerity to deliver an original speech in Greek and even in Hebrew. The social tone of these gatherings was always of the highest, and the religious note was never lacking. All the ladies of the faculty were present at these joint celebrations. A custom which continued down to the first decade of the present century was the serenade each professor received on his birthday. A quartet or octet of students would gather below his windows after breakfast and would sing a choral or other religious song. At such times it was expected of the professor that he not only acknowledge the honor by words of appreciation, but that he make a donation of ten or fifteen dollars toward the necessities which had to be provided for the testimonial gathering in the evening. In those early days the school would be dismissed for the entire student-body on each birthday. As the number of faculty members increased, the free day was limited to the celebrant. Later only the afternoon was free for the classes of the celebrating professor, and in recent years there has been no more omitting of lectures on these occasions. However, the Friday after Thanksgiving has been made a free day as a joint "faculty birthday."

It appears that the young Professor devoted the first semester of his first year strictly to the business of preparing his lectures for the classes assigned to him. These were delivered in Latin, later to an increasing extent in German. Only gradually articles from his pen began to appear in the official organs. His first contribution to the *Lutheraner* appeared in the issue of April 1, 1879. Strangely enough, this article, while merely noting the attitude of the General Synod towards Luther's Catechism, sets forth in the concluding sentence a truth which Dr. Pieper never ceased to emphasize in his classroom and in his literary work: —

> Errorists against whom the Lutheran Church must contend do not only attack the highest points of the structure of Christian doctrine; they have ever attacked the simple, fundamental truths of Christianity as they are summarized in the Small Catechism of Martin Luther.

His next article appeared May 1. It was a notice of resolutions adopted by St. Matthew's Church, New York City, against secret orders. From this time onward the *Lutheraner* regularly carried editorials and articles from the pen of Professor Pieper.

His first theological article was contributed to *Lehre und Wehre* of 1879. In the July issue of that paper Professor Pieper reviewed a dogmatic work by Pastor D. Zahn. He finds fault with Zahn for teaching man's ability to convert himself and for his rationalistic view of faith and redemption. The article is an incisive criticism of the modernistic theology of fifty years ago.

Upon arriving at St. Louis, Professor Pieper joined Immanuel Church, of which the Rev. John F. Buenger was then pastor. Rev. Buenger was really a remarkable man, who not only was the founder of the Lutheran Hospital of St. Louis, the Orphans' Home, and the Old Folks' Home, but who gave the first impetus in our Synod to missions among the colored people of the South. Professor Pieper was from the beginning assistant pastor of Immanuel, communed in that congregation to the last, and had many personal friends there. His remains rest in the cemetery of Immanuel Church.

When Professor Pieper came to the Missouri Synod, this body consisted of 693 congregations, of which number 359 held voting membership, while 334 were unaffiliated. Statistics for those years are incomplete, but Rev. E. Eckhardt estimates the number of souls in 1878 at 150,000. They were served by 558 pastors.

IV. Controversy.

Dr. Walther had many times expressed the hope that finally might come "the realization of one united Evangelical Lutheran Church of North America." This, in fact, was the goal of his life. That it was not reached was due, in part, to the attacks of enemies who brought about the controversy on Predestination, or Election. We do not regret this controversy, however bitter it was. It did not check the outward growth of the Missouri Synod. In the ten years which followed the outbreak of this controversy the Missouri Synod doubled its numbers. Furthermore, the greatest building project up to that time attempted by any American Lutheran Church, the new Concordia Seminary, was carried through while the controversy was raging. Moreover, the spiritual gain was great. Not only were pastors and people confirmed in their confession of the truth regarding this particular doctrine of Election, but the heart ache and turmoil of this controversy strengthened many characters that had once been weak and made men grateful for the possession of that truth which is the Lutheran heritage.

Dr. Walther had some presentiment of impending trouble. A pastoral conference had congratulated him on receiving the title of Doctor of Divinity from the Ohio Synod Seminary at Columbus, O. Dr. Walther, in his reply, said: "The cycle in which I have hitherto lived consists in this, that God sometimes has humbled, sometimes exalted me, so that I always knew, when an exaltation came, a deep humiliation would promptly follow." Two years later the very synod which had created him a Doctor, publicly accused him of being a heretic.

The doctrine of Predestination (or Election, the two words meaning the same) had been discussed by Dr. Walther at a convention of the Western District in 1877. One of the theses which he defended was this: "The Lutheran Church teaches that it is false and wrong to teach that not the merit of God and the most holy merits of Christ alone, but that in us also there is a cause of the election of God for the sake of which God has elected us unto eternal life." Upon the basis of this paragraph it was declared: "God foresaw nothing, absolutely nothing, in those whom He resolved to save, which might be worthy of salvation, and even if it be admitted that He foresaw some good in them, this nevertheless could not have determined Him to elect them for that reason; for as the Scriptures teach, all good in man originates with Him." Accordingly, Dr. Walther also rejected "the unfortunately selected terminology" of the dogmaticians of the seventeenth century "that God elected 'in view of faith' (*intuitu fidei*)."

In January, 1880, Prof. F. A. Schmidt, a former student of Dr. Walther, violently assailed the statements made by his former teacher, and in his new magazine, *Altes und Neues*, declared that he must "sound the alarm" against the new "Cryptocalvinism" of Missouri as expressed in the synodical report of the Western District of 1877. On September 29, 1880, a public conference was held at Chicago at which five hundred pastors of the Missouri Synod were present and took part in the discussion. A proposal on the part of Dr. Walther not to carry on the controversy publicly was flatly refused, as Professor Schmidt declared that he had been commanded by God to wage this war; whereupon Dr. Walther replied, "Since you desire war, you shall have war."

So, there was war, and from 1880 to 1884 the conflict raged with unabating ardor on both sides, the main controversialists of Missouri being Dr. Walther, Professor Pieper, and Rev. Stoeckhardt, and those of Ohio, Professors Stellhorn and Schmidt and Pastors Allwardt, Doermann, and Ernst, former members of the Missouri Synod. Also, the Iowa Synod and the Norwegian Lutherans became involved in the strife.

Now, what were the doctrines involved in this controversy? The central point at issue was: Is the salvation of man solely due to God's grace or also, in part, to the merits and powers of man? The Missourians emphatically stated: "We deny that God in His election took into consideration anything good in man, namely, the foreseen conduct of man, the foreseen non-resistance, and the foreseen persevering faith." They protested against the doctrine that the election of the children of God depends not only upon the grace of God and the merits of Christ, but also upon the foreseen conduct, the foreseen non-resistance, and the foreseen faith of man. This was really the decisive issue; for if election depends on man's good conduct or non-resistance, then salvation is no longer of faith, but of works. The Missourians were said to teach that God does not desire the salvation of all men. This charge was followed by another, they being accused of teaching that God does not seriously and effectively offer to those who are lost His divine grace. Both of these charges were vigorously denied, the Missourians rejecting any agreement with the heresies of Calvin, who taught that God would not have all men to be saved. To give unto God all praise and glory for having, out of pure grace in Christ Jesus, elected, redeemed, called, converted, and sanctified His saints; to teach salvation by grace alone, *sola gratia*, and at the same time, grace for all sinners, *gratia universalis*; to magnify Christ and not themselves, *solus Christus*; and to preach, not their word, but God's Word, *sola Scriptura* — that was the steadfast aim and invariable purpose of our sainted Dr. Walther and his coworkers.

Professor Pieper's first article on the doctrine of Predestination was in a note in *Lehre und Wehre*, of March 1880. Commenting on an expression of the German theologian Thomasius, he wrote: —

Again the doctrine of Election has become the subject of public discussion. Contributions are either promised or under way treating this theme. Very well, let everyone study this doctrine eagerly in order that the superficial and popular constructions of this doctrine may disappear, and the heart may become strong in its reliance on the Word of God. First of all, let us become quite clear on the question where *not* to seek the solution of this problem. The solutions suggested by the German theologian are not available. No light is to be brought into this doctrine by teaching man's free decision for or against salvation. Man can indeed really decide against salvation, but he has not the power to accept it. God Himself decides for salvation by making, through the act of conversion, out of an unwilling a willing one. Since there is no self-decision of man in the work of conversion, it is wrong to operate with this non- existent thing in the doctrine of Predestination.

In the same issue of *Lehre und Wehre*, Professor Pieper defends a quotation from Dr. Walther's Postil which had been assailed by a General Synod writer as Calvinistic. In this article Professor Pieper explains with great clearness the difference between the doctrine of Calvinism and that of the Lutheran Church regarding God's decree of election.

The chief articles in this volume of *Lehre und Wehre* on the doctrine of Election were contributed by Dr. Walther and by Pastor Stoeckhardt, then minister of Holy Cross Church. Their articles ran through the rest of the volume and were really fundamental to the entire controversy as representing the Missouri Synod viewpoint. However, they did not in any essential go beyond the views set forth by Professor Pieper in the same volume. We see these three protagonists for the Scriptural truth fight side by side, each according to his own endowments and all with a conviction which rings true from every line, for the maintenance of sound Lutheran doctrine regarding the way of salvation.

The controversy was at its height in 1881, and in *Lehre und Wehre* of that year Professor Pieper's power as a writer, who could speak clearly and with profound knowledge on a difficult subject, became clear to all those who followed the argument. For a man in his early thirties the force and ripeness of the articles which appeared from his pen in this volume of *Lehre und Wehre* were truly amazing. The introduction to that volume is like the challenging call of a bugle. It announces the need of insisting that the Scriptures alone can establish articles of faith. In connection with this teaching, so self-evident to Lutherans, he enters into a discussion of the assurance of faith resting upon the doctrine of Predestination. The choice which Dr. Walther had made when he asked for the election of young Pastor Pieper as his assistant was vindicated to the entire Church in the latter's essays. Not only was there a perfect unity of doctrine and conviction, but there was also in the articles of the young Professor — only three years in his theological position, less than six years in the ministerial office — a fulness of theological learning and acquaintance with Luther and the older teachers of the Church which was truly astonishing. We have also compared the replies which were issued by the opponents in 1881, and among all the mass of citation from the Lutheran classics presented by Professor Pieper in the elaboration of his arguments not one was ever attacked as a misquotation or as inaccurate. This same exactness of quotation and reference was evident in all the later work of Dr. Pieper and in no small measure accounts for the unquestioning confidence with which all his writings were received by the brethren.

Returning again to the essays of 1881, we notice that two men who later became members of the St. Louis faculty contributed articles. There was the familiar signature W., which marked all of Dr. Walther's articles. This is followed by one signed F. P. But immediately after Professor Pieper's contribution we notice a seven-page article with the signature G. St., which stands for George Stoeckhardt, and this, again, is followed by a fourteen-page essay signed E. W. K., the later professor of Church History at Concordia Seminary, E. W. Krauss. Among the Norwegians, Prof. H. G. Stub of Madison, Wis., is represented with an essay on Predestination, translated by Prof. A. Craemer. Rev. J. A. Huegli of Detroit and Rev. G. Goesswein were other members of the clergy who fought out of a full and well-rounded scholarship for the position of our Church in these essential doctrines.

V. "The Pen of a Ready Writer."

For the commemoration of the 350th jubilee of the Augsburg Confession, Professor Pieper in 1880 wrote a treatise entitled *Das Grundbekenntnis der evangelisch lutherischen Kirche* (The Fundamental Confession of the Ev. Luth. Church). The essay was chiefly of a historical nature, relating the events that led up to the Diet of Augsburg and the composition of the statement there submitted by the Lutheran representatives in 1530 and since known as the Augsburg Confession. After this essay followed the text of the Augsburg

Confession, to which Professor Pieper subjoined explanatory remarks, notable alike for their clearness and for their brevity. The book was long out of print, but in 1930, his last active year at the Seminary, Dr. Pieper had the almost unparalleled experience of republishing, after an interval of fifty years, the jubilee volume of 1880, now commemorating the four-hundredth anniversary of the presentation of the Augsburg Confession. Thus, it was the first and the last book to appear from the pen of Dr. Pieper.

Among the most valuable contributions of his pen to the literature of our Church are the synodical essays read by him at District and national conventions between the years 1883 and 1930. According to the custom introduced into our Church from the beginning, the synodical conventions are not exclusively occupied with business matters, but as a rule devote several hours of each morning session to the discussion of a religious essay treating some subject of Christian doctrine or life or significant events in church history. The reports of the Missouri Synod and its Districts containing these essays are extremely valuable. Also Dr. Pieper's essays possess abiding value. He addressed the following conventions: Southern District, 1883 and again in 1889 and 1891; Iowa, 1885; Nebraska, 1885; Kansas, 1892; Minnesota and Dakota, 1907; Southern Illinois, 1916 and again 1921; Atlantic, 1919; North Dakota and Montana, 1921; Oregon and Washington, 1924; Alberta and British Columbia, 1927; Western, 1927; Eastern, 1930. He also read a paper before the Synodical Conference in 1888 and a number of dogmatic and inspirational addresses before the national conventions of our Synod. We pass in review a few of his significant essays.

In 1885 he submitted to the Iowa District an essay on "The Certainty of Our Salvation Viewed in Its Importance for Spiritual Life." This, too, was a fruit of the controversy on Election which revolved about the point of this paper, namely, our assurance that we shall be finally saved. In his essay Dr. Pieper pointed out the fact that such assurance belongs to the a-b-c of Christianity. It is the very essence of faith. In all their troubles the Christians are comforted in Scripture through the hope of eternal bliss. Both the wickedness of doubt and the danger of carnal security are then pointed out. Contrary to the opinion of Modernists, who believe that the hope of eternal life will make a Christian careless in the affairs of this present temporary existence, the essayist showed that the spiritual life of the believer receives its true form, its power, from this very doctrine. Especially will it encourage us in our sanctification and in the avoidance of the lusts of this present world. "Where your treasure is, there will your heart be also," Luke 12:34. Even in this present life the believer has conquered death.

In the month of August 1888, the Synodical Conference met at Milwaukee, Wis. Among those present were many whose names are notable in the history of our Church — Pastor C. Gausewitz, Prof. O. Hoyer (who had graduated with Professor Pieper from Watertown), Rev. F, Bente, then president of the Canada District; Rev. Succop of Chicago, President F. Sievers, Dr. H. Duemling, Rev. J. Herzer; from the Wisconsin Synod, President John Bading, Prof. A. Ernst, Prof. A. Hoenecke, and Prof. W. Notz; among the advisory members, Rev. L. Fuerbringer, Rev. Th. Buenger, Rev. F. Lochner, Rev. W. Hagen, Rev. B. Sievers, Rev. F. W. Herzberger; Prof. E. A. W. Krauss (then of Addison, Ill.), Director Baepler of Fort Wayne, Ind., Prof. A. L. Graebner (who had been elected to Concordia Seminary the previous year and delivered the sermon in the closing exercises of the convention), Director A. C. Burgdorf of the Lutheran High School in St. Louis (later Walther College), Professors Kroening, Huth, Hamann, Hattstaedt, and Mueller of Milwaukee; of the Wisconsin Synod Teacher F. W. H. Graebner (later treasurer of this synod and also of the city of Milwaukee), and Prof. G. Thiele (successor to Professor Graebner at the Wisconsin Synod Seminary in Milwaukee). The convention adopted resolutions of condolence and respect to the memory of Dr. C. F. W. Walther, who had died the previous year. The doctrinal essay was read by Prof. F. Pieper on the theme "The Unity of Faith." He emphasizes that unity of faith involves agreement in all the doctrines of Holy Scripture, and this in spite of the fact that we acknowledge the presence of Christians also in erring church-bodies. The possibility of such unity was demonstrated by pointing out that Holy Scripture contains clear statements regarding all "articles of faith." The Word of God is so constituted that we not only are able, but also compelled to find the true doctrine in it if we only stick to the sacred text. If anyone wants to err, he must first reject the clear statements of Scripture and willfully cover up its meaning with human interpretations. "God demands unity in the faith and strictly prohibits our departure from the revealed doctrines of the Gospel." From all of this a twofold conclusion was drawn: that those who agree in the faith are to proclaim such agreement by acknowledging one another as brethren in the faith and that they are to endeavor to keep inviolate these treasures of orthodox doctrine. The essay was a notable one and for many years sounded the keynote of expression on the same point in our Missouri Synod publications. It was one of the joys of the venerable Doctor's concluding years that the Missouri Synod — now grown to a body of more than 1,200,000 souls — in all its Districts, yes, in all its pulpits fully upholds the doctrine concerning church union and fellowship so masterfully outlined by him in his essay of 1888, read in Trinity Church, Milwaukee.

Another fundamental doctrine was treated by him in 1889 at the meeting of the Southern District, which at that time still included the State of Texas. He had been requested to discuss "The Difference between Orthodox and Unorthodox Churches." The outward form of the Church that God alone desires is her confession of the truth; God wants an orthodox Church, one that is the true bride of Christ and avoids all false prophets. Hence it is the duty of Christians to join that Church which they recognize as teaching the Scriptural truth. They are able to distinguish between this Church and such churches as deviate from the truth if they keep close to the Scriptures. An interesting topic, raised by a question from the audience, was that concerning our cooperation with non-Christians in works of charity. The essayist answered this question by pointing out that in a purely civil field we may cooperate with others. Another raised the question of standing sponsor at a baptism performed in a non-Lutheran church. The answer of Dr. Pieper was that such sponsorship should not be accepted, as it would imply the assent to the false doctrine of that church. In a concluding section of the essay the high privilege of membership in a Church of the true confession was pointed out.

At the Atlantic District meeting in 1919 Professor Pieper led the discussion with a paper on "The Ecumenical Character of the Lutheran Church in Doctrine and Practice." In his paper he emphasized those doctrines in which the Lutheran Church confesses the belief of all who are truly Christians, emphasizing the universality of divine grace and the salvation by grace alone. Also, this paper dwelt upon unity in belief as essential to church union. And throughout, the subject announced in the title is kept in view, namely, that the Lutheran Church has, properly speaking, no distinctive doctrine, but confesses that which is evangelical truth and professed as such by true believers the world over.

"The Inspiration of Scripture" was his theme at the meeting of the Southern Illinois District in 1921. He discussed it under the following heads: "1. The Scriptures differ from all other books in this, that they are God's own Word. 2. The Scriptures are God's Word through inspiration, that is, through the fact that God inspired the sacred penmen to write the Scriptures. 3. All objections to the inspiration of Scripture are void." This paper shows Dr. Pieper at his best as a dogmatician, and it abounds in practical applications of a doctrine seemingly far removed from Christian life and practice.

The paper delivered on "Unionism" at the 1924 convention of the Oregon and Washington District has been reprinted in English translation in pamphlet form. It once more summed up all the reasons why we maintain a separate existence as a Lutheran denomination and as a synod within that denomination. The paper is especially interesting on account of its side-lights on contemporary history and its testimony against the lodge, particularly, however, because of its refutation of the objections commonly raised in defense of unionism, namely, that we "must have patience with the weak," that it is "contrary to Christian love to deny church-fellowship to others," and that "it is arrogance when individuals or entire church-bodies declare: 'We are in possession of God's truth, and they who teach any other doctrine are in error.'"

Among the most impressive essays delivered by Dr. Pieper were the themes submitted at the conventions of the Delegate Synod. None of us, who, for instance, attended the meeting of our Synod at Fort Wayne in 1923 failed to be impressed by his three lectures on *Die christliche Weltanschauung*. At the convention in St. Louis, in 1926, we heard him speak eloquently on "The Christian Religion in Its Relation to All Other Religions." At the last synodical session which he attended, the convention at River Forest, Ill., in 1929, he spoke on "The Open Heaven," a subject which seemed to give to all the transactions of that synodical convention a tinge and glory of other- worldliness and which will not be forgotten by the thousand and more delegates and guests who were privileged to hear on that occasion for the last time the teacher to whom our Church owes so much.

We have the opportunity in this brief sketch to mention only two of the more significant volumes that issued from his pen.

Conversion and Election, published in 1913, grew out of the Norwegian union movement. It was concerned chiefly with the "Articles of Agreement" adopted at Madison, Wis., in 1912. These articles were almost unanimously adopted by the United Norwegian Church, which consisted of the opponents of Missouri in the controversy on Election, and also by the Norwegian Synod, which had stood with Missouri and was in fellowship with that body.

The articles adopted at Madison did not bring out clearly the Scriptural doctrine but gave equal right to synergistic views by which in some way the conduct of man and not only the grace of God is responsible for our conversion. Dr. Pieper's treatise was an effort to preserve the unity of the Synodical Conference. It was evident that the Norwegian Synod could not continue in fellowship with the Missouri and the Wisconsin Synod if these "Articles of Agreement" remained unmodified. On account of the importance of the issue involved the faculty of the St.

Louis Seminary had an English translation of the book printed immediately after the German original had seen the light under the title *Zur Einigung*. This translation was furnished by Theo. Graebner, then pastor of a congregation in Chicago.

The tone of this book is extremely irenical, or peace-loving. The author said in his introduction: "Our aim is to aid, on our part, toward the recognition and maintenance of the doctrinal position of the Formula of Concord as the only one which is in accordance with Scripture and correct from the theological point of view. Our wish and our prayer to God is that the Norwegian Lutherans of America in their union, which is most desirable, would place themselves upon a platform which fully corresponds to the glorious confession of the Lutheran Church in the Eleventh Article. When they have done this, all other Lutherans of America, whether they speak German, English, or any other tongue, should follow the example of the Norwegian Lutherans." And the closing sentiment brings this heart-searching appeal: "Before we close, we beg leave to assure the reader once more that in our discussion we have had no intention of offending anyone personally. We would serve the cause of union in the truth of our glorious Lutheran Confession. Would that the entire American Lutheran Church also in its public teaching might occupy the position which all Lutheran Christians, indeed all Christians on earth and all theologians, so far as they are Christians, even now occupy in their relation to God! It is the position stated by Scripture in the words: There is no difference, for all have sinned and come short of the glory of God, being justified freely by His grace, through the redemption that is in Christ Jesus.' Away with 'dissimilar conduct' as affording a means of explaining why some are converted and saved and others are not! Back, in simplicity of faith, to the Lutheran Confessions, which state with utmost clearness: If those who will be saved compare themselves with those who will be lost, they must confess that they, too, conducted themselves ill and are in equal guilt. At the same time, they know from the Word of God that those who will be lost will perish, not by reason of any deficiency of divine grace, but through their own guilt. Whatever transcends these two truths must remain a mystery during the present life. The Calvinistic solution, by denying, or at least detracting from, universal grace, is contrary to Scripture. Likewise, is the synergistic solution contrary to Scripture. Let it be said once again, — it is but necessary that all concerned confess with their lips that which they already believe in their hearts before God. May the Lord of the Church graciously grant this through the workings of His Spirit!"

The first volume of Dr. Pieper's *Christliche Dogmatik* appeared in the year of the Reformation Jubilee, 1917. Of the completed work it was entitled Volume II, this being issued first because "the wish had been expressed that the opening volume should be that containing the doctrine of God's Grace in Christ, of Christ's Person and Work, and of Justification." The two remaining volumes (I and III) issued from the press later, the entire work being completed in 1924. It contains a restatement of Scriptural teaching as confessed by the Lutheran Church and treats the modern perversions of the Gospel with great fulness, in each case supplying the Scriptural proof for the teachings confessed in Lutheranism. Regarding the general purpose and method of his work, Dr. Pieper said in the introduction to the concluding volume: —

I have made an effort to give in these volumes an objective presentation of the subject. If in a number of passages harsh expressions have been used, it was only because they seemed to be demanded by the importance of the matter under consideration. The purpose in view has been to demonstrate that a theology which attempts to develop Christian doctrine not only from the Scriptures, but also out of the ego of the theological thinker will be neither Christian nor scientific, but the opposite of both. That I recognize a theological inconsistency as a result of which a man may believe in his heart and before his God otherwise than his writings indicate has again been noted in this volume.

We American Lutherans of a strictly confessional tendency have not the slightest reason for exalting ourselves above others. Without doubt we should be swimming in the same misdirected current if divine grace had not placed us amidst an entirely different church environment. We — the second and third generations — have received our theological training under the most favorable conditions conceivable. We were not only introduced to the sources of the theology of the ancient Church, of the Reformation and of the dogmaticians, but have been made acquainted also with the character and results of modern theology. Add to this the continual warnings uttered by our teachers not to permit any human authority, be it even that of Luther and the confessional writings, to usurp the place which belongs by divine right to the Scriptures. The admonition given to us in our last seminary year was this: 'Do not enter the ministry if you are in doubt regarding the Scriptural character of any teaching of the Lutheran Confessions. Should there be anyone troubled by such doubt, he ought to discuss it frankly with any one of his teachers.' Again, in our first seminary year, when preparing our first sermon, we were instructed to eliminate all high-sounding theological phrases and elaborate rhetoric, and this with the reason that the didactic use of Scripture has the place of first importance. We were impressed with the duty so to teach and to preach that as concerns the pastor his object must ever be to awaken the carnally secure through the preaching of the Law and to assure terrified consciences by preaching an unmodified Gospel offering the grace of God and salvation. Another aid towards keeping us doctrinally sound was the presence of enemies round about us, ranging from Rome, fanatical sects, and unfaithful Lutherans to Unitarianism and Christless lodgery. These conflicts compelled us to make an intensive study of Christian doctrine, not only for our congregational work, but also in pastoral conferences and at synodical sessions.

We are not so blind as to ignore those weaknesses which attach to us as a religious body. We have experienced, and experience today, difficulties in maintaining correct practice in individual congregations. We have suffered losses that have caused us to be deeply humbled. On the other hand, we are by the grace of God altogether convinced that the doctrine which we teach is the doctrine revealed in Scripture and in the Lutheran Confessions and is therefore entitled to make an undivided claim upon our acceptance. From this point of view also the present *Christliche Dogmatik* desires to be judged both in its thetical and antithetical presentations. *Soli Deo Gloria!*"

To the last Dr. Pieper kept himself well informed on the details of church events at home and abroad and also on the secular currents of thought. As notable examples one may refer to the article on "The Great Offensive against the Christian Church" in *Lehre und Wehre* of April 1927. His last essay on the subject which had been treated by him with such power and clarity during the years of controversy — "How may a Christian Become Certain of His Eternal Election?" — was published in *Lehre und Wehre* of 1928. To the end he maintained especially his interest in *Lehre und Wehre*, of which he became editor-in-chief after the death of Dr. Bente. Even the last volume published under his editorship, before the paper was combined with the *Theological Monthly* and the *Homiletic Magazine* into the *Concordia Theological Monthly*, was replete with editorials and articles from his pen, and there was no abatement in the clearness of his vision and the trenchant power of his expression. In the new publication, the *Concordia Theological Monthly*, he was editor of the German articles, and one need only consult his eight-page article on Adolf Harnack written upon the death of that German Modernist to realize the splendid endowment of this man of 78, an age at which most men have ceased to be active in a literary way.

The last message to his students was his address delivered at the opening of the school year 1930-31. He emphasized a reverent fear of

God's Word as the primary requirement of a Lutheran theologian. The last words of his address (printed in the November 1930, issue of the *Concordia Theological Monthly*) were these:

> We shall conquer if we, by the grace of God, retain our reverence for the Word of God. If by our own guilt we permit ourselves to lose this fear of God's Word, the major offensive directed against us may gain the victory by penetrating our front, sides, and center. May God grant us, by His grace, continued reverence for His Word! Amen.

The methods of Dr. Pieper's literary work were peculiar. He never had student help, such as Dr. Walther requested and received as early as 1870, nor did he ever employ a secretary. This was not altogether to the advantage of his correspondence, although it rarely happened indeed that letters remained unanswered. Most of these were written with pencil, as Dr. Pieper found this the only means of retaining a carbon copy. He never learned to use the typewriter. For his contributions to the church papers and for the manuscript of his books he consistently used the reverse side of the galley proofs which come in such large quantities to the faculty. While heavily interlined and sometimes supplemented with little slips containing additions or footnotes, his hand, whether in German, English, Greek, or Hebrew, was ever clear, and the typesetter had no reason to complain on the score of legibility.

Advice was sought from the Doctor on many a problem of doctrine and practice, and he usually submitted these inquiries to the faculty for an opinion. He did not spare himself when an inquirer seemed to have an anxious desire for enlightenment. To a pastor in Minnesota, he addressed within four months three letters on a doctrinal subject, and two of these at least were written with all the care of a contribution to *Lehre und Wehre*. One of these letters covered eight pages, another twelve pages, and contained the closest reasoning, together with quotations from Scripture, the confessional writings, and Luther. To the last year of his labors he gave the same unstinted measure of attention to every inquiry bearing on the teachings of our Church.

VI. A Grateful Church.

The year 1887 came. Discussions of the doctrines of Conversion and Predestination had been arranged in order, if possible, to heal the breach which had been made by the controversy. Dr. Pieper took part in all these discussions, which extended to the year 1906, but failed to bring the opposing bodies closer together. Early in 1887 one of these meetings was arranged in Milwaukee. Dr. Walther was unable to attend, having been bedridden since October. His younger colleague substituted for him. Gradually Dr. Walther's condition became worse, until finally one day Professor Pieper remarked to his wife, "Only his eyes are living." Previous to this the "*junge Kraft*" had taken over all of Dr. Walther's class work. When the great leader was released by death on May 7, 1887, his mantle naturally fell upon the shoulders of the colleague whom he had himself selected and trained for this position.

Two entirely new plants of Concordia Seminary were built during the years of his professorship. Even the Synod of 1878 had taken notice of the crowded condition of Concordia Seminary. In 1882 the old building, once dedicated with such pride and rejoicings, was torn down and during 1883 the beautiful structure was erected which to an entire generation of Missourians was known as Concordia Seminary. It was dedicated September 9 and 10. During Dr. Pieper's administration as president a large fireproof building was added 1907 and the new Concordia Seminary buildings at Clayton in 1923-26. The enrolment of the school at the time of Dr. Pieper's death was 534, of which number 432 were in attendance. The following men joined the faculty after 1878 and labored as colleagues of Dr. Pieper: —

Stoeckhardt, G., D. D.	1881-1913
Graebner, A. L., D. D.	1887-1904
Bente, Fr., D. D.	1893-1926
Fuerbringer, L., D. D.	1893—
Mezger, G., D.D.	1896-1923
Dau, W. H. T., D. D.	1905-1926
Krauss, E. A. W., D. D.	1905-1924

Pardieck, E.	1912-1924
Graebner, Theo., D.D.	1913—
Mueller, J. T., D. Theol.	1920—
Fritz, J. H. C., D. D.	1920—
Sommer, M.S.	1920—
Arndt, W., D.D.	1921—
Maier, W. A., Ph. D.	1922—
Kretzmann, P.E., Ph.D., D.Th.	1924—
Boeder, O.	1925-1930
Polack, \V. G.	1925—
Engelder, Th., D. D.	1926—
Heintze, R. W.	1926—
Laetsch, Theo.	1927—
Friedrich, E. J.	1930—
Hoyer, Theo.	1930—

To mention the various boards and committees on which Professor Pieper served during his long life would carry us beyond the limits of this sketch. He maintained, even in his later years, a particular interest in Colored Missions. From 1882 to 1899 he served on the Board of Colored Missions, holding the office of secretary. His contacts with our Foreign Mission work were intimate and some of his most impassioned pleas uttered in conference were those on behalf of bringing the Gospel to the heathen world. At the last meeting of the Board for Distribution of Calls attended by him, in May 1930, he pleaded for larger support of our work in India and China, declaring that we cannot expect the mercies of God to remain with us if we neglect our duty towards the pagan world.

Professor Pieper was elected President of the Missouri Synod in the convention of 1899. A committee had reported that arrangements could be made for properly coordinating the duties of professor and synodical officer. Dr. H. C. Schwan, whom Professor Pieper succeeded, was given a pension of $1,000 annually. As synodical officer it was the duty of Professor Pieper to visit the District synods when assembled in convention. On these occasions he contributed largely to the doctrinal discussions, and much of the sustained respect for his theological leadership was due to these trenchant and unfailingly popular discussions of Christian doctrine heard from the floor of our District synods. The writer of this sketch, when a pastor of the Illinois District, heard him make at one of the conventions his oft-quoted remark: "A pity for every dollar that is not given for God's kingdom!" Always he showed a respectful attitude, not only towards the District officers and the clergy, but also toward the lay delegates, with whom he stood in great favor. Throughout his four terms as President he remained democratic, a humble servant of Christ, anxious to serve to the limit of his ability.

Twice he visited the land of his birth. His first European trip, in 1898, included a visit to the home of his ancestors and his own birthplace. His second trip, in 1911, was made necessary, like the first, by the condition of his health. The burden of the synodical presidency had proved too much. For some time it had been noted that his usual buoyancy had been wanting, especially in his appearance on the floor of District synods, but also in his work as instructor. It was therefore resolved by the Synod of 1911 to sever the general presidency from any pastorate or professorship. Dr. Pieper had not been able to attend the sessions, his official report being read by First Vice-President Rev. F. Pfotenhauer. The convention voted the thanks of Synod for his many years of service and also the sum of $1,500 and a year's leave of absence in order that he might take a trip to Europe for the recovery of his health. He was accompanied this time by Mrs. Pieper, returning in October, but resting from his lecture hall duties the rest of this and also the following year. When he returned to his classrooms, he was restored to perfect health. It was the wise provision made in 1911 for a furlough that, humanly speaking, accounts for the almost twenty years of uninterrupted activity as teacher, author, and editor which followed. As a matter of fact, his visits of 1898 and 1911 were the only interruption in Dr. Pieper's long career as theological teacher.

When the Theological Seminary of the Wisconsin Synod celebrated its twenty-fifth anniversary September 8, 1903, Professor Pieper attended as representative of the Missouri Synod, and on this occasion the honorary degree of Doctor of Divinity was conferred upon him by Northwestern College in Watertown.

Three weeks later his twenty-fifth anniversary as professor of theology was celebrated by Concordia Seminary with a service of thanksgiving conducted in the chapel. The celebration also included Prof. A. L. Graebner, who had served the same number of years. The Wisconsin Synod was represented by Prof. Dr. Hoenecke and President von Rohr. Prof. Olaf Brandt of St. Paul, Minn., represented the Norwegian Synod. The latter brought rejoicing to the guests assembled when he conferred on behalf of Luther College, Decorah, Iowa, the honorary degree of Doctor of Theology upon both celebrants, Professors Pieper and Graebner, and also upon Professor Stoeckhardt.

The fiftieth anniversary of Dr. Pieper's ordination was celebrated May 17, 1925, with a special service and banquet. Holy Cross Church was filled with a festive audience, among which were the Electoral College and the Building Committee of the new Seminary, the District presidents and the general officers of the Missouri Synod (gathered in St. Louis for the distribution of calls), and the Synodical Board of Directors. Dr. C. C. Schmidt read the Scripture lesson, and addresses were made by Dr. F. Pfotenhauer and President R. Kretzschmar. The students sang the *Te Deum*. On behalf of the Wisconsin Synod an address was made by President G. E. Bergemann and for the Norwegian Synod by Pastor J. A. Moldstad. Dr. Pieper at this time was seventy-three years of age and still at the height of his powers. He not only addressed the audience with words of lofty sentiment in appreciation of the honor of which he was the recipient but was also able to enter into the spirit of the banquet which followed. Many congratulatory resolutions and letters, telegrams, cablegrams, and radiograms were read. Among the representatives who spoke was President E. E. Kowalke of Northwestern College, Watertown, the alma mater of the jubilarian and the school which had conferred upon him the title of Doctor of Divinity twenty years previously.

The students, the faculty, and the board of Concordia Seminary, on October 19, 1928, gathered in the Assembly Hall of the institution for a service of praise and thanksgiving. The occasion was the rounding out of half a century of service by Dr. Pieper as professor of theology. At five o'clock in the afternoon the faculty and the board of the Seminary as well as the Board of Directors of Synod filed into the Assembly Hall, where the students and a large number of ministers from the surrounding territory had gathered. The address was made by Dr. F. Pfotenhauer, who based his thoughts upon Joel 2:23 (marginal translation). President Pfotenhauer pointed out the fact that Dr. Pieper's fifty years of service as professor constituted a period in the history of our Church and country which was beset with many perils, on the one hand, but, on the other, was also a period of signal blessings. Dr. L. Fuerbringer had charge of the liturgical part of the service. Hymns of praise were sung by the gathering, and the students sang the *Te Deum* in antiphonal chant.

Dr. Pieper responded to the President's address by disclaiming any personal worthiness and merit, which was followed by an eloquent appeal to our Synod and its ministry to stand unshakenly loyal on the truths won in so many bitter conflicts.

At 7 o'clock the same evening, a testimonial dinner was tendered the venerable Doctor by a number of his friends. Some 150 of these were gathered in the banquet hall of Hotel Roosevelt. Addresses were made by President F. Brommer of our normal school at Seward, Nebr., and by two vice-presidents of the Missouri Synod, Rev. W. Dallmann, D. D., and Rev. F. Brand, D. D. These speakers extolled the blessings which God has vouchsafed our Church through the ministration of Dr. Pieper in her educational work and through the printed page, especially in her past conflicts. Shorter addresses were made on behalf of the Synod at large by Vice-President F. J. Lankenau; on behalf of the Board of Control, by the chairman, Rev. R. Kretzschmar; on behalf of the faculty, by Prof. Th. Graebner; on behalf of the preparatory schools, by President Burhop of Concordia College, Fort Wayne; on behalf of the Missouri Synod clergy, by Rev. Theo. Walther of St. Louis; on behalf of

Concordia Seminary, Springfield, Ill., by Dr. Louis Wessel; on behalf of the student-body of Concordia Seminary, by Mr. Wm. Schroeder, '29.

A Latin congratulatory address, bound in royal morocco and containing the signatures of the majority of the Missouri Synod clergy, was presented to the jubilarian, as also an engrossed Latin address by Concordia Publishing House.

Dr. Pieper celebrated the day in excellent health and buoyant spirits, his posture erect as usual and his ruddy complexion and flashing eye betraying no signs of age.

The text of the dedicatory address, prepared by Prof. Th. Graebner, read as follows: —

> Propugnatorem nominis Christi atque praeclarum et egregium veritatis Christianae praeconem te, Dr. Theol. Francis Pieper, salutant fratres subscripti, pastores et professores Synodi Missouriensis. Quinquaginta annos tibi, Professor noster, vir doctissime, gratia est data a Deo et Salvatore nostro studiosos theologiae sacrae ducere in divina arcana ea, quae circa salutem humanae gentis per fidem in Christum Iesum versantur. Remota doctrina salvifica evangelii, quid ipsi nostro seminario, imo quid ecclesiae universali futurum? Nulla demum est pars theologiae sacrae, quae nostrae ecclesiae plus roboris addat quam dogmatica, in qua docenda quinquaginta annos hie rem gessisti. Ante omnia gratias agimus Deo, qui tibi fuit custos et scutum in certaminibus ecclesiae Lutheranae occidentalis. Scimus te hoc animo de Inspiratione, de Ecclesia, de Ministerio Ecclesiastico, de Praedestinatione et Conversione, de Sola Gratia cum oppugnatoribus divinae veritatis disputasse et eos argumentis gravibus et certis refutasse, ut doctrina Christi salvifica et huicce aevo conservetur et eis gentibus nostris auxiliis efferetur, quae non habent, quo foedis vinculis err oris et mentium caligine liberentur. Ibi enisus es et contendisti quantum potuisti, ut quam plurimos ad partem

Christi traxisses. Tuae quoque diligentiae magna ex parte imputandum est, quod in nostra schola omnia tranquillo tenore procedebant. Tanta onera qui toleravit, praesertim cum per quinquaginta annos cognita sit et iterum ac saepius probata eius ortbodoxia, sine dubio dignus est, quem hisce αυτογράφοις omnium (fere) clericorum Synodi Lutheranae Missouriensis honoremus.

(The undersigned brethren, pastors and professors of the Missouri Synod, greet you, Francis Pieper, D. D., as a defender of the name of Christ and a notable and excellent herald of Christian truth. Fifty years you, our professor and learned friend, have received the grace of God, our Savior, to lead students of sacred theology into those divine mysteries which are concerned with the salvation of the human race through faith in Christ Jesus. Without this saving doctrine of the Gospel what would be the lot of our Seminary and the Church Universal? Nor is there any other part of theology from which our Church receives greater strength than from dogmatics, which you have now taught here for fifty years. Above all things we thank God, who has been your Protection and Shield in the conflicts of Western Lutheranism. We recognize that you have in such a manner defended the doctrines of Inspiration, of the Church, of the Ministry, of Predestination and Conversion, and of the doctrine of Free Grace against its adversaries and that you have refuted their arguments with such strong reasoning in order that the saving doctrine of Christ might be conserved to the present generation and that help might come to those peoples who have no other means of setting their minds free from the bonds of error. This has been your goal — to draw as many as possible towards Christ. Let us express our gratitude also to you for your supervision, to which has been due the quiet progress of our institution. One who has borne so many burdens and who has for fifty years stood forth as an orthodox teacher is worthy of the honor which is attested to by the signatures herewith affixed by almost the entire clergy of the Lutheran Missouri Synod.)

Among the many telegrams and letters of congratulations was the following poem from the pen of Pastor L. M. Wagner of Fredericktown, Mo.: —

> And the things that thou hast heard of me among many witnesses, the same commit thou to faithful men, who shall be able to teach others also. — 2 Tim. 2, 2.

Though our Lord on high ascended,
    He His Church doth not deny;
Pastors by Himself commended
    Sendeth He to edify
That His saints may perfect be,
One in faith, in unity.

Faithful to the great commission:
    "This commit to faithful men,"
He, our teacher, gave instruction
    As instructed he had been
That the Church be edified
And her Master glorified.

This command our sainted teacher
    Hath with diligence obeyed
As a conscientious keeper
    Of the trust to him conveyed;
From him others rise to spread
Tidings of our living Head.

Faithful, earnest, modest, able,
    Model leader of the flock;
In the doctrine firm and stable

As the adamantine rock:
Blessings be upon his head;
In his footsteps may we tread!

VII. In Home and Classroom.

Professor Pieper became a naturalized citizen August 6, 1884. From that oath of allegiance to the United States he never swerved. He not only loved his adopted country but took an unusual interest in the political affairs of the state and the nation. To the end of his life he was proud of the navy button on his lapel which he carried as member of a national patriotic organization supporting the naval program of our country. At social gatherings he almost invariably discussed civic and national affairs, often with a good deal of humor and with an acute appraisal of men and issues.

Good humor and wittiness were traits which impressed friends and strangers alike with their genuineness and with their refinement. Whether discoursing on the personal character of the old dogmaticians, whether discussing the latest events in Congress, or whether entertaining the company with incidents of his own experience, a gentle humor played over all his remarks. He would often talk "shop" at birthdays and other parties, but always entertainingly, and interlard his speech with the salt of wit, sometimes ironical, rarely sarcastic, never personal.

He was a man of moderation. He enjoyed a good cigar but was also able to accept and smoke a bad one graciously. His manners were refined and, while never pompous, had a certain reserved dignity.

His diversion was reading. He had little comprehension for American sports, and the motion picture had no attraction for him. He had escaped the restlessness which seizes upon so many who do a good deal of official traveling and renders them unfit for steady, serious labor, that obscure drudgery without which the really great and enduring work of the Church cannot be done. Nor had he partaken of "flash-light poison," in spite of his many public appearances and his prominence at synodical meetings. He had no craving for publicity regarding his person. Never advertised himself. Accepted compliments humbly and was generous in his remarks upon the labors of those who strove seriously, though inefficiently, to perform some work for the kingdom of Christ.

His home life was ideal. Some of us have had glimpses of the lingering of the Doctor with his family over the supper table, of the prayers there spoken free from the heart. Even a casual visitor could not fail to take note of the affectionate relations which bound that household into a family.

Of the sons of Dr. and Mrs. Pieper three are serving in the holy ministry. They are Francis of Cleveland, Theodore of San Francisco, and Eric of Rockville, Conn. Six daughters are living: Paula (Mrs. Julius Cloeter), Lucie, Clara (Mrs. Rudolph Ressmeyer), Emma (Mrs. George F. Schmidt), Else (Mrs. L. Blankenbuehler), and Irene (Mrs. George C. Koenig). Two of the sons, George and Arthur, entered secular callings. Two children preceded their father in death, Julia, age 6, who died in 1908, and Ada, whose death occurred in 1926.

To visitors the Doctor was ever cordial. On such occasions he seemed to have unlimited time. Frequently he was visited by men from other Lutheran bodies, who would report to their friends and also in their church-papers on the gracious reception they had met. In December 1916, a contributor signing himself "Germanicus" (we recognize him as Dr. G. U. Wenner of the United Lutheran Church, then of the General Council) wrote in the *Lutheran Church Work and Observer* on a visit to St. Louis. He remarks upon the memorable evening which he spent with Professor Pieper and some of his colleagues. "It was most gratifying to attend such a free conference and to exchange frank expressions of opinion on matters of preeminent interest in the Lutheran Church. On the following morning, in response to a gracious invitation, I visited the Seminary and attended four of the lectures. When Professor Pieper introduced me to his class, two hundred stalwart young men rose and greeted me. It was the finest body of young men I have ever seen together in America. Altogether, the students of Concordia number 353. No one is admitted unless he has been graduated from a college, and no one can be graduated unless he is master of both German and English. Forty per cent of the students are sons of ministers. 'Our ministers get small salaries, and their families know what privation means, but the sons are proud to follow in the footsteps of their fathers in the ministry,' was the statement of one of the professors. You may recall the proud boast ascribed to Professor Pieper, that, if a thousand additional ministers were required, they could doubtless be obtained within a reasonable time from their parochial schools. In Professor Pieper's lecture I noticed that five languages were used with startling fluency. In another room I attended an examination in philosophy. The answers had to be written on the spot, and the papers had to be handed in at the close of the hour. Apparently, the work was very thorough." After attending services at Holy Cross Church, where "Pastor Schmidt preached a simple, evangelical, and very edifying sermon," the visitor again met at a social gathering with Professor and Mrs. Pieper. "I am afraid we talked shop at the table, but the ladies graciously assured us that they were accustomed to such conversation and that no apology was needed. Before, during, and after the dinner we discussed with zeal the things that lie close to the thinking of all who have at heart the interests of the Lutheran Church of America." The report closes with the remark: "It was worth while crossing the Mississippi to form the acquaintance of such distinguished representatives of one of our greatest synods and to obtain at first hand a presentation of their attitude and point of view. I appreciated their courtesy and bade them farewell with high regard and genuine affection."

And now a few remarks on Francis Pieper the Teacher.

Those penetrating black eyes of Dr. Walther had recognized in the young student the gift of clear thinking and clear speech. This gift characterized his coworker through all the years of his teaching at the Seminary. He possessed a ringing voice, a beautiful enunciation. But this was not all. It was the soul which spoke from his features and eyes that made his lectures so impressive, the earnestness of conviction, the liveliness of imagination, the eagerness to be understood that shone forth from voice and mien, — these characteristics made him after the death of Dr. Walther the most influential teacher by word and pen that our Church has had.

He spoke rapidly, but rarely became involved in his sentence structure, and there were few lectures in which he did not rise to eloquence in the presentation of his thoughts.

His knowledge of the Scriptures was astonishing, quotations from the original Hebrew and Greek being interlarded with great frequency and utmost ease. Luther was ever at the command of his tongue, and the pages of *Christliche Dogmatik* will convey an idea of the scholastic learning and acquaintance with the old dogmaticians which made his lectures, as it were, a connecting link between the present age and that of the fathers and founders of Lutheranism. But he was equally versed in the principal writings of the Reformed theologians. He would quote from memory pages of Hodge and Shedd. His English, let it be said, was fluent, grammatically correct, and idiomatic.

All in all, his lectures even to the last remained a treat, as his most recent graduates will testify. He was able to accommodate his speech to the gradual decline in the knowledge of German among his students.

Sometimes hearty bursts of laughter would rise from his classroom. Dr. Pieper's humor played about the most solemn subjects, though ever reverently. The knowing smile and the humorous twinkle of his eye would accompany such remarks made in lighter vein, and the effect, so artlessly achieved, was never wanting.

If one learned nothing else from the lectures of Dr. Pieper, it was at least the dogmatic method, in which he was supreme. His every assertion was buttressed with Scripture texts, and no stone was left unturned to present such evidence in the way that would overcome doubt and skepticism. After submitting the proof from Holy Writ, he was accustomed to enter into the logical argument, first setting forth the contradiction of those who deny the truth under discussion and then demonstrating that even from the standpoint of reasoning the opponents' position was an untenable one. Who can tell to how great an extent the doctrinal firmness of our preaching, the unyielding insistence on Scriptural practice that characterizes our work, is due to the example given to so large a number of our ministers in the classroom of Dr. Pieper?

He created nothing new. He introduced no methods or principles that had not the approval of Lutheran custom. But he carried on marvelously the tradition of our Church under the changing sky of modern belief. The principles he enunciated, while derived from his predecessors, have become, through his emphasis, part of our synodical life and give tone to our work and to that of the churches affiliated with us in other lands.

He was a great teacher, a sound theologian, a true Lutheran, a sincere Christian.

VIII. The End.

The venerable Doctor's physical decline was first noted at the beginning of the school year 1930-31. He gave the address at the opening convocation but delivered it with difficulty. He was not his own self. The address was short. It will be found in the first volume of the *Concordia Theological Monthly*, No. 11, p. 801. But the weakness seemed to disappear after the opening of the school year, and the Doctor met his classes regularly and did not spare himself in what must have been a severe effort to overcome the advancing weakness of his constitution. Very probably the gastric trouble which ended his life was even then developing. At faculty meetings we noted for the first time an apparent lack of interest in the proceedings. He would sometimes be unable to follow the thread of the discussion. But let a question of dogmatics arise, and he was still alert, his judgment keen, and his memory unimpaired.

During the winter of 1930-1931 his life at home continued much as usual, although a growing lassitude became noticeable to his family. He had for many years been in the habit of taking solitary walks between eleven and twelve o'clock at night. He then would return to his study, and the light was kept burning until one and two o'clock. This continued well into the winter. The Doctor's last lecture was held March 5. An operation was found necessary, which revealed the serious nature of his trouble. Friends offered him and his wife trips to Florida and Cuba, but he was too weak to attempt the necessary travel. The *Doctrinal Statement*, which we might call his testament to the Missouri Synod and to the Lutheran Church, still received some final touches from his hand, and he would write an occasional note to a friend. Then came long weeks of decline. At the annual spring festival held on the Seminary grounds in May he was still able to greet a number of his friends on the lawn of his residence. He was up and about, though in a weakened condition, until a few days before the end. He suffered no pain, except for a brief spasm during the night in which his final release came. This was on June 3, at 1:20 a. m. His beloved wife, his son Francis, and his daughter Lucie were at his bedside.

The school year had just come to a close, and the Middle and Junior classes had been dismissed. The usual closing exercises, held June 4 at 10 a. m., were given a memorial character. They were attended by the Faculty and the Senior class and by many District presidents, who had been in St. Louis for the distribution of calls. The chairman of the College of Presidents, Rev. Henry Grueber, acting on a resolution of that body, made a memorial address. After the exercises the graduates visited the residence and viewed the mortal remains of their departed teacher.

June 6, after a brief service at the home, attended by the family and the faculty, Rev. J. Oppliger and Dr. W. Dau officiating, the remains were transferred to Holy Cross Church. The funeral exercises were held in the afternoon at 2 o'clock. Addresses were made by Dr. F. Pfotenhauer, President of Synod and one of the first to sit at the feet of Professor Pieper when called to Concordia Seminary. The text of his sermon was

John 17:10. Dr. L. Fuerbringer, now senior of the faculty and during the spring semester acting president, spoke as representative of the faculty and of the educational institutions of our Synod. Dr. R. Kretzschmar addressed the mourners as representative of the Seminary board and Rev. J. Oppliger as pastor of the sainted Doctor. The congregation sang suitable hymns, among these a favorite of the deceased, "Jerusalem, Thou City Fair and High," a hymn which at various times he had caused to be sung when conducting the funeral ceremonies over the remains of his colleagues — Walther, Schaller, Lange, Guenther, Graebner, Stoeckhardt, Krauss, and Bente. The Holy Cross choir sang an anthem. Members of the faculty served as pallbearers.

Burial was in Immanuel Cemetery, St. Louis, where his mortal remains, with those of two of his children, now await the glorious resurrection.

Dr. Francis Pieper the Churchman[1]

W. H. T. Dau

[In a Lecture given to the 1893 Synod of Delegates of the Synod of Missouri, Ohio and Other States, Francis Pieper said:]

There is no such thing in the Christian Church as mere teaching; all teaching is to be reduced to practice. The Christian Church is not a philosophers' school, where only teaching is done, but a society of people who by faith in the Gospel and mortification of the flesh are traveling on the way to everlasting life and are commissioned to lead others into this way. True, there is also teaching done in the Christian Church, and this is done first and ever continued. Doctrine is the basis for every activity of the Church. However, teaching is not the end, but only a means to the end. For the Word of God which is proclaimed in the Church must bring about the doing of that which each particular word requires of the hearers. The Gospel is to be received believingly and held fast by the individual hearers, and the Law, too, is to be applied by them in its threefold use. Moreover, not only each person for himself is to see to it that he yield obedience to the Word, but in accordance with God's arrangement the Christians are to lend a helping hand to one another in this task. Everyone is to be his brother's keeper. In particular the pastor, by reason of his office, must see to it that his entire congregation and its individual members not only hear the Word, but also reduce it to practice. Briefly, since only *that* person is saved who with his heart believes the Gospel and does not cast out

---

[1] W. H. T. Dau, "Dr. Francis Pieper the Churchman," *Concordia Theological Monthly*, II.10 (October 1931), 729-736 (no copyright claimed by Concordia Theological Monthly).

faith by living in sin, it is incumbent on the Church — on each member, according to his capacity and in the divinely established order — to see to it that the Word of God is practiced. In the Church nothing is mere theory. The Church is the most practical institution in the world.[2]

This conviction was voiced, with the plerophory[3] of tried faith, on the floor of the Delegate Convention of the Missouri Synod in 1893. It filled the hearts of the delegates with grateful satisfaction; for, together with the entire paper which the speaker had for days read before the convention, it showed plainly the continuity of confessional attitude which for half a century was to mark the administration of Dr. Pieper as it had marked that of Dr. Walther, whom Pieper had succeeded, in 1887, in the presidency of the Synod's foremost school at St. Louis. Six years later, in 1899, the Synod put an emphatic ap-approval on the above sentiment by electing the speaker President of the Missouri Synod, as his predecessor at Concordia Seminary also had been for many years.

In the view of both Walther and Pieper teaching theology in a professional school and administering the practical affairs of a great and growing church body were not really two offices of a conflicting character, except as far as the laborious and time consuming duties connected with both offices might overtax the strength of a single individual; but they were regarded as two intrinsically coherent and harmonious phases of the activity of a leader in Lutheran church work. The theologian, even when he held no other office in the Church, was to be a practical man of affairs, not merely a theological savant and learned theorizer; and the administrator of the externals of the Synod's work with its ramifying interests and the determining of its policies in given instances, even when that was his sole occupation, was

---

[2] F. Pieper, *Unsere Stellung in Lehre und Praxis* [*Our Position in Teaching and Practice*], (St. Louis: Concordia Publishing House,1896), 42.

[3] Ed.: complete assurance.

nevertheless to be a man fully trained in the Scriptures and the confessions of the Church and capable of discerning false and questionable trends in doctrine and practice and of maintaining his ground over against them. Such was — and, I trust, still is — the sound persuasion of the entire ministerium of the Missouri Synod, of the teachers in its congregational and synodical schools, and of its well-informed laymen. It has been expressed innumerable times, thetically and antithetically, in the literature of the Synod and orally at great official or casual gatherings of its members.

In their definition of theology the great teachers of the Missouri Synod, without a single exception, for nearly a century, have harked back to the old Lutheran view, *viz.*, that theology is the "practical, God-given aptitude" (*habitus practicus* θεόςδοτος) of believingly accepting, expounding, and applying Holy Scripture for the creation, clarification, invigoration, and preservation of genuine Christian faith in the individual believer and for the upbuilding jointly in truth and love of the entire body of believers, the one holy Christian Church, the communion of saints. The effort of defining theology thus began with Walther's epochal series of articles in the early volumes of *Lehre und Wehre* on the subject *Was ist Theologie* (What is theology?) and in his annotated edition of Baier's *Compend of Positive Theology* Walther's annotations in the chapter on the definition of theology culminated a significant and epochal antithesis which was directed against the philosophical concept of theology embraced by modern scientific theologians. All subsequent utterances on this topic within the Missouri Synod — specific treatises, critical remarks, and controversial references to phenomenal evolutions and vagaries in the theology of our times that are scattered throughout the literature of the Missouri Synod — are but faithful echoes of the clarion call that Walther raised on the Western border of American civilization in days that were dark indeed for the Lutheran Church. Pieper, with his remarkable clarity of perception and his concise and pregnant style, has been the most forceful, eloquent, and convincing champion of the time-honored, Scripturally oriented view of theology that is part of the badge of honor and an heirloom of the Church of the Reformation. In inculcating this view upon their students, both Walther and Pieper impressed a distinct character and gave definite tone to the church work of nearly four generations of the Missouri Synod's workmen. Though well aware of the hostility which they faced in the theological world of their day with their "repristinating" theology, they were conscious also of the fact that the best minds among their theological contemporaries were with them. Repeatedly I have heard both Walther and Pieper cite with relish Rudelbach's dictum (quoted from memory) : "*Praktisch ist die Theologie durch und durch, praktisch in ihrem Anfang, Mittel und Bezuegen*" (Theology is practical through and through, practical as regards its origin, means, and relationships.)

It used to be customary in theological circles in Germany, and to some extent in America, to denounce Missourians as *Wissenschafts-verächter* (contemners of science). A few well-disposed critics of the unscientific attitude of Missouri Synod theologians were inclined to apologize for the lack of appreciation which our theologians showed towards the theological labors of university men by pointing to the immense amount of intensely practical church work which was demanded, not only of our pastors and schoolteachers, but also of the professors at the colleges and seminaries of our Synod. A great Lutheran church organization doctrinally trained and confessionally conscious of its denominational identity amidst the multitude of American sects had to be built up out of the rough from ignorant masses of immigrants who had flocked to our shores without any previous training in the management of the affairs of a soundly Lutheran congregation independent of the state. Incessant preaching and catechizing on the fundamentals of Christianity, patient and persistent explanation of doctrinal differences for the purpose of retaining the divine means of grace pure and unadulterated, an untiring zeal in bringing church practice into ever greater harmony with church doctrine, a clear and convincing presentation from the Scriptures of the divinely bestowed rights and spiritual authority of every local congregation and the duties resulting therefrom, the definition of what constitutes the Church and of the qualifications for church-membership, the explanation of why we may and must speak of the Church invisible and visible — these and a host of cognate discussions characterize the work of the churchmen who built up the Missouri Synod and the Synodical Conference in the North American Republic and amazed the Lutherans of the world by the success of their enterprise, unparalleled even in the days of Luther himself. For the first time in the history of the Church it was shown by the work of these churchmen that the principles of Christian church work for which the Reformation had battled could really be carried out on a large scale.

Naturally, labors of this kind left little time and energy for the pursuit of mere learned studies, for academic disquisitions, and intellectual feats of evolution in scientific theology. But this does not explain adequately the Missourian aversion to mere theological learning for learning's sake. One reason for this aversion has been stated at the head of this article in Dr. Pieper's own words. True Christianity, in the belief of Missourians, represents a life, not a system of creedal formulas or a compend of religious teaching. Even orthodoxy, which Missourians have always valued as the only permissible form of teaching in the Church, is regarded as worthless, yea, as the more damnatory to the possessor, if it is not lived. There is no room in the Missouri Synod for dead orthodoxy, though she is again and again charged with it. Faith is viewed by Missourians as that lively, energetic, ever-active and productive thing in men as which Luther characterized it in his Introduction to Romans. With what joy and power Dr. Pieper taught this fact is evidenced not only by many tracts and papers which he read at synodical conventions and articles which he contributed as editor to the periodical literature of the Synod, but most emphatically by the soteriological section in his *Christliche Dogmatik*. All the contents of the preceding sections of Bibliology, Theology Proper, Christology, are exhibited in their practical bearing on Christian life in the individual believer and in any community of believers. The dogma assumes a marvelous shape and form in the conversation of those who have sincerely accepted it by a genuine faith of the heart. When you lay aside this volume you say to yourself: "These Missourians certainly are not satisfied with intellectual attainments, oratorical feats, and solemn declarations of their church councils; like the proverbial Missourian they want to be 'shown' that the faith professed is actually lived."

The period beginning with Dr. Pieper's presidency of the Seminary at St. Louis in 1887 is marked by a wonderfully intensified activity along every line of church work throughout the Synod. One might call it an era of aggressive work and expansion. The Synod's statistics will bear this out fully. After the last great controversy on election was practically closed, the Synod, undismayed by predictions of its speedy discomfiture, quietly settled down to the enlarging of its mission fields and colleges and seminaries and began something like systematized charity work on a larger scale. These things did not simply happen in accordance with some mystic law of cycles, but they were the normal outworking of genuine faith. After the principles of correct teaching and proper church practice had been patiently inculcated and intelligently grasped, the believers in the Missouri Synod proceeded to work them out in the form of endeavors which were the fruits of their faith. These endeavors are not claimed as the exclusive merit of Dr. Pieper, but he was the enthusiastic and optimistic leader of the Synod during this period of expansion, and his word and personal example cheered the people in their enlarged task. Above all, this period of the Synod's work has shown, I think, that it is, again, a wise method, first to be sure that you are right and then to go ahead, also that a church body which stands foursquare on a sound doctrinal basis need not worry, even in a hostile world, whether Christ will have enough work for it to do.

To churchmen who hold views such as these and are determined to regulate their church activities in accordance with them the aspect of a professional theologian who is content with ransacking libraries in research work to establish an abstruse thesis or who sits in his study philosophizing on religious relativities, spinning religious theories from his reflecting mind, starting new "trends" of theological thought, and building up a new "school" in theology, is a wearisome object of contemplation. He exemplifies to them that labored futility of "ever learning and never being able to come to the knowledge of the truth" against which Paul warned Timothy, 2 Timothy 3:7. When such men speak in terms of depreciation, and even disgust, about "learning," they do not despise the acquisition of real knowledge, a liberal education, or special training, but only that inane quality of "the bookful blockhead, ignorantly read, with loads of learned lumber in his head," that "noisy jargon of the schools, and idle nonsense of laborious fools who fetter reason with perplexing rules," which has been satirized *ad nauseam* in the world's literature.

True learning has always been highly esteemed and eagerly cultivated by Missouri Synod churchmen. Not a few of the founders of the Synod had received university training. Their writings show the wide range of their reading and their scholarly skill in assertion and argument. Men like Walther and Pieper accumulated very respectable private libraries, were enthusiastic book lovers, and made their homes dwellings of culture and Christian refinement. To listen to Pieper in his genial and spirited conversation was an intellectual feast. From their teachers at the seminaries the pastors and schoolteachers of the Missouri Synod derive, amongst other things, their love of learning, their desire for ever wider and profounder knowledge, and their studious habits. Even the humblest parsonage and teacherage in the Synod has always boasted a study with a library within the means of the owner and honest studying has been done in these sanctums. Pieper's desk and table were constantly littered with the evidence of his varied literary pursuits. It is a marvel that he accomplished what he did without the aid of a regular secretary and with a simple filing system all his own. On any important theological matter his memory rarely failed him. All the knowledge and erudition, however, which he and his pupils acquired was at the service of the Church and was put to work immediately in the upbuilding of the Church.

There is, however, another reason for the legendary Missourian aversion to learning. Dr. Pieper touched on this in the opening remarks of his paper at the Delegate Convention in 1893, when he said: "We Missourians, so-called, are well aware that we are opposed in principle to the aims of modern theology. Nor is the fact hidden from us that we are *persona ingrata* with the greater part of the ecclesiastical public."[4] The principle to which Dr. Pieper refers is this: Theology is not a science in the strict sense of the term. Some Lutheran theologians have classified theology as a science; but whenever this was done by a gnesio-Lutheran teacher, the term "science" was used in a wide sense. Science is derived from *scire*, to *know*. Inasmuch as theology operates with the revelation of God, or with what God wants men to know, it deserves to be called science. In that sense anything else that men know, even most trivial facts, could be called science. But when science is defined as the sum total of facts which the human mind has discovered by research and established by correct reasoning, it is plain that theology does not belong in the same category with philosophy, jurisprudence, and medicine, which have created systems of thought and methods of ratiocination in certain domains of human knowledge. Theology is absolutely *sui generis*, in a class by itself, because, in the first place, it does not create its facts by processes of thinking and drawing conclusions from discovered facts, but receives them on the authority of God in the Holy Scriptures. Reason has no other function with regard to these facts than to apprehend the meaning of the terms in which God in His Book has chosen to express them. (*Usus ancillaris* or *ministerialis* of reason.[5]) It does not determine the validity of the facts by exhibiting their reasonableness. (*Usus magisterialis* of reason.[6]) Even an incomprehensible mystery is a theological fact if it has been revealed as such. In the second place, the manner and method employed in theological work is by accepting unquestioningly the statements of Holy Scripture, not by testing them against other known facts outside of theology or by universal laws governing the existence

---

[4] Pieper, *Unsere Stellung*, 3.

[5] Ed.: ministerial use of reason.

[6] Ed.: magisterial use of reason.

of things. In other words, the standard and exclusive instrument for any genuine theological activity is faith, while every science strictly so called must operate only with the logically correct and established convictions of human reason. In the third place, all scientific work terminates when the knowledge sought has been attained by experiment and logical deduction. What is to be done with the knowledge obtained is more or less a side issue to pure science, and is now relegated to what is called applied science. The end of every theological labor, however, is the glory of God, which is magnified as fact upon fact is exhibited and believingly grasped from the divine revelation.

Trouble for the Church, most serious trouble, arose when the old *triga academica* of the pure sciences was increased to a *quadriga* by hitching theology as the fourth horse to the academic chariot and making it run a race with philosophy and the other sciences under the whip of the charioteer, Magister Reason, Ph.D., LL.D., M.D., and now also D.D. What became of theology in this unwarranted yoking together of incongruents and disparates became apparent through the rise of rationalism, first at Halle and thereafter gradually at every other university. Theology had allowed itself to be stripped of its distinct quality, and by making itself the equal had become the inferior of the other sciences because it simply could not, in fact, was never meant to, do its God-appointed tasks on the basis, by the method, and for the end which were proper to the sciences properly so called.

Dr. Pieper took up Walther's critique of the theology of such men as Kahnis, Hofmann, Luthardt, and others, whose rationalistic tendencies were dominating the Lutheran Church. The able polemics in which he, together with his older colleagues, engaged against this hybrid theology have stamped him a churchman of exceptional valor to his age. The labor which he performed directly for the Missouri Synod, and indirectly for the entire Church, is a perennial task for loyal churchmen. How much we in the Missouri Synod really love Dr. Pieper will have to be shown in the years to come by the use we shall make of the literary heritage which he and his theological forebears have left us.

    Valparaiso, Ind.   W. H. T. Dau.

Chapter One

The Doctrine of Christ's Work[1]

Outline

Preface

The theological seminary at St. Louis teaches Dogmatics by dictating an overview of Dogmatics to the students. Further instruction is based on the extensive dogmatic material which has been collected with great care by the late Dr Walther in his edition of the *Compendium* of Baier. For several years now a wish has been expressed to print the overview, which used to be dictated, in order to avoid the laborious dictation and leave more time for the lecturer's verbal explanations. The undersigned decided to respond to this wish by publishing the dictation about some

---

[1] Franz Pieper, *Die Lehre von Christi Werk: de Officio Christi (Baier III, 100-133)*, (St. Louis: Concordia Publishing House, 1898), trans. Susanne Russell, eds Neil Carlson, Marcus J. Baikie, and T. R. Halvorson (2024).

of the *loci* in print.

In case that these papers fall into the hands of readers who are not students of the local theological seminary, they would do well to remember that this is not a complete dogmatic but an overview for lectures about dogmatics. Further teaching can be found in the quotation of Baier´s *Compendium*, which are referenced throughout. This should be noted with reference to all the individual quotes. If it says, for example: Kromayer III, 102, it references the quote as printed in Walther's edition of Baier, Vol III, p. 102. For those who wish to read the quotes by the authors themselves, refer to the reference following each of the quotes used by Walther.

In some places, the overview is supplemented by other material than that offered by Baier. This occurs in those parts where needs of the present time require further exemplification. Furthermore, the overview refers to the practical importance of particular dogmatics or parts thereof.

F. Pieper

The Doctrine of Christ's Office

Christ's office in general

Christ is such a wonderful person, in fact God and human, who does such wonderful work, by being the mediator between God and humans (1 Timothy 2:5) to save man, Luke 19:10: "For the son of man came to seek and to save that which was lost." In the natural order of things, the doctrine of Christ's office or works follows the doctrine of Christ's person. Christ's works of office (*officium Christi*) is defined by everything Christ, the Son of God, who was made man, did or does for the salvation of mankind.[2]

Christ's office is in short expressed in the names "Jesus" and "Christ". Scripture itself interprets these names for us, Matthew 1:21, John 1:41,

---

[2] Compare Kromayer III, 102 and Quenstedt p. 103.

and John 4:42. These are a Gospel *in nuce* (in a nutshell). About the names "Jesus" and "Christ", as well as the correct interpretation of the anointing, see Baier § 1, nota b, III, 101; Kromayer and Gerhard p 101.

Since when has the son of God incarnate been in his ministry as the redeemer?

Since well before the Baptism through which his public involvement was solemnly inaugurated, but from his becoming man which coincides with his humiliation. Christ was a Christ *for us*, not since his becoming visible in public but in his conception, birth, circumcision, and childhood obedience. This has been previously elaborated in the state of humiliation. Compare Baier III, 83-86. See Kromayer III, 26: "Christ went through all stages of human age, so He would heal our impure conception and birth from the ground up." Luther talks about this very impressively in the *Church Postil* (*Kirchenpostille*), sermon at Christmas, St Louis edition XI, 124,127; Sermon at Christmas Eve mass XI, 2022 ff. About the doctrine of Christ's salvation in his circumcision, compare XI, 291 ff. About the same point, *House Postil* (*Hauspostille*) XIII, 1534 f.: "For his own person He had no need of circumcision, the same as He had not needed for himself to be obedient to his mother or to die on the cross. For his own person, He was rightly not bound by the Law. He does it for our sake, because we are in need of such a man who would be without sin, who fulfilled the Law for us and also satisfied the wrath of God, or else we would have to remain under the curse of the Law for eternity. This is why He subjected himself to the Law, and obtained by his works and his office our freedom from the Law; as Saint Paul says in Galatians. 4:4-5: 'But when the fullness of time had come, God sent his son, born of a woman, born under the Law, in order to redeem those who were under the Law, so that we might receive adoption as sons.'"

We have already exposed the point of view that Christ would have become man even if mankind had not sinned as a useless and a dangerous philosophical speculation in the Doctrine of the State of Christ. Baier III, 18,19. Scripture names no other use of the Son of God

Incarnate than the salvation of sinners. 1 Timothy 1:15: Christ Jesus came into the world ἁμαρτωλοὺς σῶσαι (to save sinners). Compare Luke 19:10. Galatians 4:4-5. Therefore, there is no other use to be found. Augustine's dictum is biblical: "*Si homo non periisset, filius hominis non venisset.*" (If man had not perished, the Son of Man would not have come.) If one made up other uses of the Son of God becoming man[3], this would have no other effect than this, that the sin of man as well as God's grace in Christ would appear diminished. Compare in this regard Gerhard, Brochmand, Ambrosius III, 101-102.

One of the *quaestiones curiosae* is this: why did God send his Son only after four thousand years and not immediately after the fall. Quite rightly Kromayer remarks in relation to this and other questions: Although probable reasons could be stated *a posteriori* ("God wanted to subject his people to the Law first, so they yearned all the more for the promised Messiah"), it is safer to answer that it also pleased God. Compare Kromayer, p. 102.

Christ's office in particular

If we ask in more detail what Christ has done, and still is doing, to save mankind, we can conveniently order the related passages in Scripture into three classes. Christ saves all people by:

- Teaching,
- Reconciling, and
- Reigning.

Even in the Old Testament, Christ is announced as a prophet (Deuteronomy 18:15.), a priest (Psalm 110) and king (Psalm 2 and 72). In the fullness of time, He will appear as the one who preaches to people (Luke 4:18, John 1:18, Hebrews 1:1, Luke 13:33), reconciles them with God (Matthew 20:28, 2 Corinthians 5:18-19, Romans 5:10) and reigns in the church and over all living creatures (Matthew 1:21, Luke 1: 31,

---

[3] Compare the list of old and new teachers who have made speculations of this kind, Baier III, 18.19.

John 18:33-36, Ephesians 1:20ff, 1 Corinthians 15:27).

Thus, Christ's office can be understood threefold:

- Prophetic,
- Sacerdotal, and
- Royal

(*Munus Christi triplex: propheticum, sacerdotale, regium*). Compare Baier §2, S. 102f and Gerhard, S. 103. The scriptures of the Old and the New Testaments have directly and clearly described Christ as prophet, high priest and king, and therefore, church fathers of all periods have taught the threefold office of Christ[4], although not necessarily in the formal order of the syllabus that is generally followed in the Lutheran Church since Gerhard. Compare Gerhard, p. 103. Hutter for example used to speak of the twofold office of Christ, the sacerdotal and the royal, but there is no objective difference. The sacerdotal included the prophetic office because a priest was also an instructor, Malachi 2:7. Quenstedt, however, remarks about his time that most of the Lutheran teachers abide by the threefold division.[5] Concerns about the order of the threefold division have been expressed here and there. We are reminded that the sacerdotal office should be ranked first because Christ's reconciliatory deeds begin with his conception, whereas the instructional work begins much later. Usually, the prophetic office is ranked first, which is why we follow the same order. It should be noted anyway that the offices cannot be divided in a successive manner. Christ is, as we will see later, in his royal office even in the state of humiliation, when He explicitly calls himself a king in the state of humiliation. John 18:37. Christ is born a king, Isaiah 9:6-7, Matthew

---

[4] As did Eusebius in *The Church History* I, 2: "All of these (the prophets) relate the true Christ, the divine and heavenly *Logos*, who alone is the high priest of the whole world, who alone is the king of all creation, and who alone is the highest prophet of his Father amongst all prophets." St Louis edition (L. Volkening), p. 8.

[5] *Systema*. 1715. II, 304. Amongst the Reformed, Calvin teaches the threefold division, *Inst*. II, 15.

2:2, 11. The reason for the objection to the teaching of the threefold office of Christ which can be found in Socinianism, Rationalism, and in the works of some more modern theologians is in the objective deviation from what Scripture teaches us about Christ's person and office.

All works of office belong to the whole divine and human person, that is to say, that Christ carries out his works in and according to both natures, as we have already seen in the third expression of the characteristics of Christ as stated. All works of office are divinely human actions (*operationes* Θεανδριχαι). If this is denied, the whole reason of the Son of God becoming human is canceled. Baier III, 70-75. Quenstedt, p. 103.

The Prophetic Office of Christ

The execution of the prophetic office in the state of humiliation

Christ teaches in the state of humiliation in his own person (αυτοπροσώπως) or directly. In Luke 4:21 Christ himself interprets the verse in Isaiah 61:1 where the Messiah is announced as the great prophet of grace: "The Spirit of the Sovereign Lord is on me, because the Lord has anointed me to proclaim good news to the poor." In Acts 3:22 Peter interprets the verse about the great prophet (Deuteronomy 18:15-19) as Christ. These verses and others like John 1:18, John 3:31-34, and Hebrews 1:1 express equally clearly that Christ was a unique prophet, unlike any other before or after him. (*Propheta* χατ'ἑξοχήν, *propheta omnibus excellentior.*) What is this uniqueness? In Christ God appeared in the flesh, and God himself teaches on earth, Hebrews 1:1: "In the past God spoke to our ancestors through the prophets at many times and in various ways, but in these last days He has spoken to us by his Son." Christ as prophet therefore differs from all other prophets regarding the source of knowledge which He confirmed in his prophetic office. While all prophets taught by virtue of the revelation which is offered to all people on earth, that is to say by inspiration, and who therefore talked "of the earth" (ἐχ της γης), like John the Baptist said of himself in John 3:31 and all other simply human prophets, Christ taught with the council of the Holy Trinity "what he has seen and heard" (ὃ ἑώρακεν καὶ ἤκουσεν), verse 32, and as "the one and only Son, who is himself God and is in closest relationship with the Father," John 1:18.[6] Christ draws from a source in his teaching from which no human, not even a prophet, can draw; because – says John when describing the uniqueness of Christ's teaching – θεὸν οὐδεὶς ἑώρακεν πώποτε, John 1:18. In other words: In his teaching in the state of humiliation, Christ confirms the divine knowledge which was in him by virtue of his divine nature, and which was communicated with him in the way of human nature. This is expressed further when Scripture says about Christ's human nature that the spirit has been given to him "without limit"(οὐ γὰρ ἐκ μέτρου), John 3:34, *quod idem est*, says Baier III, 57, *ac sapientiam immensam seu infinitam ei secundum humanam naturam, in qua locutus est, esse datam* (that he was given immense or infinite wisdom according to the human nature in which he spoke). Therefore, one should not talk about an inspiration of Christ for the purpose of his ministry as a teacher[7], nor fantasize with the Socinians

---

[6] The words: "in closest relationship" (literally: in the bosom of the Father), ὁ ὢν εἰς τὸν κόλπον τοῦ πατρός, are not to be understood as Christ being raised up, as it is the understanding of modern kenotics, but instead the words state the unique source of knowledge for Christ's preaching on earth (εξηγησατο). While the Son of God taught on earth, He still remained εἰς τὸν κόλπον τοῦ πατρός. That the Son of God in his human form should have given up the divine "being and works" is an invention of the modern kenotics. Scripture attributes most clearly the divine "being" (John 10:38, 14:10, 10:30) as well as "works" (John 5:17) to the Son of God incarnate, even in the state of humiliation.

[7] A. H. Strong is right in saying this: Christ found the sources of all knowledge and power within himself. The Word of God did not *come* to him, – He was himself – the Word. And Martensen: The source of Jesus' teaching was "not inspiration but incarnation." Jesus was not inspired, – He was the inspirer. (*Systematic Theology*, p. 389.) Philippi: "The source of his (Christ's) being a prophet did not come from external inspiration, but all the fullness of the deity resided in him, Colossians 2:9. God's omniscience itself has become the omniscience of Jesus the man." And before that:

(Antithesis, p. 104) about the rapture of Christ into heaven for the purpose of instruction. Compare A. Osiander, p. 104. Even the masses of people got the impression that Christ, entirely different from other teachers, taught in his own divine power, compare John 7:46, Mark 1:22, Matthew 7:29 (ἦν γὰρ διδάσκων αὐτοὺς ὡς ἐξουσίαν), Luke 4:32 (ἐν ἐξουσίᾳ ἦν ὁ λόγος αὐτοῦ), compare Baier §3, nota d, S.106. If Christ is called a prophet like Moses, Deuteronomy 18:15, the point of comparison is the mediation of a covenant. As Moses was the mediator of the old transient covenant, Christ is the mediator of the new permanent covenant. Hebrews 12:18-28. The fact that Christ will be greater than Moses is one that Moses says himself most clearly in Deuteronomy 18, because he points the people from himself towards the prophet who the Lord will raise up later, verses 16-19.

Considering the content of Christ's teaching that He proclaimed during the days of being in the flesh, He not only showed salvation as present[8] but as present in his person.

He asked of everyone, by their faith in him, to take salvation from him. John 6:35: "I am the bread of life. Whoever comes to me will never go hungry, and whoever believes in me will never be thirsty." John 6:40: "For my Father's will is that everyone who looks to the Son and believes in him shall have eternal life, and I will raise them up at the last day." Christ preaches himself, while the apostles who follow preach about him, 1 Corinthians 2:2. This causes grumbling and opposition. But Jesus remains steadfast that we would have to receive life from him. John 8:24: "I told you that you would die in your sins; if you do not believe that I am He, you will indeed die in your sins." Christ inculcates in them that Moses, John 5:46 and all of Scripture, John 5:39 point to

"Like his miracles, his instructions and prophecies had their source and origin in him himself... So it is his own knowledge that anything He saw from the beginning from his Father He has proclaimed to us. Nobody has ever seen God. The incarnate son, who is at his Father's side, proclaimed him to us, John 1:18."(*Kirchliche Glaubenslehre* [*Church Doctrine*] IV, 2., S. 18-19.)

[8] Matthew 4:17: ἤγγικεν γὰρ ἡ βασιλεία τῶν οὐρανῶν.

him, the giver of life. In fact, his sermon consists of the proclamation of salvation and the Gospel according to Luke 4:18-21, Deuteronomy 18:15-19, John1:17; He teaches the Law *"propter evangelium"* (because of the Gospel), that is to say, to get to his actual office, the proclamation of the Gospel, through the proclamation of the Law, Matthew 22:34-46.[9]

Papists and Socinians make Christ into a new lawgiver. They maintain that Christ gave new laws, better ones than Moses. They say so in order to sell their pagan doctrine of office in the name of Christ. Likewise, they claim that no one who followed the works offered by Moses had found salvation, which can only be found by following Christ's perfect laws. Similarly, in our times, the sectarian preachers of Arminianism describe the belief in Christ as the attempt to keep Christ's commandments. We have to state against this: Christ does not teach a new law but Moses´ Law, as He himself explains in Matthew 22:34-44. In the Sermon on the Mount, Matthew 5-7, Jesus does not argue against Moses but against the twisting of the Mosaic Law by the scholars. The commandment of charity, which the Rationalists appear to miss in the books of Moses in the Old Testament, is clearly laid out exactly there, for example, in Leviticus 19:18, compare Matthew 22:34 ff, which reasonable Israelites, for example the legal scholar in Luke 10:27, knew all along.[10] The Papist "evangelical councils" (*consilia evangelica*) are no completions of Moses´ laws. They contain the same divine commandments that are contained in Moses´ Law; and what is not contained in Moses´ Law is not taught by Jesus but made up by the Papists. More about this in Kromayer, S. Schmidt, Quenstedt, S.105-

---

[9] Mayer is of the opinion that Christ has followed up the question about the Law with the question about the Messiah, in order to accuse the Pharisees of "their own theological bafflement ... and to dispense with their participation" However, exegetes with more intellect say with Bengel that Christ wanted to lead the Pharisees from the Law to the Gospel. Compare Luther XI, 1710.

[10] The church fathers say in short: *Christus quidem fuit legis doctor, sed non legislator.* (Christ was indeed a teacher of the law, but not a legislator.)

106.

The execution of the prophetic office in the state of exaltation

In the state of exaltation, Christ carries out the prophetic office through mediators. Even in the Lutheran Church, the prophetic office of Christ has been narrowed to the state of humiliation (so Calov[11]) and then also subsumed those doctrines of present days on this earth under the royal office of Christ. However, this is just a formal distinction. Christ is presented as a king when teaching is subsumed under the royal office, a king who teaches through his servants or ministers. However, there is good reason for those Lutheran scholars who with Gerhard and Quenstedt follow the teaching method that they attribute the prophetic office to Christ also in the state of exaltation. The reason lies in Scripture itself, to understand the teaching which is carried out now in and by the church as a continuation of Christ's teaching on this earth. John 20:21: "As the Father has sent me, I am sending you." According to the apostle Paul, Christ says, as Paul reminds us emphatically in 2 Corinthians 13:3: "Since you are demanding proof that Christ is speaking through me."[12] It is secondary whether the teaching of Christ in the state of exaltation is categorized within the prophetic or the royal office. It is, however, important to state that in all teaching carried out by and in the church, Christ is the one who does the teaching. Preachers have to be seen as instruments. Only the Word of God, and not the word of man, must be taught in the church until the day of judgment. Peter 4:11: εἴ τις λαλεῖ, ὡς λόγια θεοῦ. Now, how did Christ ensure that his Word would be taught on earth even after his exaltation? He gave his Word to the apostles, John 14:26 and 16:13-15, not only to be preached verbally but also to be written down, 2 Thessalonians. This is how He made his apostles into infallible teachers of the whole earthly kingdom. Furthermore, He gives the church teachers and preachers until judgment day, Ephesians 4:11; but in their teaching they are

---

[11] Baier speaks waveringly about this, §5 and nota b, p. 106f.

[12] ἐπεὶ δοκιμὴν ζητεῖτε τοῦ ἐν ἐμοὶ λαλοῦντος Χριστοῦ

bound by the infallible Word of the apostles, and therefore Christ's own Word. John 17:20.[13]

Finally, He fills all his Christians with the wisdom and the knowledge of the Spirit, so that they can teach and admonish each other, John 7:38-39, Numbers 11:29; but even this instruction and admonition is not expressed through an independent word of an individual, but through the Word of Christ: "Let the message of Christ[14] dwell in you richly",

---

[13] When Christ says here "My prayer is not for them alone" (the apostles), "I pray also for those who will believe in me through their message" (the apostles), He names the infallible apostolic Word as the source and the foundation of the church's faith until judgment day. When souls come to faith through the service of preachers, it happens because these preachers proclaim the inspired Word of the apostles.

[14] Luther talks about this point powerfully: "If someone wants to preach, he must be silent about his own words that hold true in this worldly government of his own house; but here in the church he must not speak any other words but those of this rich landlord, else it would not be the true church. Therefore, it should be called: God speaks. This is how it goes in this world. If a prince wants to reign, his voice must ring out in his lands and in his house. This is how it goes in this wretched life, how much more must we ring out the Word of God in this church and in eternal life. ... Although there is so much chatter outside the Word of God, this prattle is not the church's yet, even if they become mad; they scream "Church, church" we are meant to listen to the pope and the bishops ... A Christian is meant to hear nothing but the Word of God. Otherwise, a Christian might hear another under the worldly rule, how to punish the bad and protect the pious, and of all things domestic. But here in the Christian Church it will be a house in which the Word of God alone rings out. Let them shout madly 'church, church', without God's Word it is nothing."(XII, 1413 f.) The point Luther makes here against Papists can equally be made against all modern unbridled enthusiasm and the "science" that claims power in the church. Think in this context also of Luther's famous dictum that a preacher, if he is a real preacher, must not look for the forgiveness of sins in his sermon. Every preacher should be able to say about themselves: "In this sermon I have been an apostle and prophet of Jesus Christ. Here it is not necessary, in fact it is not good to ask for the forgiveness of sins,

Colossians 3:16. This is how Christ is, through his Word, the only teacher in and through the church until judgment day. This is why the Word used by the Christian community in their mission is "the word of the Lord", 1 Thessalonians 1:8: "The Lord's message [lit. The word of the Lord] rang out from you" (ἀφ' ὑμῶν γὰρ ἐξήχηται ὁ λόγος τοῦ κυρίου). All teaching that is not purely proclamation of the Word of Christ is false doctrine, pseudo-prophetism, and simply forbidden in the Christian church.[15]

The truth that Christ is the actual teacher in church is of utmost practical importance. It lies in the powerful admonition, as already indicated, that human beings should not undertake preaching their own word in church; because this is an imposition on Christ's prophetic, respectively royal office; Christ wants his Word alone proclaimed in the church. All false doctrines are a crime against his majesty. It is not only the Papists (compare Gerhard, S.106) but all who preach "without and against the Word of God" in the church because they are part of a rebellion against Christ. All false teachers are called

---

as if it was taught badly; this is God's Word and not my word which God should not, nor would be able to forgive, but confirm, praise, crown and say: You taught well, because I spoke through you, and this Word is mine. Anyone who cannot proudly say this about their sermon, should give up preaching, because surely they deny and blaspheme God." (Walch XVII, 1685). Strong rightly says as well: "All modern prophecy that is true is but the republication of Christ's message – the proclamation and expounding of truth already revealed in Scripture." (1.c., p. 389) Philippi: "From Montanus to Irving attempts have been made to assert a new prophethood in the Christian Church. They all turned out to be false. ... There are only teachers and preachers of the Word of God, through which the Lord receives his prophethood which is once and for all perfect, which can be called the preservation of the prophetic Word and his illuminating spiritual effect, but also as the continuation of Jesus Christ's prophetic office, in the same way as the *conservatio mundi* was called the *creatio continua*."(1.c., S.22)

[15] ο λόγος του Χριστού, the Word of Christ, "the word spoken and proclaimed by him."(Boise)

ἀντίχριστος (antichrist). This must be stated in the face of modern underestimation of false doctrine. Thereupon lies the truth that Christ is the actual teacher in the church. [It is] a great comfort to all listeners and readers of the Word of God that Christ himself deals with them in his Word which is brought to them by human instruments. Equally, the Word of God which is offered through human instruments is an admonition. "Whoever listens to you listens to me; whoever rejects you rejects me", Luke 10:16.[16]

Finally, it must be pointed out that even before his incarnation, in the Old Testament, the Son of God is the person of the Holy Trinity who spoke with people and mediated for them. Scripture gives evidence,

a. that the prophets spoke through Christ's Spirit, 1 Peter 1:11 and

b. that it was the Son of God who went about among the people, Isaiah 6, compare John12:41, who dealt with Israel in the desert, 1 Corinthians 10:4.

Compare B. Mentzer, p. 107, Luther II, 800. Furthermore, see the extensive explanation in the report of the Central District of the Synod of Missouri, Ohio and other states, 1883, in particular p. 59ff.[17]

---

[16] Luther says "that human nature is so twisted and corrupt that we, unfortunately, do not believe that we hear the Word of God when He speaks to us through a man. We judge the Word in relation to the greatness and fame of him who speaks: the man who speaks we listen to as a mere man and think that it is the word of a man. And this is why we reject it and become tired of it, when we should thank God that He puts his Word into the mouth of a man or servant, who is like us, who can talk with us and comfort and raise us up ... But it is not the word of a pastor, neither Saint Peter's, nor the word of any other servant, but it is the Word of the divine majesty itself." (II, 905.)

[17] Here, the following thesis was put forward: "Our Lord Jesus Christ is the person in the Holy Trinity who first reveals himself in the old covenant." In the explanation it says: "If you open the Bible (the Old Testament) and read: God spoke, God did this, and ask ' Which person is meant by this?', the answer is: First, the Son of God. This is not to say that the Father or the Holy Spirit are not revealed in the Old Testament. The thesis only says that it is our Lord Jesus Christ who appears first and mainly in the Old

The Sacerdotal Office of Christ

The grace which Jesus proclaims as a prophet, He gained for us as a priest. We must keep an eye on this close connection between the prophetic and the sacerdotal office. The sacerdotal office provides the content for the prophetic. If, in his sacerdotal office, Christ caused only a quasi-reconciliation of mankind with God, then in the same way, in his prophetic office proclaims only a quasi-reconciliation. On the other hand, [since in truth] Christ has brought about a real, perfect, and objective reconciliation of all mankind with God through his substitutionary life and suffering, that makes the Gospel now into a message of grace which people only have to accept through faith in order to gain possession of the grace gained by Christ. One might say that the Socinians or Rationalists and others accept only the prophetic office of Christ because of their denial of Christ's vicarious satisfaction. In fact, this is not precise enough. By denying the sacerdotal office, the prophetic office in the biblical sense is denied as well. This leaves Christ in his prophetic office not as the guarantor of grace for a world of sinners who are under the curse of the Law, but as a moralizing

---

Testament, as an acting and talking divine person, who is first Jehovah revealing himself. Not only did Jesus Christ reveal himself in particular appearances, but He is the God of the Old Testament, unless it is clear in context that it is the Father or the Holy Spirit." Luther says: "In nearly all places in the Old Testament, Christ is revealed when God's name is mentioned." (II, 853) Hengstenberg: "The doctrine of the angel of the Lord is like a red thread through all the Old Testament, his mediation everywhere." In the first two of the passages mentioned (Genesis 16:13, 32:31) we can prove in particular that God was seen through mediation of his angel. Genesis 16:7 goes ahead: 'The angel of the Lord found her [Hagar].' And according to Hosea 12 it was the angel of the Lord who Jacob struggled with in Penuel. By the way, the 'invisible God' 1 Timothy 1:17 is not mediated twice, under the old covenant by the angel of the Lord, under the new covenant by the incarnate Son, ... but the *Logos* presents himself in the angel of the Lord in a prelude to his incarnation. The Old Testament itself presents this understanding when in Zechariah and Malachi it prefigures that the angel of the Lord appears to his people in the Messiah. John follows this idea when he says in John 1:11 that the Messiah came to that which was his own, and in chapter 12:41 that Isaiah saw Christ." (*Commentary on the Gospel of Saint John* I, 61f.)

preacher who teaches and appeals to people to acquire salvation by their own striving for virtue. So much depends on the correct understanding of the sacerdotal office of Christ!

But what is the sacerdotal office of Christ exactly?

The Sacerdotal Office of Christ

The sacerdotal office in the state of humiliation

Christ, who is expressly called a "priest" in both the Old and the New Testament,[18] reconciled all of humanity with God in the state of humiliation. 2 Corinthians 5,19: "God was in Christ, reconciling the world to Himself." It has to be said that Scripture does not only report reconciliation to be a fact, but it also describes the manner of reconciliation (*modus reconciliationis*) or the medium through which reconciliation is achieved (*medium reconciliationis*). Christ reconciled mankind with God by offering himself up for sacrifice: John 17:19 "And for their sakes I sanctify myself"; 1 Timothy 2:6: "who gave himself a ransom for all"; 1 John 2:2: "And He Himself is the propitiation (ἱλασμός) for our sins, and not for ours only but also for the whole world." Herein lies the difference between the exemplary sacerdotal office in the Old Testament and the unique sacerdotal office of Christ in the New Testament: *in Veteris Testamenti sacrificiis offerebantur victimae a sacerdotibus distinctae, Christus semet ipsum sacrificavit* (in the Old Testament sacrifices were offered separately [from themselves] by the priests, Christ sacrificed himself), Baier, §8, p. 109. In the New Testament, Christ is priest and victim at the same time, Hebrews 7:27.

According to Scripture though, this self-sacrifice of Christ contains two parts:

1. Christ gave himself for us in his holy life (*obedientia activa* [active obedience]), Hebrews 9:14: "who through the eternal

---

[18] Compare Psalm 110:4 כֹּהֵן לְעוֹלָם; Zechariah 6:13: כֹהֵן עַל־כִּסְאוֹ and accordingly in the New Testament ἱερεύς, ἀρχιερεύς, ἱερεύς μέγας and others, compare the passages in Baier, §6, nota a, p. 107.

Spirit offered Himself without spot to God" (ἑαυτὸν προσήνεγκεν ἄμωμον τῷ θεῷ);[19] Hebrews 7:26, and

2. also in his suffering and dying (*obedientia passiva* [passive obedience]), Ephesians 5:2: Christ "has given himself for us as an offering and a sacrifice" (θυσίαν, sacrifice).

Once and for all, God is reconciled with mankind through the sacerdotal office which Christ fulfilled on earth; this means the grace of God is given to all people, Hebrews 9:12: διὰ δὲ τοῦ ἰδίου αἵματος, εἰσῆλθεν ἐφάπαξ εἰς τὰ ἅγια, αἰωνίαν λύτρωσιν εὑράμενος. This is what Scripture teaches us about the fact and the medium of reconciliation through Christ's self-sacrifice. The finer points will be explained later.

The following needs to be added here: People are reconciled with God through Christ's sacrifice; or, which is the same [thing], the debt of sin of all people is fully paid to God. This also means that through this sacrifice, all people are saved from the terrible *consequences* of sin, [namely,] from death and from the power of the devil. Scripture describes this *effect* of the reconciliation which was achieved through Christ's sacrifice extensively and in many places. The force of death is overcome by Christ, 2 Timothy 1:10: Christ "has destroyed death and has brought life and immortality to light through the gospel." See also: Psalm 68:21, Hosea 13:14, 1 Corinthians 15:55-57. The force of the devil, *who gained it through God's judgment over mankind*, is destroyed, Hebrews 2:14: "Since the children have flesh and blood, He too shared in their humanity so that by his death He might break the power of him who holds the power of death, that is, the devil ;" John 12:31, 14:30, 16:11, Colossians 2:15.

Mankind is saved from the rule of sin through Christ's sacrifice, Titus 2:14: "who gave himself for us to redeem us from all wickedness (ἀπὸ πάσης ἀνομίας) and to purify for himself a people that are his very own, eager to do what is good." 1 Peter 2:24, 1 Peter 1:18-19, Romans 7:1-6.

---

[19] The being "without spot" (or unblemished, sin free) must not be downplayed. Being without spot means to be obedient toward the divine law.

This must be impressed through the strength of Scripture, so it is understood that we are saved from all evil by Christ's sacrifice, but in a way that Christ's sacrifice brought about the extinction of all our sins once, [that this] will remain in the foreground forever, and that it will be taught as the cause and the source of salvation from death, from the devil and from the rule of sin. We are saved from death because our debt of sin has been paid.[20]

An ecclesiastical expression for Christ's sacerdotal office in the state of humiliation is "vicarious satisfaction", *satisfactio vicaria*. The idea of this expression is that Christ achieved satisfaction substitutionally (meaning in the place of mankind) so that God, who was angered by human sinfulness, turned his wrath into mercy towards all people. This expression is not biblical. However, the meaning of it is the same as the doctrine of atonement through Christ in Scripture. This ecclesiastical term can be paralleled with [another ecclesiastical term, one about the incarnation] ὁμοούσιος [same in being or essence, e.g, in the Nicene Creed, being of one substance with the Father]. The biblical doctrine of the true divinity of Christ is expressed in this one-word ὁμοούσιος, in the same way as "vicarious satisfaction" summarizes, in the face of false doctrines, everything Scripture teaches about the salvation through Christ. Compare Baier §9, nota b, p. 111.

Scripture reveals clearly and unambiguously two truths in the term "*satisfactio vicaria*":

I. In God, there is an immutable justice, which demands perfect fulfillment of God's Law from all people, and who directs his wrath at

---

[20] Th. Harnack argues quite rightly against von Hoffmann: "The main focus and emphasis of salvation is not the annulment of death but the annulment of the divine judgment and the human condition of sinfulness which are the cause and the force, and therefore the deadliness of death. This is why, as we are taught by our creed in accordance with Scripture, the annulment of the condition of sinfulness precedes the annulment of the governance of death." (*Das Bekenntnis der Lutherischen Kirche von der Versöhnung* (*The declaration of belief in atonement of the Lutheran Church*) by G. Thomasius, with an afterword by Dr Th. Harnack. Erlangen, 1857, p. 138f.)

those who trespass his Law by condemning them for eternity (*justitia Dei vindicativa*). The first is expressed in Matthew 22:39, 40: "You shall love the Lord your God with all your heart, with all your soul, and with all your mind.[...] You shall love your neighbor as yourself."; the latter in Galatians 3:10: "Cursed is everyone who does not continue in all things which are written in the book of the Law, to do them." Romans 1:18. The consequence of this is that *all* people are indeed under the wrath of God and under the curse of the Law because they neither comply with the demands of God's Law (Romans 3:9-18), nor are able to comply (Romans 8:7). Romans 3:23: "for all have sinned and fall short of the glory of God [...]" Romans 3:19: "that . . . all the world may become guilty (ὑπόδικος) before God"; Romans 5:10: "when we were enemies ἐχθροὶ we were reconciled to God through the death of His Son";[21] Ephesians 2:3: "we . . . were by nature children of wrath (τέκνα φύσει ὀργῆς)."

II. Christ willingly fulfilled the divine council of salvation for all mankind and the divine Law, given to all people, and accepted the punishment for their breach of the Law as his. This fulfillment of the Law given to all people in their place is testified in Galatians 4:4-5: "God sent forth His Son, born of a woman, born under the law, to redeem those who were under the law." Matthew 5:17; 3:15. Isaiah 53:6 teaches about the transfer of the debt of sin from mankind to Christ: "And the Lord has laid on Him the iniquity of us all." 2 Corinthians 5:21. Psalm 69:6. The vicarious suffering is testified in 2 Corinthians 5:14: "One died for all." 1 Peter 3:18: "For Christ also suffered once for sins, the just for the unjust." Galatians 3:13. Christ did not only suffer for the benefit of all people but in place of them.[22]

---

[21] See Meyer and Philippi.

[22] We should rather say: It is "for the benefit" because it is "in place of." It cannot be denied that ἀντ has the meaning of *in place of* and *instead* when reading passages like Matthew 20:28 and 1 Corinthians 1:15. Meyer says about Matthew 20:28: "ἀντί

III. Because of Christ's actions and suffering, God *is* reconciled with mankind. This means that God's wrath against all people is changed into mercy towards them. Romans 5:18: "through one Man's righteous act *the free gift came* to all men." Galatians 4:4-5, Romans 5:10: "For if when we were enemies we were reconciled to God through the death of His Son." 2 Corinthians 5:19: "God was in Christ, reconciling the world to Himself."

According to Scripture, there is an objective reconciliation of all people with God, not only one brought about by Christ 1900 years ago. Reconciliation exists; it existed before all human actions and independent of them. It is a perfect truth, like the creation of the world. This – and nothing but this – is the doctrine of Scripture. Romans 5:10: "we were reconciled to God through the death of His Son," therefore, at that time, when Christ died, our reconciliation with God occurred. Christ's death is in the past, [and] in the same way our reconciliation was brought about in the past. 2 Corinthians 5:19: "God was in Christ reconciling" (that is to say, then, when Christ lived and died on earth) the world to Himself." The κατηλλάσσιεν in Romans 5:10 and 2 Corinthians 5:19 does not describe a change of heart of mankind but a process in God's heart. God let go of his wrath when Christ offered himself up for sacrifice. This is explained further when the apostle says: "God was in Christ reconciling the world to Himself" and adds: μὴ

---

describes the substitution. The ransom that is given takes the place of (instead of) those who are to be redeemed with it. The λυτρον is a ἀντίλυτρον (1 Timothy 2:6), ἀντάλλαγμα (Matthew 16:26). Also, ὑπὲρ carries the meaning of *loco*, instead of, in 2 Corinthians 5:14: εἷς ὑπὲρ πάντων; 1 Peter 3:18: δίκαιος ὑπὲρ ἀδίκων. Steiger aptly remarks about the last verse: "The stark juxtaposition of these two predicates leaves no doubt to anyone with an ounce of sense of language that by the use of ὑπὲρ a change of pronouns is expressed, through which the apostle says that we are the unjust who deserve suffering because of our sins, that Christ did not deserve any suffering but has taken it on, by suffering when sinners should have suffered, therefore instead of them and to their benefit." Luthardi would do well not to say (*Compendium*, 9th edition, p. 230): "Substitution is not directly expressed, but it underlies the whole idea and presentation (and the ὑπὲρ)" instead he should say something like: "Substitution does not only underlie the whole idea, but it also is directly expressed."

λογιζόμενος αὐτοῖς τὰ παραπτώματα αὐτῶν, not imputing their trespasses to them, that is to say, as early as that, God forgave the world all their sins in his heart and justified the whole world. "Not to impute their trespasses" in the parlance of Scripture (Romans 4: 6-8) means to "forgive sin", and to "justify" the sinner. So, therefore, the truth of Christ's raising from the dead is in Romans 4:25 a true absolution or an objective justification of the whole world of sinners. Scripture clearly defines the objective reconciliation of all people with God by the reconciliation effected by Christ once and for all![23] The Gospel

---

[23] Meyer explains 2 Corinthians 5:18.19 correctly: "Mankind was afflicted by God's holy wrath because of their unpaid sin, εχθρούς Θεοῦ. Romans 5:10, *Deo invisi*; but because God caused Christ to die, He effected the redemption of their sins, which ended God's wrath. The same thought is contained in Romans 5:10, although in the passive voice ... The redemption of all people happened objectively because of Christ's death." This point is discussed extensively in the report of the Southern District of the Synod in Missouri, 1883, p. 20ff. It says there: "Christ's work has effected God's perfect reconciliation with mankind. Christ's work as ΄mediator΄ (1 Timothy 2:5) between God and people pleases the Lord; see Ephesians 5:2 about Christ who has "given Himself for us, an offering and a sacrifice to God for a sweet-smelling aroma" "For He made Him who knew no sin *to be* sin for us" (2 Corinthians 5:21) which means God counted people's sins as his own, and in the same way He looked upon Christ's atonement as if people had atoned themselves. The Holy Spirit writes through St Paul in 2 Corinthians 5:14 "we judge thus: that if One died for all, then all died." Through Christ's suffering and dying, all sins of mankind have been so perfectly atoned, as if a thousand million people had suffered the pains of hell themselves. The result is: God is reconciled with all and every single person. Nobody needs to do or suffer anything to reconcile with God, to obtain righteousness or blessedness. This is testified extensively in Scripture. We read in 2 Corinthians 5:19: "God was in Christ reconciling the world to Himself." This means, that 1900 years ago, when Christ fulfilled the Law for all people and bore the punishment for the violation of the Law by mankind, God reconciled all people with himself. We must contemplate these simple, clear words and take them in. We do know

proclaims this message of this objective reconciliation, which has already happened, which is why it says in 2 Corinthians 5:19 τὸν λόγον τῆς καταλλαγῆς. This is the reason why people will gain access to the already effected reconciliation only through faith (*sola fide*) or will have to be reconciled with God individually (subjective). In other words: We are only reconciled with God by faith because the reconciliation through Christ's atonement is already in existence and described and proclaimed in the Gospel. Paul confesses on behalf of all Christians that

---

very well what it means to be reconciled with someone. We describe someone as reconciled when he lets go of all the anger that he had felt in his heart for whatever reason. In the same way, because of Christ's work, God let go of all his anger that He felt because of the sins of mankind. This is expressed in the words: "God was in Christ, reconciling the world to Himself." In Christ, God now feels about people as if they had never insulted him with their sins, as if there had never been any separation between God and mankind. This is the so-called objective doctrine of redemption. If God is reconciled with mankind through Christ, He has nothing against them anymore, He has absolved them in his heart from their sins, and He looks upon them as righteous for Christ's sake. The justification for Christ's sake, which has already occurred, is well documented with expressive words when the apostle says "God was in Christ reconciling the world to Himself" and adds "not imputing their trespasses to them" ′Not imputing trespasses to them′ is the same as ′justification′ as we know it from Romans 4:6-8: "just as David also describes the blessedness of the man to whom God imputes righteousness apart from works: ′Blessed *are those* whose lawless deeds are forgiven, And whose sins are covered; Blessed *is the* man to whom the Lord shall not impute sin.′"

"According to Scripture, there is a reconciliation of God with mankind, and a justification for mankind in faith. Christ died for us and atoned to divine justice, because we were still sinners, yes, before we were born. God accepted Christ's work, which was done for us. In the same way, God is reconciled with us through Christ, even before we were born, and absolved us of our sins for Christ's sake. This can be seen in the circumstances of Christ's death. Christ's cry "It is finished!", the darkness until the ninth hour, when Christ died (in the 9th hour the sun broke through as a picture of the sun of mercy which rose for us through Christ's death), the tearing of the temple curtain (because in this wonderful event God explained that every sinner has free access to him)."

we "now" – that is to say, when coming to faith and in reconciliation – "have received the reconciliation."[24]

It is of crucial importance for the whole of Christian teaching that it holds on to objective reconciliation. Any oversight here cannot be remedied later. When we hold on to the fact that mankind is fully reconciled with God through Christ's works and suffering, there remains no room for the heresy which has occurred in many forms, that people must obtain reconciliation with God fully or in part by themselves. This undermines all rationalistic, Papist, and modern-theological doctrine of works.[25] This objective reconciliation of all people with God, which was brought about by Jesus, forces us toward the correct understanding of the Gospel and of faith. The Gospel can be nothing other than the proclamation and presentation of the forgiveness of sins, gained for us by Christ;[26] and the salvation-bringing faith can be nothing other than the simple acceptance of the forgiveness of sins gained for us by Christ.[27]

---

[24] Philippi remarks about Romans 5:11: "The καταλλαγὴν is present, we receive it through faith, so that καταλλαγὴν ἐλάβομεν equals δικαιοσύνη, compare 2 Corinthians 5:21: καταλλάγητε τῷ θεῷ.

[25] Luther's argument against the Papist doctrine of works is the perfect work of Christ. He writes: "As it is written in the article the children pray: I believe in Jesus Christ, crucified, died and so forth. It is no other than Jesus Christ, the Son of God, who died for our sins. No other than Jesus, the Son of God; again I say, no other than Jesus, has saved us from our sins. This is true and is the whole of Scripture. And even if all devils and the world should tear themselves apart and burst, it is still the truth. But if it is Jesus alone who takes away our sins, then we are not able to do the same by our works." (E.A.25,76).

[26] Luther about Luke 24:46.47: "On the other hand, we must preach the forgiveness of sins in his (Christ's) name; this is nothing other than our duty to preach the Gospel, which proclaims to all the world, that the sin of the whole world is devoured, and that He sacrificed himself, in order to take away our sin, and that He was raised from the dead, so that He devours and destroys our sin."(XI, 693)

[27] Luther: "Works are not part of the Gospel, because the Gospel is not the Law, but

Old and new false doctrines attempt to interpret salvation-bringing faith as a human achievement, good human conduct, and so on. This is easily recognizable as false teaching in the light of the objective reconciliation brought about by Christ.[28] On the other hand: When the doctrine of Scripture about the perfect reconciliation through Christ's vicarious satisfaction is not recognized or is dismissed, the consequence naturally is a rationalist, Papist, remonstrant, modern-theological doctrine of works. If Christ has not, or has only partially, atoned for all people, the people would have to do what Christ failed to do. In that case, only a quantum or an outline of the righteousness of works is worth considering. [In that case] the Gospel is not τὴν διακονίαν τῆς καταλλαγῆς, 2 Corinthians 5:18, λόγῳ τῆς χάριτος, Acts 20:32, but is demoted to a mere instruction [about] how people can please God because of their own deeds. The Gospel becomes *eo ipso* law. Accordingly, faith is then not only acceptance of the salvation through Christ, but a human accomplishment to appeal to God.

It is the purpose of dogmatics to explain Christian teaching as it is revealed in Scripture, and to do this first and foremost by stating the objective, perfect reconciliation as it is given by Christ, and to hold fast against all misinterpretation and weakening of the message. As soon as the perfect, vicarious satisfaction of all people through Christ is

---

faith alone is part of the Gospel, because the Gospel is a free offer of God's grace. Those who believe will receive grace." (XI, 84) Furthermore: "Faith holds its hand and sack wide open, and only receives benefit. God is a giver who gives freely through his love, and we are the receivers through our faith, that does nothing but receive what is so freely given. It is not caused by us, and we cannot earn it with our deeds; because it is a gift, freely given; all you need to do is open your trap or rather your heart, and be still and be filled, Psalm 81:11." (XI, 1103f).

[28] Walther reminds us that the objection against absolution is founded in the fact that it is not possible to see Christ's salvation of the world of sinners. He writes (*Pastorale*, p. 157): "Someone who does not believe that Christ has saved the whole world perfectly already, and that the good news of the Gospel is nothing but an absolution based on the already accomplished salvation, which only requires for salvation the belief in it or the acceptance of it ...: he will never be convinced of the precious nature of private confession and absolution."

surrendered, dogmatics loses its Christian character and becomes a pagan doctrine of works. All of this doctrine is immediately rendered practically useless, because no conscience, that understands God's Law correctly, can find peace until it is wholly founded in faith and on salvation as it is ensured by Christ and proclaimed in the Gospel. We have already discussed the rationalistic objections against the reconciliation which is effected by Christ through vicarious satisfaction in the doctrine of grace when describing the salvation-bringing grace as a grace in Christ. Compare III, p 12-15. The following points are reviewed for further elaboration.

I. Some said God could forgive sins because of his omnipotence without vicarious satisfaction rendered by Christ for all people.

Reply: Speculations about what God could achieve in his omnipotence are useless and foolish because God declared in Scripture that He forgives sinners their sins solely based on Christ's satisfaction, διὰ τῆς ἀπολυτρώσεως τῆς ἐν Χριστῷ Ιησοῦ, Romans 3:24. Compare Luther's stern rebuke of the foolishness of those who philosophize about God's ability, when Scripture clearly states what God actually does and intends to do, Baier, III, 14. However, ἀπολυτρώσεως, Romans 3:24, does not mean a general liberation (like Socinians and like-minded people have argued), but a price in the form of a ransom is undoubtedly clear in the fact that Scripture explicitly names the ransom, namely Christ himself. 1 Timothy 2:6; Christ's life, Matthew 20:28; Christ's blood, 1 Peter, 1:18 and others. Compare Baier, §9, nota b, p. 111. Quenstedt, pp. 111-112.[29]

---

[29] Meyer about Romans 3:24: Within the word ἀπολυτρώσεως is contained the meaning of "paying a ransom" (Ephesians 1:7, 1 Corinthians 6:20, Galatians 3:13.), which is not to be translated freely as "liberation" in general because the λύτρον or ἀντίλυτρον (Matthew 20:28. 1 Timothy 2:6.) which Christ provided, ... was his blood which was the sacrificial blood of atonement. ... While, ἀπολυτρώσεως can contain the general meaning of "liberation" that is to say, in the Christian sense of messianic salvation (Romans 8:23); but where it is mentioned in connection with Christ's death

II. Some said that it is an unworthy idea of God to present God [as being] so angry with sinners that He could only be reconciled through Christ's substitutionary suffering and dying.[30]

Reply: We can only learn through God's revelation, that is to say in the Holy Scriptures, what are worthy or unworthy ideas about God. However, in the Holy Scriptures, God is angry in his righteousness with all sinners, Romans 1:18: "For the wrath of God is revealed from heaven against all ungodliness and unrighteousness of men, who suppress the truth in unrighteousness"; Galatians 3:10: "Cursed be everyone who does not continue in all things which are written in the book of the law, to do them;" Romans 5:10. Psalm 5:6. Everyone feels within his conscience that God is angry with all people because of their sins; none of the philosophical speculations about the impossibility, the irrationality etc. of the wrath of God can calm his conscience. The wrath of God against human sinfulness becomes clear as day in the fact of death that is inflicted on man, Hebrews 2:15. Galatians 3:13 teaches clearly that this real wrath of God about the sinfulness of man has been poured out upon Christ, was appeased in Christ, and turned into grace by Christ: "Christ has redeemed us from the curse (κατάρα) of the law, having become a curse for us." Calov III, 113.

III. Some said God's love is revealed in the fact that Christ died for mankind, Romans 5:8: "But God demonstrates His own love (ἀγάπην) toward us, in that while we were still sinners, Christ died for us."

---

as it is here and in Ephesians 1:7, it means the sacrificial blood of atonement as a ransom price (not so Ritschl), this is clear in Matthew 20:28. 1 Corinthians 6:20, 7:23, Galatians 3:13 and others.

[30] This objection is not only voiced by Socinians, general rationalists, Ritschl and others but also by many American evangelists of our time. Many are too timid to preach to the sensitive souls of our time about the wrath of God against the world of sinners. Even in "Lutheran Evangelist" of the 24th of December 1897, we find the following remark: "Possibly in the pew and in the pulpit are some yet deaf to the love story which enters in the Christmas. Have we ceased to teach and to hear that harsh theology which so misinterprets the Christmas as to make the gift, suffering, and death of the only begotten and well-beloved Son necessary to appease the wrath of our loving Father?"

Therefore, we could not speak of a reconciliation of God's wrath through the death of Christ.

Reply: According to Scripture, both are revealed in the death of Christ: God's love and God's wrath. This is clearly expressed in the following passage in Romans 5:8-11: ἐχθροὶ ὄντες (*Deo invisi* = being under the wrath of God) κατηλλάγημεν τῷ θεῷ. It is love that moves God to reconcile with us through the death of his Son, that is to say, to satisfy his righteousness [or, the demands of his justice]. According to Scripture, God's will to love does not exclude a confrontation [or, settlement] with God's justice, rather it includes it. Calov, p. 115.

IV. Some said there is an obvious injustice in presuming that the innocent Christ was punished instead of sinful people.

Reply: God's deeds are just. Scripture testifies clearly that:

a. God imputes the guilt of mankind to the innocent Christ, Isaiah 53:6. 2 Corinthians 5:21. John1:29. Psalm 69:6 and others;

b. God did, as a matter of fact, let the innocent Christ suffer instead of all guilty people, 1 Peter, 3:18: "For Christ also suffered once for sins, the just for the unjust" (δίκαιος ὑπὲρ ἀδίκων). Galatians 3:13: Christ "having become a curse for us."

We can remain calm and forget all worries concerning the justice of the process. All human critique regarding injustice must remain silent in the face of the facts so clearly stated in Scripture. Calov III, 114-115. Incidentally, there is no lack of examples in history where a human stands up for their people by his deeds and suffering (Codrus, Decius, Zaleucus, et al.). But one should not be tempted to try to use these examples to evidence justice in the divine process regarding Christ's suffering in terms of human reason. The one sufficient proof is this: "It is written." Human reason will keep finding new objections to the substitutionary suffering of Christ. This is also valid in relation to the cause, that Christ suffered voluntarily, and that therefore there is no injustice in his substitutionary suffering. Quenstedt, p. 110. It is indeed true: Christ was not forced but freely took the place of the guilty sinner,

Psalm 40:8, John 18:4-11. Immediately, human reason is ready to object that we will declare any earthly judge unjust who will convict and punish with death an innocent person who presents himself voluntarily in the place of a convict sentenced to death. The safest option therefore is to simply refer to God's revealed will when we consider the justice of God's doing because God reconciled the world with himself through Christ's vicarious satisfaction.[31]

V. Some say Christ did not suffer what mankind should have suffered, that is to say eternal punishment in hell; therefore, the term of substitutionary suffering was null and void.

Reply: Scripture says clearly that Christ suffered exactly the punishment that mankind should suffer according to their sins. Because of their sins, all human beings are under God's curse, Galatians 3:10: "Cursed is everyone who does not continue" etc. Christ is under exactly this curse, Galatians, 3:13: "Christ has redeemed us from the curse of the law, having become a curse for us" (γενόμενος ὑπὲρ ἡμῶν κατάρα). The saying by the church fathers that the life of Christ, limited in time as it was, is worth as much as the eternal suffering of all people because Christ's suffering was the suffering of the Son of God[32] is not dogmatic invention but the teaching of Scripture. Scripture deliberately emphasizes that it was the suffering of the Son of God, when describing the power and the value of Christ's suffering, 1 John 1:7: "the blood of Jesus Christ His Son cleanses us from all sin." Acts 20:28. (His own blood) etc. Judging by Scripture, there are indeed "equivalent punishments" in Christ's suffering.

VI. It has been said, and is still being said, that the whole idea of God reconciling all people with himself through Christ's vicarious satisfaction was too "juridical" and not "ethical" enough.

---

[31] Compare "*Lehre und Wehre,*" 1883, S.354-356.

[32] Dorscheus: *Quod apud homines aeternum fuisset, ipsa majestate et excellentia personae (Christi) compensatum est.* III, 87. (What would have been eternal among men was compensated by the very majesty and excellence of the person (Christ).)

Reply: that can be refuted easily! According to Scripture, all the factors that are to be considered are "juridical". God's Law is juridical, which demands complete obedience from all people. Juridical are also God's wrath and the curse of the Law, which is cast upon all who violate the Law. Juridical is the transfer of the guilt of sin from mankind to Christ, Isaiah 53:6, 2 Corinthians 5:21. Juridical is the justification of all people through faith in Christ. In order for people to obtain salvation, everything needs to be "juridical" because there is no ἦδος or comeliness [or, good qualities] in human beings because of which God could offer them salvation, Romans 3:9-18, 23, 24, 28. God's "ethics" are not neglected either, because in this awesome exchange God's justice comes into its own through the punishment of all sin in Christ, and equally God's grace through the justification of all sinners who believe in Christ, Romans 3:25-26. So, all is well, as long as we use the appropriate yardstick to evaluate this process, that is to say the divine yardstick as it is offered to us in Scripture.[33]

The teachers of false doctrines have over the course of time either completely denied the vicarious satisfaction of Christ or mutilated it. Refer to this point in Antithesis, pp. 116-117 for further explanation and characterization.

The vicarious satisfaction of Christ is completely denied by those false teachers across all times who consider Christ a mere human, such as the followers of Photinus, Socinus, and all rationalists in general. For them Christ is but a mere human, and therefore, consequently, they deny the vicarious satisfaction of Christ. The only importance they attach to the life and suffering of Christ is that it inspires people in their

---

[33] Th. Harnack argues quite rightly against von Hofmann: If it (the doctrine of atonement of the Lutheran confession) should be accused that it has, by using the term of satisfaction, introduced a legal [or, juridical] dimension to the redemption of the world, this accusation, as far as it is founded, goes back to Scripture... The statement of our symbols can only be eliminated after all the following have been eliminated from Scripture: justice and holiness of God, of the Law and of conscience, guilt, punishment and judgment, of the Mediator, the ransom and imputation. (in another place, p. 139f).

own efforts to live virtuously, which would lead to reconciliation with God.

Abelard (died in 1142) must be counted amongst the deniers of vicarious satisfaction. According to Abelard, the Son of God did not become flesh to satisfy God's justice, but to offer the world the highest evidence of the love of God by his teaching and his life (and therefore also by his death), and to awaken mankind to requited love. It is through this awakened love for God that mankind is reconciled and justified. Abelard calls the doctrine that God is reconciled with the world by the blood of the innocent Christ "cruel and unjust."[34]

In our time, it is Albrecht Ritschl (died 1889) who closely follows

---

[34] Abelard says in his exegesis of St Paul's letter to the Romans: *Nobis videtur quod in hoc justificati sumus in sanguine Christi et Deo reconciliati, quod per hanc singularem gratiam nobis exhibitam, quod filius suus nostram susceperit naturam et in ipsa nos tam verbo quam exemplo instituendo usque ad mortem perstitit, nobis sibi amplius per amorem astrinxit, ut tanto divinae gratiae accensi beneficio, nil jam tolerare propter ipsum vera reformidet caritas* ... Redemptio itaque nostra est illa summa in nobis per per passionem Christi dilectio, *quae nos non solum a servitute peccati liberat sed veram nobis filiorum Dei libertatem aquirit, ut amore ejus potius quam timore cuncta impleamus, qui n obis tantam exhibuit gratiam, qua major inveniri, ipso attestante, non potest.* (We believe that we are justified in the blood of Christ and reconciled to God, that through this singular grace shown to us, that his son took on our nature and in it, both in word and in example, led us all the way to death, bound himself to us through love, so that inflamed by such a great benefit of divine grace, true charity now fears nothing for his sake... Our redemption is therefore that highest love of Christ in us through his passion, which not only frees us from the bondage of sin but acquires for us the true freedom of the sons of God, so that we may fulfill all things with his love rather than fear, who has shown us such great grace that, as he himself testifies, greater cannot be found.) Against vicarious satisfaction he says: *Quam crudele at iniquum videtur, ut sanguinem innocentis in pretium aliquod quis requisierit aut ullo modo ei placuerit innocentem interfici, nedum Deus tam acceptamfilii sui mortem habuerit, ut per ipsam universo reconciliatus sit mundo?* (How cruel and unjust it seems that someone would seek the blood of the innocent as payment or in any way be pleased with the killing of the innocent, let alone that God would have the death of his own son so acceptable that through it the whole world would be reconciled.) (See Schmid, *Dogmengeschichtge* [*History of Dogmatics*], 4th edition, pp. 259, 258.)

Abelard's doctrine of a revelation of God's love through Christ without vicarious satisfaction. Ritschl teaches: In God there is no anger about the sins of the world. Therefore, there is no need for a vicarious satisfaction on the part of Christ. Christ's works and suffering serve the purpose to reveal God's paternal attitude to all people, so that they do not need to fear God because of their own sinfulness. Reconciliation is achieved when people are convinced of this. Here, the objective reconciliation has been entirely changed into a subjective one. Böhl says aptly in his description of Ritschl´s doctrine of reconciliation: "Holding Ritschl´s hand, we are conveniently placed to know no divine wrath anymore."[35] Böhl calls Ritschl "*Socinus redivivus*".[36]

Others belong to a category in which the vicarious satisfaction of Christ is mutilated because they deny the internal [or, intrinsic] and eternal value of Christ's atonement by teaching that Christ's works and suffering were not in themselves (*ex interna sua perfectione*) a perfect ransom for the sins of the world, but they were only accepted by God as such (*per liberam Dei acceptionem, per gratuitam Dei acceptationem*). Amongst the Scholastics, these are particularly the representatives of Scotism. Anselm (died 1109) himself taught, of course, in his *Cur Deus Homo* resolutely that Christ, the God-Man ("*Gottmensch*") achieved complete atonement by offering up his life to the divine justice for the sins of the world, which [sins] were a violation

---

[35] *Dogmatik*, p. 412.

[36] Ritschl summarizes all of his doctrine when he says about the title of his *opus magnum* "*Christian Doctrine of Justification and Reconciliation*," "The order of these two terms is certainly unusual. One would expect them to be the other way around, Reconciliation and Justification, by thinking first of the reconciliation of God through Christ, and accordingly, of the justification through him. ... The title Justification and Reconciliation is put like to indicate that the true presentation of the subject must be along lines that *exclude the idea that God is brought around from wrath to mercy through Christ.*" (I, 2). Compare the extensive description and interpretation of Ritschl´s doctrine in "*Lehre und Wehre*"1894, p. 218ff; 1895, p. 97ff.

of the divine majesty and therefore implied eternal indebtedness.[37] Duns Scotus (died 1308) on the other hand taught that Christ's achievement only has a finite value, but has been accepted by God as infinite[38] in his freedom of divine omnipotence. This not only applies to the actual Scotists but also for Thomist theologians like Durandus. Thomas himself laid the foundation for this theory of Acceptilation despite his "*satisfactio superabundans*," because he taught that God is able to forgive sin even without satisfaction because He is Most High.[39] The acceptance theory[40] has later been picked up by the

---

[37] *Vides igitur quomodo vitae haec* (namely the God-Man) *vincat omnia peccata, si pro illis detur.* II,14. (You see then how this life (namely the God-Man) overcomes all sins, if it is given for them.) And just before that: *Anselm: Cogita etiam, quia peccata tantum sunt odibilia, quantum sunt mala; et vita ista tantum amabilis est, quantum est bona. Unde sequitur; quia via vita ista plus est amabilis quam sint peccata odibilia. Boso: Non possum hoc non intellegere. Anselmus: Putasne tantum bonum tam amabile posse sufficere ad solvendum, quod debetur pro peccatis totius mundi? Boso: Imo plus potest in infinitum.* (Think also, because sins are only hated as much as they are evil; and this life is only lovable as much as it is good. Therefore, it follows; because this life is more lovable than sins are hateful. Boso: I cannot fail to understand this. Anselmus: Do you think that such a great and lovable good can be enough to fully pay what is owed for the sins of the whole world? Boso: Yes, it can do infinitely more.) There will be further mention of Anselm's denial of *obedientia activa* when covering the *obedientia activa* of Christ.

[38] Duns Scotus says (cited III, 19): *Quod attinet ad meriti sufficientia, fuit profecto illud finitum, quia causa ejus finita fuit, videlicet voluntas naturae assumtae et summa gloria illi collatga. Non enim Christus quatenus Deus meruit, sed in quantum homo. Proinde si exquiras, quantum valuerit Christi meritum secundum suffientiam, valuit procul dubio quantum fuit a Deo acceptatum. Siquidem divina acceptatio est potissima causa et ratio omnis meriti.* (See Schmid, on the date indicated, 1st edition, p. 103). (As for the sufficiency of merit, it was definitely finite, because its cause was finite, namely the will of the assumed nature and the highest glory conferred upon it. For Christ did not merit as God, but as man. Therefore, if you inquire how much Christ's merit was worth in terms of sufficiency, it doubtless was worth as much as it was accepted by God. Indeed, divine acceptance is the most powerful cause and reason for all merit).

[39] Compare Gerhard III, 13.

[40] The church fathers refer to this as acceptilation theory (in German: *Acceptationstheorie*).

Remonstrants.[41] Calvin, too, is thrown back to the acceptance theory by his false doctrine of predestination. For Calvin, Christ's merit, as a human's merit, only gains full value through predestination. Compare Antithesis No. 7, p. 117, Calvin's words in Gerhard III, 75.[42]

---

[41] Limborch polemicizes against the *satisfactio plenaria* thus: *Satisfactio Christi dicitur, qua pro nobis poenas omnes luit peccatis nostris debitas, asque perferendo et exhauriendo divinae justitiae satisfecit. Verum illa sententia nullum habet in Scriptura fundamentum. Mors Christi vocatur sacrificium pro peccato; atqui sacrificia non sunt solutiones debitorum neque plenariae pro peccatis satisfactiones; sed illis peractis conceditur gratuita paccati remissio.* (*Theol. christ.* III, 21,6). (The satisfaction of Christ is said to be that by which He paid all the penalties owed by our sins for us, and by enduring and exhausting, He satisfied the divine justice. However, this opinion has no foundation in Scripture. The death of Christ is called a sacrifice for sin; but sacrifices are not payments of debts nor complete satisfactions for sins; but after they are offered, free remission of sin is granted). Christ's sacrifice suffices: *primo, respectu voluntatis divinae, quae ad generis humani liberationem nihil ultra requisivit, sed in unica hac victima acquievit.* (22,5). (First, respecting the divine will, which required nothing more for the liberation of the human race, but was content with this one victim.)

[42] The quote in context Inst. II, 17, § 1: *Equidem fateor, si quis simpliciter et per se Christum opponere vellet judicio Dei, non fore merito locum, quia non reperietur in homine* (Calvin nestorianizes here the same as Scotus) *dignitas, quae possit Deum promereri. [...] Nam Christus non nisi ex Dei beneplacito quidquam mereri potuit. Sed quia ad hoc destinatus erat, ut iram Dei sacrificio suo placaret suaque obedientia deleret transgressiones nostras, in summa, quando ex sola Dei gratia (quae hunc nobis constituit salutis modum) dependet meritum Christi non minus apte quam illa humanis omnibus justitiis opponitur.* (In fact, I admit that if someone wanted to compare Christ simply and by himself against the judgment of God, He would not be worthy in that place, because no dignity can be found in man (Calvin Nestorianizes here the same as Scotus) which can earn God's favor. ... For Christ could earn nothing except by the good pleasure of God. But because He was destined for this, to appease God's wrath with his sacrifice and to blot out our transgressions by his obedience, in conclusion, when the merit of Christ depends solely on God's grace (which has established this way of salvation for us), the merit of Christ is no less apt than all human justice is opposed to it.) Against this it should be said: It is true that God did not force, but in his free mercy, gave Christ to the world as their Savior; but to deduce from this that Christ's merit has no value in itself, but only obtains value through God's pleasure or ordinance, is conjecture and incompatible with Scripture. Where the Bible says that

The Papists mutilate the atonement in many ways. They claim that all people must serve their temporal sentence [or, do penance] for all their sins which they have committed after their Baptism, either in this life or in purgatory. Therefore, they deny that through Christ's merit all debt of all sins of mankind is covered. Furthermore, what they do accept of Christ's merit is supposed to only benefit people because of their own improvement and sanctification. This way, they render all of Christ's merit useless. Furthermore, the Papist sacrifice of the Mass, in which supposedly the body and blood of Christ must be sacrificed in an unbloody way forevermore, is a denial of the sacrifice of Christ given once and given absolutely. The Papist excuse that the sacrifice of mass is a medium of acquisition of the all-sufficient sacrifice of Christ is not valid because the benefit of the sacrifice of Christ is administered through the Gospel and the Sacraments, and it is received by people through faith. Although Papists talk of "overflowing merit" (*satisfactio superabundans*), they give this "overflowing merit" to the pope for safe-keeping, who shares some of it with the people under his terms. Papists also parallel Christ's merits with those of Mary and the saints, "that the saints free us from the temporal punishments for sins, and also from the punishments of purgatory."[43] Thus, the *satisfactio Christi vicaria* is

---

we are purified by Christ's blood, the blood of the Son of God, from all our sins (1 John 1:7. Acts 20:28 and others), it ascribes infinite value to Christ's blood.

[43] See Bellarmin. Compare Quenstedt, *Systema* II, 661. He replies shortly and to the point: *Solus (Christus) ita nos redemit, ut castigatio sit super ipsum, et nos pacem habeamus, Isaiah 53:5. Ergo etiam redemit nos a poenis peccatorum nostrorum temporalibus. Nisi enim et hae essent per Christum solutae et sublatae, nondum pacem haberemus cum Deo. Quidquid enim justificatis hominibus immittitur afflictionis, id non amplius est maledictio et τιμωρία, sed castigatio et paterna δοκιμασία.* (He alone (Christ) redeems us in such a way that the punishment is upon him, and we have peace, Isaiah 53:5. Therefore, He also redeemed us from the temporal punishments of our sins. For if these were not also removed and taken away through Christ, we would not yet have peace with God. For whatever affliction is inflicted upon justified men, it is no longer a curse and punishment, but rather correction and paternal testing.) It is well-known that in Roman Catholic practice the difference between temporal and eternal

being denied by Papists in many ways. Papacy is and remains the one great devilish institution through which vicarious satisfaction is dismissed and mocked under outwardly Christian frills. Compare against the Papists Quenstedt, Antithesis No. 6, pp. 116-117; also Quenstedt, p. 116, second quotation.

In the United States, Hugo Grotius' theory has found widespread attention. According to Grotius (died 1645) God punished the innocent Christ instead of the guilty people not to satisfy his justice but to make an example of Christ, thus to uphold the authority of the Law before mankind and to deter all people from sin.[44] This theory is known as "Governmental theory" and has been incorporated especially into the "New England theory."[45] This theory at least still faintly recognizes satisfaction rendered by Christ – Grotius himself retains the term *satisfactio* – but others carried on to deny any satisfaction rendered to divine justice and to see the nature of reconciliation merely in the moral

---

punishments is often dropped completely in favor of quite simply basing the forgiveness of sins on the merits and intercession of the saints.

[44] Grotius says: *Deus ... cruciatibus et morte Christi uti vlouit, ad statuendum exemplum grave adversus culpas immensas nostrum omnium, quibus Christus erat conjunctissimus, natura, regno, vadimonio.* (*De satisfactione* IV, §18) (God ... wanted to use the sufferings and death of Christ to set a serious example against the immense sins of all of us, with whom Christ was most closely connected, by nature, kingdom, and pledge [or, as a surety]. And before that about the same point: *Poenas infligere et a poenis aliquem liberare ... non est nisi rectoris, in universo Dei.* (II,1.) (To inflict punishment and to free someone from punishment ... is only for the ruler in the universe of God.)

[45] Hopkins, Edwards, the younger, E.A. Park von Andover and others. Hugo Grotius' "Governmental Theory" can be found in essence in the works of German Supranaturalists Stäudlin, Flatt, Reinhard etc. Even Storr cannot avoid it. He calls the "appeasement of God's wrath" through the life and suffering of Christ a "false delusion." "Rather it was intended" (through the punishment of sins in Christ) "to confirm the idea of the holiness of the law, which is true and quite beneficial not just for men in general, but for the purest and most insightful of minds."(*Compendium of Christian Dogmatic* (*Lehrbuch der Christlichen Dogmatik*), ed. Flatt 1803, §91, footnote 9.)

influence which Christ's teaching and example have on people (moral-power view of atonement, moral influence theory).[46]

A great number of thinkers define Christ's teaching and example in varied ways, one example is this: Christ is the representative of mankind and has confessed and repented[47] the sins of mankind perfectly and thus caused God to be inclined to forgive the sins of mankind, as long as they follow Christ in his confessing of sins and repentance.[48] It is hardly worth the effort to present the deviations from the Christian doctrine of reconciliation in detail. As soon as the objective reconciliation of all men through Christ's substitutionary life, suffering, and dying is denied, it becomes obvious that the foundation of Christian doctrine is abandoned. With that denial, one can design [or, formulate] and name his ideas about reconciliation as one will, but that which Christ alone accomplished is always fully or in parts attributed to the actions of mankind. Then, salvation out of grace and for the sake of Christ, Christ's honor as the Savior, and the firm solace of mankind — it is all over once and for all!

It is opportune to mention von Hofmann's doctrine of reconciliation

---

[46] In particular, Horace Bushnell (died 1876) in "Vicarious Sacrifice" Bushnell states: "His (Christ's) work terminates, not in the release of penalties by due compensation, but in the *transformation of character*, and the rescue, *in that manner*, of guilty men from the retributive causations provoked by their sins." (In Hodge, *Systematic Theology* II, 568.) Bushnell concedes, however, that his "moral view" of reconciliation would have no effect on mankind if it was not clothed in "language of the altar," that is to say, if it was not describing Christ as the sacrifice for our sins. Hence, Hodge says about Bushnell: "Toward the end of his book, however, he *virtually* takes it all back." Bushnell says in a later publication, "Forgiveness and Law" God was not able to forgive sins without "making cost to himself." This is why God is willing to pay with the life of his Son; but not in a way that He demanded satisfaction for his justice, but in the same way that a man is only able to truly forgive the one who offended him if he has sacrificed himself for him. Quite rightly, a critic of Bushnell says that this theologizing treats God as if "God were made in the image of man."

[47] Christ is the great Penitent (Campbell in England).

[48] See "*Lehre und Wehre*" 1883, p. 305 ff. 345 ff.

at this point. Hofmann's doctrine is presented on page 117 in his own words. First, Hofmann denies the substitutionary sufferings of Christ, which is what the old theologians call *obedientia passiva*. He appears to place all emphasis on the *obedientia activa* of Christ. It only seems that way. Hofmann's "obedience of Christ" is not the fulfillment of the Law given to mankind, fulfilled in mankind's stead, but it is only Christ's self-conservation in his calling to be the savior. Indeed, truly Hofmann denies all the substitutionary works of Christ, not just the *obedientia passiva* but also the *obedientia activa*. The consequence of this denial of the substitutionary character of the works of Christ is that Christ did not directly gain forgiveness of sins for men. As long as one maintains with the Christian Church, with Scripture as the Church's foundation, that Christ vicariously took on man's duty and punishment, one accepts that Christ brought to light the forgiveness of all mankind in his resurrection, that it is proclaimed in the Gospel and that it is received by man in faith (Luke 24:46-47). In Hofmann's doctrine of reconciliation, there is no trace of this immediate result of Christ's life and suffering. According to Hofmann, Christ was not judged by God in mankind's place; equally [or, consequently], Christ did not bring forgiveness of sins forth from the grave. All He did for the "benefit" of mankind, by means of his self-conservation "even under the most extreme consequences of sin" was to make in his person a beginning of a new holy humanity. For Hofmann, the Gospel gains different content, as well as saving faith obtains a different object. The immediate content of the Gospel and therefore the immediate object of faith is not the forgiveness of sins achieved by Christ, but a piece of history, which is this, that Christ held onto his oneness with God until the end, and has, by doing so, in his person made a beginning of a new, holy humanity. The guilt of sin and the forgiveness of sins fade into the background. This has consequences for the understanding of justification and sanctification through faith: faith is not understood as the appropriation of the forgiveness of sins brought into the light by Christ, but rather, faith is mankind's reception of the message about the restoration and completion of mankind through the "archetypal purpose of the world" [*das urbildliche Weltziel*, the archetypal world-goal] (Christ). Forgiveness of sins is not the immediate objective of faith, but it only makes an appearance in the progress into the new community of life founded by Christ. Even in Hofmann's understanding, it becomes clear that one cannot deny the objective reconciliation achieved by Christ's vicarious satisfaction without mixing [or, confusing] justification and sanctification. Dorner says quite rightly in his characterization of Hofmann's doctrine: "At bottom, sanctification is the principle upon which we have reconciliation"[49] Hofmann's doctrine of the works of Christ is also stated substantially by Frank. Compare the critique of Frank's doctrine in "*Lehre und Wehre*", 1896, pp. 137ff. Further, there is an understanding of sin at the basis of Hofmann's doctrine which is not scriptural. Hofmann sees sin not as trespass against God, and therefore guilt before God, but as an act of losing oneself in the physical world [i.e., the opposite of Christ's self-conservation] and therefore being trapped by some ill [or, evil]. See Hofmann's *'Ansprachen über die Sünde'* (Talks about sin), Baier II, 292-294. Hofmann, when considering reconciliation, is concerned with the overcoming of the power of sin, and not with the cancellation of the judgment [of guilt] and the sentence [of condemnation]. He has no need for the Savior who, instead of mankind, takes on God's wrath and punishment and annuls God's sentence and judgment over mankind. Rather, in accordance with his doctrine of sin, he constructs a Savior who breaks the power of sin in his person, by his self-conservation, even under the extreme consequences of sin, and who makes a beginning for a new holy humanity and thereby guides the stream of humanity back to God. One cannot deny the similarities between Hofmann's theology with that of Menken and Schleiermacher: their essence is the "mystical substitution of the subjective salvation instead of objective reconciliation."

Hase remarks about the modern deviations from the church's doctrine

---

[49] *System der Christlichen Glaubenslehre* (*Systematic Christian Doctrine*), II, 587.

of reconciliation: "Church doctrine expresses the deepest sense of sinfulness together with the highest trust in the eternal mercy of God. Most modern objections are based on a superficial notion of sin. It is easy for someone who does not ponder the extent of his own guilt to argue against the atonement. Someone who is aware of the futility of saving oneself by oneself from evil will gratefully receive the merit of the divine Redeemer."[50]

The Active Obedience of Christ (obedientia Christi activa)

As mentioned before, part of the vicarious satisfaction achieved by Christ is that Christ keeps the Laws given to mankind in their place. In other words: To satisfy God's justice, Christ did not only accept the punishment for the breach of the Law by all people, but He also obeyed the divine Law with his holy life, when it is mankind who should but will not obey. Our guilt as well as our duty have been imputed to Christ. It is opportune to particularly discuss this part of vicarious satisfaction at this point, because it has been pushed into the background or even been ignored in presentations of the doctrine of salvation.

See the following examples:

a) Even Anselm says in *Cur deus homo* II, 11 that Christ's obedience in life is not part of the satisfaction achieved for mankind because Christ, like any other rational being, owed this obedience himself;[51]

---

[50] *Hutterus redivivus*, 6th edition, p. 251.

[51] Philippi draws attention to the fact that Anselm looks beyond his scholastic theory in his life of faith and in his reflections and prayers when he says, for example: "While I did not want to obey, you atoned for me with your obedience; I indulged while you were thirsty" and by saying this, Anselm explicitly attributes the active obedience of Christ to the vicarious satisfaction. Anselm's incorrect statement in *Cur Deus Homos* is this: *Anselmus: Quaerendum est nunc, cujusmodi haec datio debebit esse. Dare namque se non poterit Deo aut aliquid de se quasi non habenti, ut suus sit, quoniam omnis creatura Dei est. Boso: Sic est. Anselmus: Sic ergo intelligenda est haec datio, quia aliquo modo ponet se ad honorem Dei aut aliquid de se, quo modo debitur non*

b) Georg Karg, General Superintendent in Ansbach (died 1576), but

---

erit. *Boso: Ita sequitur ex supra dictis. Anselmus: Sic dicimus, quia habit seipsum ad obediendum Deo, ut perseveranter servando justitiam subdat se ejus voluntati, non erit hoc dare, quod Deus ab illo non exigat ex debito. Omnis enim rationalis creatura debet hanc obendientiam Deo. Boso: Hoc negari nequit. Anselmus: Allo itaque modo oportet ut det se ipsum Deo aut aliquid de se. Boso: Ad hoc nos impellit ratio. Anselmus: Videam us, si forte hoc sit vitam suam dare sive ponere animam suam sive tradere seipsum morti ad honorem Dei. Hoc enim ex debito Deus non exiget ab illo; quoniam namque non erit peccatum in illo, non debebit mori, ut diximus.* (Anselm: We must now inquire what kind of offering this should be. For he will not be able to give himself, or something about himself, to God as if God did not have it [already], so that it might be God's own, since every creature is God's. Boso: So it is. Anselm: This offering must be understood, because in some way he will give himself, or something about himself, to the honor of God, in some way that it would not already have been due. Boso: Yes, it follows from what was said above. Anselm: Thus we say, because he commits himself to obey God, by persistently submitting himself to God's will in upholding justice, it will not be to give what God does not demand from him out of debt. For every rational creature owes this obedience to God. Boso: This cannot be denied. Anselm: Therefore it is necessary that he offer himself or something of himself to God. Boso: Reason drives us to this. Anselm: Let us see if this means to give his life, or to lay down his soul, or to surrender himself to death for the honor of God. For God does not demand this from him out of debt; for since there will be no sin in him, he will not have to die, as we have said.) Anselm clearly excludes the active obedience of Christ from the vicarious satisfaction. The biggest mistake in Anselm's work (*Cur Deus homo*) is, by the way, this: it does not present the doctrine of reconciliation straight from Scripture, but endeavors to develop it with reason. This is also connected with a cumbersome train of thought which has an unpleasant impact. The simple and clear doctrine of the Scripture is strapped onto the torture rack of theological speculation. Anselm's method should not be presented to students of theology as a good, but rather as a cautionary example. We should not overestimate the meaning of Anselm's work for subsequent periods. Although generally accepted, it is misleading to assume that the basic ideas of Anselm's theory have been adopted in the Reformation (an example of this is in the *Handbook of Theological Science* by Zöckler, III, 137, and also in Luthardt, *Comp.*, p. 236). Luther did read Anselm. He calls him "*monachissimus monachus*" (most monk-like monk) *Exeg. opp. lat.*, Erl. XXI, 238. One should still not assume a particular influence of Anselm's on Luther. All that is correct in Anselm's *Cur Deus Homo*, is more approachable and better in the Bible.

who recanted in 1570;[52]

c) A group of theologians of the reformation, by name Joh. Piscator (died 1625);

d) There are more recent theologians who want to limit the active obedience of Christ to the fact that Christ gave himself willingly to be the savior, who suffered willingly, but who deny that Christ fulfilled the Law given to mankind in the place of mankind.[53] See Antithesis, p. 119f.

The *Formula Concordiae* speaks clearly and adroitly (S.D.III, 14-16, p. 612f.) about the *obedientia Christi activa* as an integral part of Christ's

---

[52] Georg Karg (Parsimonius), a Philippist, comes from this sentence: "The law either binds with obedience, or with punishment, but not with both at the same time." It will be demonstrated, shortly, in how far this sentence is misleading. Karg, however, deduces from this sentence: "Because Christ suffered punishment for us, He rendered obedience for himself." Karg's doctrine provoked universal objections, which proves how clearly the truth was seen within the Lutheran Church that the *obedientia activa* is a part of Christ's vicarious satisfaction. Karg was suspended. He travelled to Wittenberg, he stood convicted of his error, moved to recant and reinstated in his office. Recantation by men in power is a relatively rare occurrence in the church, which is why we quote Karg's recantation literally: "Up until this moment, I have been in dispute with many about the essential article of our holy Christian faith about the justification of the sinner before God, the understanding of the imputation of Christ, our mediator of both righteousness and obedience, but now I have been graciously corrected and repudiated by the venerable and expert theologians and doctors in Wittenberg that in the office of mediator his innocence and righteousness in divine and human nature neither could nor should be divided from the obedience in the suffering and the total humiliation of the Son of God, our Lord and Savior Jesus Christ because his death and sacrifice is valued and loved by God, the Father, because of the dignity, the sanctity and the righteousness of the person, who is God and human and innocent: I thank God, the eternal Father of our Lord Jesus Christ, and his incarnate Son and the Holy Ghost, and the venerable Doctors for such fatherly report, and I promise heartily and by the grace of God, that I will refrain from now on from such disputations, and that I will use common and customary speech according to the spirit of God with other Christian teachers with the help and grace of God, according to this recantation, as it happened here in Wittenberg between myself and the mentioned venerable doctors, the 10th of August 1570."

[53] See "*Lehre und Wehre*" 1896, p. 137.

satisfactorial merit when it states: "Because Christ is not alone human but God and human in one indivisible person, He was not under the Law" (that is to say, not obliged to keep the Law, *legi subjectus*), "because He was a lord of the Law and did not suffer and die for his person's sake. His obedience not only in suffering and dying, but also in putting himself, out of free will and in our stead, under the Law, and fulfilling it with such obedience, was all imputed to us in justice, so that God forgives us our sin for the sake of such absolute obedience which He achieved in his works and suffering, in life and death, for us and to God, who renders us pious and just and grants us eternal salvation." Here, the limitation of the *obedientia Christi activa* in terms of "the spontaneous acceptance of suffering" is explicitly rejected.

The doctrine of the *Formula Concordiae* is the doctrine of Scripture. Two things are clearly obvious in the passages in Galatians 4:5-5 and Matthew 5:17ff:

1. That it is about the Law which was given to mankind; here, "law" is not "will of God" addressed at Christ.

2. That Christ was put under this Law, given to mankind, and that He fulfilled it for the salvation of mankind.[54]

---

[54] Philippi is certainly right when he remarks about Galatians 4:4-5: "Israel was ... subjected to the *nomos* [Law] and its statutes, which demanded fulfillment, thus the work of salvation of the Son of God has to be seen as substitutionary fulfillment of the Law" (IV, 2, 300). Just as Stöckhardt: "The Law, under which Israel stood, is the sum of all demands of God from mankind, especially from Israel, all that God wants mankind to do or not to do. And it is the same Law which Christ was subjected to, and He has taken it on, and therefore He has fulfilled all the commandments of God. And it is this obedience that has served our salvation." (L.u.W., 1896, p. 137). In agreement with most of the old theologians, we hold on to Matthew 5:17 as evidence for the *obedientia Christi activa*. To fulfil the Law, τὸν νόμον πληρῶσαι, to reduce this to "with doctrine" does not fully express the phrase. It is arbitrary to restrict δικαίωσιν in Romans 5:18 to merely mean Christ's obedience in suffering. Adam's offense παράπτωμα is contrasted with the δικαίωσιν righteous act of Christ, the very thing through which Christ – in contrast with Adam – presented himself as righteous, the

When more recent theologians, while describing the works of Christ, juxtapose the fulfillment of the Law and the fulfillment of God's will, it includes a *petitio principii* (begging the question). First, one has to understand what the will of God, which Christ has to fulfill, actually is based on Scripture. This will of God does not only, according to Scripture, refer to obedience by suffering but also to vicarious obedience of living, to a positive fulfillment of the Law in the place of mankind. Based on Scripture, the following has to be stated with regard to the righteousness of Christ's life: Christ's righteousness in life is not only a model for us — although it is that, too, since we are to follow Christ, 1 Peter 2:21 — it is also not only a prerequisite for the suffering obedience — although it is that, too, since only the death of a perfect saint has the power for atonement, 1 Peter, 1,:19 — it is an integral part of the merit Christ has offered vicariously to the just God for the reconciliation of humanity. This is the dogma from Scripture in the quoted passages; to recognize and to state this in practice for a Christian life of faith is of the utmost importance, as can be seen in the following words of Luther. Luther says this about Christ's substitutionary fulfillment of the Law: "He satisfied the Law, He fulfilled the Law completely; because He loved God with his whole heart, his whole soul, with all his strength, with his whole mind, and his neighbor like himself" etc., and He carries on "Therefore, when the Law comes to you, brings charges against you, that you have not kept the Law, point to Christ and say: There is the man who did it, I cling to him, He fulfilled it for me, and gave me his fulfillment; so be still" (E.A. 15, 61-62). We pointed out above how Anselm was led forward in his life of faith from his theoretical denial of the *obedientia Christi activa*.

---

obedience of Christ (the ὑπακοη, v. 19) without limitation. Quenstedt says clearly and sharply: δικαίωσιν opponitur παράπτωμα. *Ut ergo* παράπτωμα *est* ἀνομία, *ita* δικαίωσιν *vi oppositionis est* ... ἐννομία *actio* ἔννομος *seu activa Christi obediential.* (Δικαίωμα is opposed to παράπτωμα. Therefore, just as παράπτωμα is lawlessness, so δικαίωμα by way of opposition is lawful conduct ... the action of lawful or active obedience of Christ.) Therefore, it does not go far enough to say like Philippi ad h.l. that there is only "the base" [or, basis or foundation] given for the dogma of the *obedientia activa*.

It remains to examine those objections which were used to exclude Christ's active obedience from being part of his vicarious satisfaction.

It was argued that:

> Christ needed his active obedience because He was bound to fulfill the Law as a true human.

> Reply: This statement denies the personal union (*unio personalis*) of God and human in Christ. It is because of the personal union that human nature is part of the person of the Son of God. The person of the Son of God, however, is not under the Law; consequently, neither is the human nature of Christ which is part of this person. Because the Son of God took on human nature, He did not come under the Law, but He did lift this human nature by making it part of his divine person from under the Law onto the throne of the divine majesty. The fact that Christ still came under the Law (γενόμενος ὑπό νόμον), happened as a consequence of a particular action which, although it coincided chronologically with the incarnation, is nevertheless objectively different from it in Scripture: the humiliation, Philippians 2:5-8. God put his Son under the Law, and his Son subjected himself to the Law for all people and for our salvation, Galatians 4:4-5, Psalm 40:7-9. This is how obedience to the Law came about (δικαίωμα, ὑπακοῆς, Romans 5:18.19) which Christ can and wants to pass on to mankind. Even in the state of humiliation, Christ explicitly declares himself as one who in his person stood above the Law, Matthew 12:8. See Quenstedt, p. 118.

> Scripture ascribes the salvation of mankind to the pouring out of Christ's blood, and therefore to the *obedientia passiva*.

> Reply: Not exclusively! Although the *obedientia passiva* is being emphasized in passages like 1 Peter 1:19, Colossians 1:14 and others, there are also passages in which salvation is ascribed to the *obedientia activa*, Romans 5:18-19, Psalm 40:7-9. None of these passages are to be understood exclusively. See Gerhard, pp. 118-

119.

Divine justice is fully satisfied through the *obedientia passiva*. God would demand too much if He demanded not only payment by Christ for the breach of the Law but also the fulfillment of the Law. *Lex obligat vel ad obedientiam vel ad poenam* (the law obliges either to obedience or to punishment).

Reply: This particular objection, which seeks to deal with this question with reason but ignores the relevant passages in Scripture, does not even do justice to human reason. Even in human law, the suffering of a punishment for the breach of law is not fulfillment of law, no *conformitas cum lege*. A thief who has served the legal punishment for his theft does not then turn into a person who has complied with the law, i.e. who has not committed theft. Even less is the serving of punishment for the breach of the divine Law a fulfillment of the Law before God. Who can say of the damned in hell who suffer the punishment for breaking divine Law that they thus fulfill the divine Law of which the sum is: to love God with all thy heart and thy neighbor as thyself? The sentence *lex obligat vel ad obedientiam vel ad poenam* is appropriate when it is necessary to emphasize that man cannot refuse obedience to the Law without penalty when considering the case before any transgression of the law has already occurred. If presenting what the Law demands of the fallen human, this must be said: *lex obligat et ad poenam et ad obedientiam* (the Law obliges both to punishment and to obedience). See Mentzer, p. 118.[55]

---

[55] Even clearer in Quenstedt, *Systema*, 1715, II, 407. Quenstedt states: *Lex obligat vel ad poenam vel ad obedientiam, nimirum creaturas rationales nondum in peccatum prolapsas, v.g. sanctos angelos obligat tantum ad obedientiam, non vero ad poenam. Adamum in statu innocentiae tantum obligavit ad obedientiam, non autem simul ad poenam (nisi sub conditione). Ubi enim nulla est transgressio, ibi poena locum non habet. Sed creaturas rationales in peccatum prolapsas lex obligat ad poenam et ad obedientiam; ad obedientiam, quia sunt creaturas rationales; ad poenam, quia sunt in*

The doctrine that Christ fulfilled the Law vicariously for all people could damage morals because nobody needs to fulfill the Law by themselves anymore.

Reply: This argument also allows one to deny the *obedientia passiva*, the vicarious suffering of punishment by Christ, whilst assuming that people are not frightened of hell anymore and therefore do no more penance when they hear that Christ has already served the sentence for all sins. This objection reveals great spiritual blindness and has been disproved *ex professo* by the Apostle Paul, Romans 6:1ff. See Gerhardt, p. 118f.; especially Quenstedt, Systema II, 407.

Christ's Sacrifice and the Sin Offerings of the Old Testament

Scripture clearly states that the sin offerings of the Old Testament are types of Christ's sacrifice.

In Hebrews 10:1 it says in relation to the annual and daily sacrifices of the Old Testament: "For the law having a shadow (σκιάν = shadow outline, image) of the good things to come and not the very image of the things (οὐκ αὐτὴν τὴν εἰκόνα τῶν πραγμάτων = not itself the image of the matters)." There is no doubt in the following verses what is

---

peccatum prolapsae. Juri pobligationis ad obedientiam per lapsum nihil quidquam decessit, quin notius nova obligatio, videlicet et poenam propter peccatum sustinendam, eidem accessit. Christus legitur et Adae et nostrum omnium loco sese sistens, legem perfecte implevit et poenas peccatorum nostrorum in se recepit. (The Law binds either to punishment or to obedience rational creatures who have not yet fallen into sin. For example it binds the holy angels only to obedience, but not to punishment. He bound Adam in the state of innocence only to obedience, but not at the same time to punishment (except under a condition). For where there is no transgression there is no punishment. But rational creatures who have fallen into sin are bound by the Law to punishment and obedience; to obedience because they are rational creatures; to punishment because they have fallen into sin. Nothing of the obligation of the people to obedience to the Law passed away through the fall, but a new obligation, that is to say, to bear the punishment for sin, was added to them. It is read that Christ, standing in the place of Adam and all of us, completely fulfilled the Law and took upon himself the punishment for our sins.)

meant by "shadow" and "image". In v 1b-14, it is explained that true atonement for sins can only be ensured by Christ's self-sacrifice and not by the sacrifices of the Old Testament. V 4: "For it is not possible that the blood of bulls and goats could take away sins;" also v11. The taking away of sins happened "through the offering of the body of Jesus Christ once for all," v10; also v12:14. The sacrifices of the Old Testament were thus only types of the sacrifice of Christ. In them the objective atonement of sins was not fulfilled, but they were an actual indication of the objective atonement which is fulfilled in the sacrifice of Christ. The sacrifices of the Old Testament have been appropriately called "prophetic acts" which means: in the same way that in many passages in the Old Testament the reconciliation of mankind through Christ is foretold, there is the same prophecy in the act in which animals were sacrificed as sin-offerings as commanded by God. The essential difference between these sacrifices and those of pagan cults lies in this exemplary character and in the prophecy of the sacrifices in the Old Testament. Pagans attributed real power of atonement to their sacrifices; the sacrifices in Israel had their significance in the fact that they were prophecies of Christ's sacrifice. There appear to be contradictory statements in regard to the power of sacrifice in the Old Testament. On one hand, we read in Hebrews 10:4f: "For it is not possible that the blood of bulls and goats could take away sins", but on the other we read in Leviticus 17:11f: "I have given it (namely the animal blood) to you upon the altar to make atonement for your souls; for it is the blood that makes atonement for the soul." The explanation becomes clear. It is not the animal expiated in itself; it is expiated typically, which means it illustrated Christ's sacrifice for the Israelites and offered them, by means of God's mercy, the atonement as it would be fulfilled by Christ. See Kromayer, p. 109. This is how a faithful Israelite received forgiveness of sins through the right understanding of the sacrifices in the Old Testament.

About the use, custom, and power of the sacrifices of the Old Testament see Baier, §7, nota b, p. 108; Quenstedt and Dannhauer, p.

108f.[56]

To Whom and For Whom Christ Offered Atonement

The question to whom Christ offered atonement has been previously answered sufficiently: namely God, inasmuch as holiness and justice belong to God. Atonement has been offered up to divine justice. Divine justice is not present threefold [or, does not exist three times]. Rather, the divine justice of the Father, the Son, and the Holy Spirit is one and the same justice.

Therefore, the early church fathers are right in saying that Christ offered atonement unto himself also. Baier: "Inasmuch as Christ offered atonement, He must be looked upon as a mediator; inasmuch as He himself demanded atonement, He must be understood as God himself, the author and the avenger of the Law who in his substance is

---

[56] The interpretation of all the separate parts of the sacrificial ceremonies in the Old Testament far exceeds the scope of a dogmatic compendium. It is worth recalling that the vicarious satisfaction (atonement) through Christ is clearly depicted in all its main points in the sacrifices of the Old Testament. We summarized above what Scripture says about vicarious satisfaction in three points: 1. God in his inviolable justice demands of mankind the fulfillment of his Law, and the transgressors of the Law forfeit life. 2. Christ, by putting himself in the place of mankind, satisfies God's justice in his active and passive obedience. 3. God is reconciled with mankind through Christ's vicarious works and suffering. All of this is clearly displayed in the sacrifices of the Old Testament, particularly in the ceremonies of the great Day of Atonement. 1. The inviolable sanctity and justice of God is expressed when God demands a sacrifice from the transgressors who breach his Law, by killing the sacrificial animals and by bringing their blood in front of him (i.e. to the altar in the inner sanctum on the Day of Atonement). 2. This was a substitutionary act, which means that it was really the person who was meant to die and not the animal. This was expressed by the person laying his hands on the innocent sacrificial animal, confessing his sins, and transferring his sin onto the animal. 3. It is obvious that God accepted the sacrifice as an atonement because He calls the blood of the sacrificial animal the blood of atonement, Leviticus 17:11: "I have given it to you upon the altar to make atonement for your souls; for it *is* the blood *that* makes atonement for the soul." This reconciliation was represented in outward signs, for example, when on the Day of Atonement the goat, after the misdoings of the people were confessed and transferred onto his head, was led into the desert and set free.

absolutely just with the Father and the Holy Spirit." Baier III, § 10, nota a, p. 120. It is a biblical understanding that the one who offers atonement, and the one who receives it are one and the same, 2. Corinthians 5:19. One must reject Origen's peculiar notion, which smacks of dualism, that Christ paid a ransom to the devil.[57]

Compare this with Quenstedt III, 112, who elaborates: by God's punishment, the devil is only the jailer of people, not their lord and judge who is due a ransom. *Soli deo, non diabolo, λύτρν, persolvendum erat.*

The answer to the question for whom Christ achieved atonement is:

a) not for himself, Baier §10, nota b, p. 120; Kromayer, p. 120; Antithesis p. 120;

b) not for the angels, neither the good nor the bad ones, Antithesis p.120, No. 1-2, but

c) for mankind, that is to say all humans, Baier §10, nota c, p. 120f.

The fact that Christ offered satisfaction for all people has already been generally discussed in the explanation of the *gratia universalis* (III, 6-

---

[57] Origen asks about Matthew 20:28 "τίνι δέ ἔδωκε τήν ψυχήν αὐτοῦ λύτρον αντί πολλῶν"and answers:οὐ γαρ δή τώ θεω. He asks furthermore: μή τι οὖν τψ πολλών and answers: οὗτος γάρ εκράτει ἡμών, ἕως δοζη τό ὑπέρ ἡμών αὐτψ λύρον, ή τού ιησού ψυχή κτλ. But that it is a great error to make this doctrine of Origen the actual doctrine of the church until Anselm is proved in "*Lehre und Wehre*" 1883, p. 308 ff. Even Origen does not merely speak of the ransoming of mankind by handing over the ransom to the devil, but also teaches a reconciliation of God, which took place through the fact that Christ, through the sacrifice of his body, made God gracious to man. About Romans 3:23. Compare Thomasius, *History of Doctrine*, I, 288. The error of the church fathers, who are afflicted by these strange Origenist ideas, lies in the fact that they add rationalist conclusion to the truth of scripture. From the scriptural truth that sinners are subjected to the power of the devil through God's just judgment (1 Corinthians 5:5; Hebrews 2:14, etc.), they concluded that the devil had gained a right over the sinners for himself and therefore could demand a ransom. The fact that merciful salvation of all people requires consideration of the holiness and justice of God, is absent in the church fathers' understanding.

10). It is easy to summarize what Scripture says about the perfection of Christ's satisfaction: The satisfaction offered by Christ is both intensively and extensively perfect. It is intensively perfect inasmuch as God is fully reconciled with mankind because of Christ's actions, and that is why there are no more actions needed from people but faith alone to be reconciled with God. Christ's satisfaction is also extensively perfect inasmuch as complete reconciliation extends not only to the blessed and the chosen ones [the elect] but also to the lost souls.

Any restriction of the extensive perfection of reconciliation or satisfaction defies Scripture, which clearly names every one of the following as atoned through Christ:

a) the whole world, John 1:29, 1 John 2:1, 2f and all people 1 Timothy 2:6f, and

b) also the lost ones, 1 Corinthians 8:11, Romans 14:15, 2 Peter 2:1f. See Quenstedt, p. 121.

Calvinist teaching is actually unbiblical because Christ's satisfaction is explicitly restricted to the chosen ones [the elect], as is the teaching of those who do talk about universal satisfaction but who restrict God's intention to grant people this satisfaction, that is to render people truly believing and blessed, to just the chosen ones [the elect]. The so-called "hypothetical Calvinists" also play with this "universal satisfaction." See further elaborations in Quenstedt, Antithesis No.6, p. 123f.

Scripture states clearly that God ensures the saving atonement even for the lost souls, Acts 7:51, Matthew 23:37. In fact, it is like this: The motivation for restrictions to the intensive and extensive perfection of the satisfaction offered by Christ is not found in Scripture but in rationalistic speculation. All of these semi-pelagian synergistic arguments against the *sola gratia* disintegrate into one argument: "If people can only be converted and saved by Christ and by God's grace, then all people would be converted and saved indeed, but this does not happen. *Ergo.*" All the Calvinist argumentation against the *universalis gratia* is founded in this sentence: "If God really wanted to convert and save all people by his grace and in Christ, then all people would be saved. *Ergo.*" This is not evidence from Scripture but rationalistic precociousness.

In all disputes about the sufficiency of the satisfaction gained by Christ, another question has arisen, namely, if a droplet of Christ's blood was sufficient ransom for the sins of the world. The Papists have answered this question in the affirmative in order to use the "surplus" of Christ's gain for trade. See Quenstedt, p. 121. Lutherans have answered this question in the affirmative, inasmuch as the blood of Christ is the blood of the son of God and therefore has infinite value in even the smallest quantity. It is not quantity but quality of the blood shed by Christ that gives it its infinite value for salvation. Others who dealt with this question in great detail and who tried to refer it to its dogmatic meaning have added that salvation can be attributed to a single drop of Christ's blood, not by itself (absolute) but respectively (respective), namely as part of Christ's suffering and death, and inasmuch as each drop of blood contains and represents the power of Christ's suffering and death. Apart from Luther, see also B. Meisener, pp. 121-122, and Joh. Hermann's hymn: "Where should I flee", *St. Louis Hymn Book*, Nr 230, V.9: "Your blood, the noble liquid", further Quenstedt, *Systema* II, 467-470, where rich historical dogmatic material has been assembled, which is partially repeated in Philippi IV, 2, pp. 95-98. Quenstedt suitably reminds us in this presentation about the principle: "*Solus Deus optime novit, quantum ad plenam perfectamque pro peccatis nostris satisfactionem requiratur et cur Filium suum unigenitum tot plagas, nec plures nec pauciores pati, nec minus sanguinis ac fuit effusum, effundi voluerti. [...] Quantum justitia Dei acceptare debuerit, on ex nostra phantasia, sed ex Dei verbo depromendum est*" (l.c.p.469). (God alone knows very well what is required for full and perfect satisfaction for our sins, and why He willed his only begotten Son to suffer so many plagues, neither more nor fewer, and to shed no less blood than was actually shed. [...] How much God's justice required is not to be determined by our own ideas, but must be drawn from God's Word.) In short, we consider all of Christ's deeds and suffering as they are described in the Bible to be the ransom through which God's justice is satisfied. If we attribute redemption to one part of the work of redemption, it can only be understood not exclusive, but inclusive of all the other parts.

Following the example of the Old Testament (Exodus 30:7-8, Leviticus16:12-13.[58]) the offering of intercessions on people's behalf is part of the sacerdotal office of Christ in the state of humiliation. In Isaiah 53:12 *intercessio* is mentioned next to *satisfactio* in its description of the work of Christ: "And He bore the sin of many, and made intercession for the transgressors." Christ intercedes for

a) all people, even the godless, whose sins He had born also. Example: Luke 23:34 (*intercession generalis*),

b) in particular for the faithful as He is the head of the church. Example: John 17 (*intercession specialis*).

The purpose of intercession is the granting of the forgiveness of sins and the preservation of forgiveness, as is shown in the quotes and examples. The apparent contradiction between Luke 23:34 and John17:9 is resolved by 1 Timothy 4:10. See Baier § 11, p.123. In the sacerdotal office of Christ during the days of the flesh [on earth], both natures work together, which has been described in the dogma of the communication of the attributes, in particular in the third genus. See Baier §12, p. 123f; Gerhard, Calov, Quenstedt, pp. 124-126.

The Sacerdotal Office in the State of Exaltation

Christ's sacerdotal office did not end at the [end of his] state of humiliation. Scripture also explicitly attributes the office to Christ in his state of exaltation. According to Hebrews 7:24 Christ has "an unchangeable priesthood (ἀπαράβατον ἔχει τὴν ἱερωσύνην)." It concludes in verse 25: "Therefore He is also able to save to the

---

[58] Philippi IV, 2, p. 340: "In Scripture, smoke [incense burning] is the symbol of prayer." Psalm 141:2, Revelation 5:8.

uttermost (εἰς τὸ παντελὲς) those who come to God through Him."

What exactly is the sacerdotal office of Christ in the state of exaltation about? It is not about the repetition of the atoning sacrifice. Scripture rejects this explicitly in Romans 6:9-10 and Hebrews 9:12, 15; 7:27. (*Intercessio Christi in statu exaltationis non est satisfactoria*), but in his intercession for the saved so that they may once and for (ἐφάπαξ) all take part in salvation (*Intercessio Christi in statu exaltationis est applicatoria*). Scripture makes this very clear in Hebrews 7:24-25. (ἐντυγχάνειν ὑπὲρ αὐτῶν who come to God through Him). 1 John 2:1 (παράκλητον ἔχομεν πρὸς τὸν πατέρα Ἰησοῦν Χριστὸν) Romans 8:34 (ἐντυγχάνει ὑπὲρ ἡμῶν). The intercession is about the gathering and the preservation of the church. Baier is purposefully unclear about whether Christ's intercession for the saved is expressed in words and pleas – obviously heavenly words and pleas – (*intercessio verbalis*), or whether it is expressed in God's continuous mercy for us which Christ gained in the state of humiliation (*intercessio realis*). See Baier §13, nota d, pp. 126-127. However, one would do well here, like always, not to stray too far from the exact wording of Scripture. According to Scripture, Christ speaks in his own words not just through his gain, Hebrews 7:25: "He always lives to make intercession for them", θεῷ, πάντοτε ζῶν εἰς τὸ ἐντυγχάνειν ὑπὲρ αὐτῶν; Romans 8:34 (literally translated): "who is even at the right hand of God, who also makes intercession for us;"[59] 1 John 2:1: "We have an Advocate (παράκλητον) with the Father, Jesus Christ." It goes without saying that this intercession is not "supplication on his knees" because it is the intercession by the one "who is at the right hand of God," Romans 8:34. One would leave Scripture behind by only hearing Christ's gain and not Christ himself. Quenstedt defines all the reductions of Biblical teaching, pp. 127-128. Regarding the Socinians and their followers, it must be said that they entirely deny Christ's sacerdotal office in the state of humiliation (the offering of an atoning sacrifice through

---

[59] The repeated use of ὅς καὶ distinguishes the intercession clearly from the sitting on the right hand of God and depicts it thus as a different act.

vicarious satisfaction). See Quenstedt, Antithesis, p. 110. They transfer Christ's sacerdotal office into the state of exaltation, which they understand to be merely Christ's assistance for mankind to achieve salvation by themselves by following Christ's Word and example and by keeping from sin and living a pious life.[60]

Papists distort the dogma of the sacerdotal office of Christ in the state of exaltation:

a) by the so called "unbloody" repetition of Christ's sacrifice in the sacrifice of mass, by which they deny the ἐφάπαξ of Scripture (Hebrews, 7:27, 9:12. Romans 6:10. Hebrews 10:14), see A. Osiander, p. 109f.,

b) by letting Mary and the saints intercede for people by their merits[61] and therefore putting aside Christ as the intercessor.

To answer the question if Christ carries on to intercede for his own people even after the Day of Judgment, see Feuerborn and Calov, p.

---

[60] *Catechesis Racoviensis,* Question 476-479. Question 479 asks: *Qui* (in which way) *expiationem peccatorum nostrorum Jesus in coelis peragit? And the answer: Primum a peccatorum poenis nos liberat, dum virtute et potestate, quam a patre plenam et absolutam consecutus est, perpetuo nos tuetur et iram Dei interventu suo quodammodo a nobis arcet, quod Scriptura exprimit, dum ait, eum pro nobis interpellare. Deinde ab ipsorum peccatorum servitute nos liberat, dum eadem potestate ab omni flagitiorum genere nos retrahit et avocat: id vero in sua ipsius persona nobis ostendendo, quid consequatur is, qui a peccato desistit: vel etiam alia ratione nos hortando et monendo, nobis opem ferendo, ac interdum puniendo, a peccati jugo exsolvit.* (How (in which way) does Jesus in heaven perform the expiation of our sins? And the answer: First, He frees us from the punishments of sins, by constantly protecting us with the power and authority which He has obtained in full and absolute measure from the Father, and in a way, He wards off the wrath of God from us through his intervention, as Scripture expresses it, when it says, He intercedes for us. Then, He frees us from the slavery of sin, by the same power drawing us away from every kind of disgraceful behavior and calling us back: this He shows us in his own person, what follows for one who desists from sin; or by other means encouraging and warning us, offering us help, and sometimes by punishing us, He frees us from the yoke of sin.)

[61] Bellarmine in Quenstedt II, 1444: *Sancti ex meritis praecedentibus impetrare possunt et sibi et aliis id, quod orando petunt.* (Based on their past merits, saints can obtain for themselves and for others what they ask in prayer.)

127. Feuerborn answers this questions with 'No', Calov with 'Yes'. Quenstedt agrees with Calov. However, the passages in Scripture which are about Christ's intercession assume the conditions before the Day of Judgment, namely the gathering and preservation of the church. There is no evidence in Scripture for Calov's and Quenstedt's views. When referring to Hebrews 7:25 where it says, "He always lives to make intercession for them", Gottfried Hoffmann (*Synopsis Theologiae*, p. 540) notes: "In this verse and the immediately preceding words, this (the intercession) appears to be restricted to the coming to God, inasmuch as it occurs with repentance and faith." One has to agree with Hoffmann.

The Royal Office of Christ

Scripture reveals the wonderful fact that the rule over all people is given over to Christ, the redeemer of mankind and all creation. Matthew 28:18: "All authority has been given to Me in heaven and on earth;" the Father "put all things under His feet," Ephesians 1:22. 1 Corinthians 15:27, Psalm 8:7, Daniel 7:13-14. Christ's royal office (*officium Christi regium*) consists of Christ being God and human, and of Christ ruling everything in heaven and on earth.

Since when is Christ the king? This is a question Scripture answers in short thus: According to his divine nature, Christ is the ruler of all things with the Father and the Holy Spirit as long as there are living beings, John 1:1-3. Colossians 1:15-17. In his human nature, Christ has been ruler since He became human through the personal union of the human with the divine nature. In other words: even in his human nature, Christ is a born king. Isaiah 9:6, Matthew 2:2, Luke 1:33, Micah 5:1, John 18:37. In the state of humiliation, there is no shortage of examples of the exertion of royal power (miracles, forgiveness of sins, the foundation of ministry, and the Sacraments, etc.). Since becoming human, Christ only entered the full exertion [or, use or exercise] of royal government in the state of exaltation, Ephesians 1:20-22. 4:10,

Psalm 8:6-10. See Baier, §18, p. 133. Calov, p. 128.[62]

More of this has been discussed in the teaching about the states of Christ, particularly under the heading "Seated at the right hand of God." Because "*Sedere ad dextram Dei dicitur, qui totum terrarum orbem, imprimis ecclesiam, potenter et provide gubernat omnibusque hostibus suis dominator* (He is said to sit at the right hand of God, who powerfully and providently governs the whole world, especially the church, and has dominion over all his enemies.), Psalm 110:1-2, Acts 2:34-35." (Baier, after the Formula of Concord, III, 97ff.) Christ's reign is divided into the kingdoms of power, grace and glory, depending on the state of the subjects,[63] and, due to this, the different ways of governing.[64] Christ rules with his power (*regnum potentiae*) those who do not believe and who have not accepted his Gospel, as well as brute animals for whom the Gospel does not exist; those who believe and who have accepted the Gospel, and who are the foundation of Christ's church on earth, He rules through his Word revealed in grace (*regnum gratiae*); those who were subjects in his kingdom of mercy in this life, He fills with his glory in the life to come (*regnum gloriae*).

---

[62] Quenstedt expresses this like this: "*Durationis terminus a quo spectatur vel secundum divinitatem vel secundum humanitatem. Secundum divinitatem terminus a quo est exestentia objectorum regibilium, juxta humanitatem vero ratione possessionis potestatis et majestatis regiae divinae nec non juris ad universale dominium primum conceptionis momentum…aut ratione universalis et incessantis imperii ac plenari majestatis regiae usus session ad dextram Dei Patris.*" (*Systema* II, 378) (The starting point is considered either according to divinity or according to humanity. According to divinity, the starting point is the existence of the governable objects, while according to humanity, on the basis of possession of divine power and royal majesty, as well as the right to universal dominion, the first moment of conception … or on the basis of universal and unceasing dominion and full use of the royal majesty, sitting at the right hand of God the Father.)

[63] *Pro diversa ratione* (state, condition) *eorum, quos rex Christus sibi subjectos respicit.* (For the different reason (state, condition) of those whom Christ the King regards as his subjects."

[64] *Pro diverso regnandi modo.* (For different ways of ruling)

With this in mind, the three distinct kingdoms are the kingdom of power for the whole universe and all creatures (see the description of this kingdom in Baier. §15, p. 129f.), the kingdom of grace for all Christians[65] which we tend to call the church (Baier, §16, p. 129f.), and the kingdom of glory which is the eternal continuation of the kingdom of mercy (Baier, §17, p. 132f.). Angels belong in this kingdom, Hebrews 12:22-23.[66] It should be recalled that, in public preaching, it is not enough to rely on the naming of these three kingdoms or sketching an outline of them when dealing with this subject, but – as our fathers used to – to "pull out all the stops." Of course, these stops are not our own but those of the Holy Bible, which is very detailed in its descriptions. In particular, one has to describe heaven in such a way that "awakens the enthusiasm in all Christians to enter heaven."

We need to consider the unity as well as the difference of these kingdoms on the ground of Scripture. These kingdoms are one, inasmuch as Christ is the one and only Lord in all of them, and He reigns them perfectly consistently, which means according to his will and by his divine power and majesty. Passages like Ephesians 1:21 and Philippians 2:9-11 point to this unity, and it is of great practical importance to keep this in mind. It is indeed a great comfort to know that sun, moon, and stars; air, fire, and weather; the devil, and all enemies are subservient to Christ, just as his church and all holy angels are. And regarding the consistent rule, Scripture reveals clearly and precisely that Christ reigns the universe in the interest of the kingdom

---

[65] There is an objective difference when some of the old Lutheran teachers name *only* Christians as the objects of the kingdom of grace, and others count all people as the object of the kingdom of grace. So, for example, Quenstedt, *Systema* II, 348. However, Quenstedt does not mix the kingdom of nature and the kingdom of grace in the way of some old and new heretics, who extend the kingdom of grace to honorable pagans, but Quenstedt wants to say that grace and the means of grace are for all people.

[66] The reign of Christ over the damned can be seen in the *regnum potentiae* (kingdom of power) or the *regnum gloriae* (kingdom of glory), see Baier, § 17, nota c, p. 133.

of grace or the church.[67] In other words: everything in heaven and on earth must serve the foundation and the preservation of church. The kingdoms of this world are the "scaffolds for the building of the church." Matthew 28:18-19: "All authority has been given to Me in heaven and on earth. Go therefore (πορευθέντες οὖν) and make disciples of all the nations;" Luke 2:1-14. Romans 8:28. Corinthians 15:24-25.[68] Baier, §14, nota b, p. 128, reminds us rightly that we must not look at the kingdom of grace and the kingdom of glory as if the use of divine omnipotence was excluded from them. Both require the omnipotent king who is all powerful in his divine and in his human nature. Scripture teaches very clearly that the gathering and the preservation of the church is equivalent to a work of divine faith and therefore also to divine omnipotence. Divine omnipotence is directly related to the church in action,

a. for the development of faith and its preservation in the individual members of the church. Ephesians 1:19: "us who believe, according to the working of His mighty power;" 1 Peter 1:5: "who are kept by the power of God through faith for salvation ready to be revealed in the last time." 2 Corinthians 4:6, Luke 11:21.22.

b. for the outward protection of the church. Matthew 16:18: "the gates of Hades shall not prevail against it" Psalm 2 etc.

We also must consider the differences of the kingdoms. Christ does indeed differentiate his kingdom of grace from the kingdoms of this world when He says in John 18:36: "My kingdom is not of this world. If my kingdom were of this world, my servants would fight, so that I should not be delivered to the Jews; but now my kingdom is not from here. (ἐντεῦθεν=ἐχ τοῦ χόσμου τούτου)." "The church is in the world but not of the world." This means: although the church is in the world (John 17:11,15, 1 Timothy 2:2), it is not like the kingdoms of this

---

[67] Quenstedt: *Regnum potentiae ad regnum gratiae est ordinatum.* (The kingdom of power is ordered to the kingdom of grace.) (*Systema* II, 383)

[68] About this Luther, St Louis edition, VIII, 1166.

world,[69] and it is not built nor reigned in the same way as the worldly kingdoms. Christ preserves the kingdoms of this world by keeping the order of worldly authority and everything belonging to it (outward righteousness, outward power, Romans 13:1-7); but Christ gathers and reigns over his church by his Word and his Sacraments. Christ effects and preserves faith in people only by these means, in which the Holy Spirit is active. (Baier, §16, S.129.) Christ offers his gifts to the church and, in particular, He instituted the office of ministry. (Baier, §16, nota d, S.132.)[70]

Everyone who wants to build the church by means other than the Word and Sacrament acts against Christ's order, and they are fools, because they do not build the church by their self-appointed means, but they destroy it. See Hollaz and A. Osiander, p. 129f. In Scripture, it is not only the kingdom of the world and the kingdom of grace that are to be distinguished. The kingdom of grace is in some passages closely connected with the kingdom of glory: John 5:25, 3:36, Colossians 3:3, Galatians 4:26, Matthew 4:17 etc. However, in other places these are strictly distinguished from each other. See for example 1 John, 3:2, Romans 8:24-25. The decisive difference between both kingdoms lies in the way of recognizing divine things. In the kingdom of grace, all understanding is conveyed by the Word and by faith (*cognitio abstractiva*), while in the kingdom of glory it happens by seeing

---

[69] Phrases "*ex mundo*" *notat id, quod est mundanae indolis.* ("'ex mundo' denotes that which is of a worldly nature" (A. Osiander, in Baier, p. 129)

[70] It is not necessary to concern oneself with whether the appointment or the administration of ministry belongs to the prophetic or the royal office, as mentioned above. See Kromayer, p. 132. The office of ministry belongs to both because Christ teaches and *eo ipso* ("rules" or "reigns in") the church through both. It is far more important to state that Christ is the *only* teacher and regent in his church because preachers can only be *causa ministerialis* who must preach not their own but Christ's Word alone. 1 Peter 4:11: εἴ τις λαλεῖ, ὡς λόγια θεοῦ. Matthew 28:20. Preachers must not teach nor reign the church by their own thoughts. Luther admonishes all preachers to study the Bible well, in particular the pastoral epistles "so that Christians are not ruled with the conceit of the human mind" (E.A. 63,148).

(*cognitio intuitiva*). 1 Corinthians 13:12: "For now we see in a mirror, dimly (ἐν αἰνίγματι), but then face to face (πρόσωπον πρὸς πρόσωπον)." Compare vv. 9-10. It is of utmost practical importance to understand this difference.

All the attempts to rise above the Word and faith in this life and to claim to be seeing are endless sources of false doctrines. It is so in Calvinism on the one hand and in Synergism on the other, as well as in all the modern constructive theology. The major difference between the kingdom of grace and the kingdom of glory lies in the outward state of the members of these kingdoms. In the kingdom of mercy one can only expect lowliness, the cross, and affliction; only in the kingdom of glory, lowliness is turned into glory, Acts 14:22, Matthew 5:10-12, Romans 8:18, Philippians 3:20-21, Matthew 16:24-26, etc. Whoever confuses the kingdoms of grace and glory in this respect turns Christian hope upside down and relies on chiliastic dreams.

The existence of the threefold kingdom of Christ is an article of faith and must therefore be impressed on people. We can recognize only Christ's objectives in the kingdom of power, at least in part, but we cannot see Christ's rule over it. Hebrews 2:8: "But now we do not yet see all things put under him." We cannot see Christ's omnipotence with our own eyes. In fact, it often seems as if "not Christ, but the devil reigns." But this is why Scripture talks so much and in so much detail (angels and devils, the enemies of Christ, brute creatures, etc.) about Christ's *regnum potentiae*, so that we may find comfort and believe it. Compare Baier, § 15, pp. 128-129. Regarding the kingdom of grace, the means of grace are visible by which Christ gathers and preserves this kingdom. But the kingdom itself is invisible; it is inside people's hearts because they believe in Christ through the Holy Spirit, Luke 17:20-21, 2 Timothy 2:19, 1 Peter 2:5. Scripture testifies that there is and always will be a Christian church on earth, Matthew 16:18, Matthew 28:18-20, Isaiah 55:10-11, etc., and because of this scriptural evidence we believe the existence of the church. Regarding the kingdom of glory, see 1 John 3:2: "It has not yet been revealed what we shall be." The kingdom of glory is the object of Christian hope. We have to wait for it in patience,

Romans 5:2, 8, 24-25. According to Scripture, it is part of a righteous Christian life to keep one's gaze firmly fixed on the kingdom of glory, 1 Corinthians 1:7, Philippians 3:20-21. As mentioned before, a servant of the church must not merely mention the kingdom of glory only in passing, but must go into great detail because of the many passages which deal with the eternal life. He should put it in front of all Christians eyes so that they may live their daily lives in the hope of Christ, feel comfort in affliction, and awaken and preserve their sense of the divine. Romans 5:2-11; 8:17-39, and others.

We point to Antithesis, p. 133 when dealing with the various false doctrines which distort the royal office of Christ. Christ's royal office is misrepresented by:

I. all followers of the Nestorian heresy. They halve [or, separate into halves or cut in half] Christ as king by excluding his human nature from the omnipresent reign in the kingdom of power and the kingdom of grace, as do the Papists, the Reformed, and the Reformed sects. This has been extensively demonstrated in the Doctrine of the States of Christ.

II. The modern Kenotics. Despite his divine nature, they exclude Christ in his divine nature from the royal office, reducing his world reign in the state of humiliation, [as if He were] without omnipotence, omnipresence, and omniscience. According to this, the Son of God renounced as the modern theological phrase goes "the divine being and mode of action," although the opposite is attested in John 5:17, John 10:30, John 14:10. This has been described in the doctrine of the States of Christ.

III. Subordination Theologians. They subordinate Christ after the divine nature to the Father ("God in the second sense of the Word"). This is the reason why they take away the reign from Christ in the kingdom of glory. See Kahnis and Hofmann, p. 133. It should be noted: Scripture attributes eternal reign to Christ, Luke 1:33, Hebrews 1:9. On the other hand, it talks of a commitment of the kingdom to the Father on the last day, 1 Corinthians 15:24. This commitment of the kingdom is the transformation of the temporal kingdom, in which Christ reigned in secret through his Word and outward means, into the eternal kingdom which is illuminated by the divine glory as it is revealed in the three persons. Therefore, it does not say about the commitment of the kingdom that "the father (ὁ πατήρ) may be all in all" but that "God (ὁ θεὸς) may be all in all." In this context, see Luther's extensive explanation, p. 130f; also Quenstedt and Dorscheus, pp. 131-132.

IV. All those who in some form or other want to set up human rule in the church. The church is a strict monarchy (Matthew 23:8: "for One is your Teacher, the Christ, and you are all brethren"), in which Christ wants to rule alone and by his Word. The office of ministry given by Christ only holds the power of the Word of God, that is to say, it can only command what is commanded by the Word of God. Those things which are not commanded by God's Word (immediate things), Christians put in order by coming to agreements with each other. The most awful interference in Christ's royal kingdom is Papacy (Antichrist κατ' ἐξοχήν, 2 Thessalonians 2:4).

Others who are transgressing against Christ's sole reign are:

a. all false teachers, insofar as they promote their own words in church (they are called ἀντίχριστοι in 1 John 2:18);

b. all Protestant church congregations with Romanizing tendencies, insofar as they want to subjugate Christians' conscience, either de iure or de facto, under a church regime instead of following the Word of God. This applies not only to the Reformed sects but also to Romanizing Lutherans, like those in Buffalo and Breslau and others, and the followers of a state church.[71]

V. All those who mix the worldly kingdom and the kingdom of grace,

---

[71] See the comprehensive presentation in the lecture "Church and church regiment" Synod of delegates 1896. Report p. 33 ff.

or state and church. Amongst them are counted the ones who:

a. want to turn church into a worldly kingdom, by building church not on God's Word but on all sorts of earthly things that belong to this world (outward power, natural morals, culture, and other things) and who thus take away the church's particular character;

b. those who want to turn state into a spiritual kingdom by intending to rule the state with God's Word and following "Christian principles" rather than reason;

c. all the old and new teachers of false doctrine who dream of the Holy Spirit's grace and mercy having an effect outside the means of grace, of saving heathens without the Gospel, and who therefore mix nature and grace, the kingdom of power and the kingdom of grace. See lately for example Hofmann, in Baier II, 302; III, 230.

VI. The Chiliasts. The thousand-year kingdom of the Chiliasts does not belong in the kingdom of grace, nor in the kingdom of glory, but it is a caricature of both; it belongs in the kingdom of imagination. It turns Christian hope upside down by directing it onto a dream-like glory here on this earth rather than toward the eternal glory in heaven (1 Corinthians 1:7, Philippians 3:20-21, John 17:24, etc.).

Concluding remarks

To summarize the whole doctrine of Christ's works: Christ in his prophetic office is the only teacher to save mankind. Any doctrine which is proclaimed in and by the church but which is not Christ's Word is pseudo-prophetism. Christ in his sacerdotal office is the only redeemer of mankind, who atoned [or, reconciled] all people with God by his vicarious satisfaction. Any reconciliation which humans aim to achieve by their own means is pseudo-reconciliation. Christ in his royal office is Lord over all the world, but in particular over the church, which He reigns alone and by his Word. All government of church which is carried out without the Word of Christ, but which ties the Christian conscience to the human word, is pseudo-government.

Chapter Two

The Reconciliation of God with Man[1]

Outline

I.   Man is in need of reconciliation with God, but is unable to effect it by his own efforts.

    1.   The realm of nature

    2.   The conscience of man

    3.   The Word of God

    4.   Wrath laid upon Christ

II.   Through Christ's vicarious atonement God has reconciled the whole world unto Himself.

    1.   A complete reconciliation with God has been effected.

    2.   A further description of the divine method of the atonement.

    3.   Human criticism of the divine method of the atonement.

    4.   All criticism of the reconciliation effected by Christ comes to nothing.

III.   Man becomes a partaker of this reconciliation through faith in the divine message of the atonement made by Christ.

    1.   Faith is necessary.

    2.   Faith alone is necessary.

    3.   How does a person come to faith in the Gospel of reconciliation?

    4.   The task of the Christian church in the world.

Reconciled to God! These words express the greatest happiness that mortal man can know. Since the Fall the life of man on earth is filled with sorrow and misery. This is taught by Scripture, and this we know from experience. But for everyone who through faith in the Gospel of

---

[1] Franz Pieper, "*Die Versöhnung des Menschen mit Gott,*" *Lehre und Wehre*, Vol. 67, No. 10, October 1921, 289-297. [A lecture to the Southern Illinois District of The Lutheran Church – Missouri Synod, Belleville, IL, October 18-24, 1916.], trans. John Theodore Mueller, from F. Pieper, *What Is Christianity? And Other Essays*, (Decatur, IL: Repristination Press, 1988, second printing in the public domain).

Christ knows that he is reconciled to God, there is really no more unhappiness on earth; for such a one has overcome the world with all its anguish and woe. That which is terrible here on earth holds no terrors for him, for even in the darkest night of tribulation he sees the heavens opened. Poverty, pain, illness, especially chronic and incurable illness, are certainly not easy to bear; but whoever has the assurance of being reconciled to God nevertheless is able to say: "Whom have I in heaven but You? And there is none upon earth that I desire besides You. My flesh and my heart fail; But God is the strength of my heart and my portion forever." (Psalm. 73:25-26)

Death also is no trifle. Against death the whole world is powerless; not even the greatest genius can escape it. The German poet Schiller confesses in a letter to Baron von Humboldt that be knows of no consolation in the face of death. But he who knows that be is reconciled to God can boldly confess even in the hour of death: "O death, where is your sting?" (1 Corinthians 15:55) Above all it is not easy to give oneself up to be stoned, beheaded, or burned. Nevertheless St. Stephen, beholding the open heaven (Acts 7:55) kept a cheerful spirit while he was being stoned to death; and John Huss at Constance confidently commended his spirit into bis Savior's hands in the midst of the flames and was even able to offer up a prayer for his benighted accusers. In discussing this subject, Luther declares: "Whoever knows that God is gracious to him walks through life along a path of roses, even in tribulation, and for him the land flows with milk, honey, and precious wine." (St. L. Ed., II, 1968, §§ 201-205.)

It is God's will that all men enjoy the blessedness of reconciliation with God. Through Christ God has reconciled the world unto Himself, and all who accept this reconciliation in faith possess it fully. (Romans 5:1-3) However, the devil, man's old evil foe, begrudges him this happiness. He endeavors to mislead man either utterly to despise the atonement of Christ or to attempt to establish his own righteousness, as a result of which Christ's reconciliation is forfeited. The consequence is that God must punish the world with dreadful plagues, wars, floods, earthquakes, and other frightful calamities to remind man for what purpose the earth still stands, namely, that he might repent and by faith accept the reconciliation with God which Christ has effected. God graciously grant that not a single one of us may despise the reconciliation which has been brought about at so great a cost — the suffering and death of His incarnate Son. To this end may our discussions at these synodical sessions[2] be of aid to us!

We shall devote our attention to three theses: —

> I. *Man is in need of reconciliation with God, but is unable to effect it by his own efforts.*
>
> II. *Through Christ's vicarious atonement God has reconciled the whole world unto Himself.*
>
> III. *Man becomes a partaker of this reconciliation through faith in the divine message of the atonement made by Christ.*

I.

Our first thesis reads: "*Man is in need of reconciliation with God, but is unable to effect it by his own efforts.*" Let us first consider the statement that *man is in need of reconciliation with God.*

1.

The fact that man is in need of reconciliation with God, or — what amounts to the same thing — that man is the object of God's wrath on account of sin, is borne out by an innumerable host of witnesses. We see God's wrath in the realm of nature, in the conscience of man, and above all in the Word of God.

The realm of nature

In the realm of nature and of human society we find nothing but confusion and chaos, for a condition of ceaseless and universal warfare

---

[2] Ed: A lecture to the Southern Illinois District of The Lutheran Church -- Missouri Synod, Belleville, IL, October 18-24, 1916.

prevails there. The irrational creatures strive against man, while men themselves are constantly engaged in warfare against one another. But this entire state of chaos is a proof of the anger of God because of man's sin, as Holy Scripture clearly teaches. In Genesis 3:17-19 we learn that the thorns and thistles that grow upon the earth as well as all things else that bring hardship and injury upon man and deprive him of his sustenance must be regarded as a consequence and punishment of sin. In Romans. 8:19-23 St. Paul teaches us that the bondage of corruption in which all creatures lie fettered is caused by the sin of man. Likewise death, the dreadful fact that body and soul are torn asunder, or that man, created unto life, must die, finds its cause not in matter itself nor in a necessary transformation of matter, as certain philosophers fancifully speculate, but in God's righteous wrath over sin. This is pictured to us most clearly and impressively in Psalm 90:7: "For we have been consumed by Your anger, And by Your wrath we are terrified."

The fact that wars are waged; that fires, floods, and tempests rage against man and his possessions; that this earth of ours quakes and trembles; that pestilences and famines plague mankind — all this is a revelation of God's hot displeasure at the sins of men. Such chastisements should impress us with the need of reconciliation with God. For this reason we should not thoughtlessly disregard these punishments, but recognize in them the evidences of God's wrath over our sin, as Luther in his writings continually admonishes us. (Cf. St. L. Ed., I, 249 ff.)

We are living in the age of the newspaper.[3] Daily we read of great catastrophes, of war and bloodshed, of robbery and murder. We Christians should not read about these calamities unthinkingly or merely with an eye to their news value, but rather fold our hands and reflect upon the dreadful revelation of God's anger at the sins of men which these accounts picture to us. Then we shall read our periodicals

---

[3] Ed: Pieper was speaking in 1916.

with devout prayer and supplication to God and with the earnest plea: "God be merciful to me and all sinners!"

We would indeed be self-righteous Pharisees if we were to think that the disasters which befall individuals, regions, and whole nations do not constitute a call to repentance for us and all men. Our Savior clearly explains this fact in Luke 13:1-5 in connection with two "news items," as it were. For one thing, a number of Galileans had been slain by Pilate while they were offering sacrifices. In another instance 18 persons had been killed by the falling tower of Siloam. These incidents provided an opportunity for the Savior to warn His hearers against the verdict uttered in a spirit of self-righteousness that the victims evidently were extraordinarily great sinners and for that reason were punished with particular severity. On the contrary, the Lord took this occasion to drive home the fact that the calamities which individuals suffer serve to remind men of what they all deserve on account of their sins. "I tell you, no; but unless you repent you will all likewise perish." (Luke 13:5)

Now that the great war is raging,[4] we should give this fact especial consideration. The current war is primarily, of course, a dreadful punishment for all the nations involved. But that is no reason for us to become self-righteous Pharisees and to regard ourselves better than those who are suffering the horrors of the war. We should bear in mind instead that before God we are all in like condemnation and that the same punishment would surely strike us if God were to deal with us according to our deserts.

True it is that in Germany, the land of the Reformation, the Word of God now is shamefully despised. But what about our own country? Ours is the land of lodges, which deny the crucified Christ. Ours is a land in which the Pope — "who ... sits as God in the temple of God, showing himself that he is God" (2 Thessalonians 2:4) — is constantly gaining ground. Ours is a land in which so-called Lutherans

---

[4] Ed: World War I or The Great War.

reproachfully term the pure Lutheran doctrine "the disturbing factor."

But what about us who are known as "Missourians"? True, we boast an excellent church organization. We possess the Word of God, as rich and pure and unadulterated as it was in the age of the apostles. But do we really love and treasure the Word of God? Do we hear and read it diligently? Are we spreading it with consecrated zeal? Alas, even among us there is so much indifference, so much apathy, so much satiety! It is only God's grace which thus far has spared us from the angry punishing-rod of war. This great war, just as every other catastrophe in the world, should therefore serve as an earnest call to repentance.

The conscience of man

The confusion and chaos reigning in the realm of nature and human society are harbingers of God's wrath from without. But there is for man a much clearer and more ominous portent of God's wrath from within — the guilty conscience. The accusing conscience is the realization of the awful fact that God — yes, the majestic, holy God — is angry with the sinner. Luther writes in his commentary on Isaiah: "A guilty conscience is the immediate consequence of sin." (Erlangen Ed., 22, 41.) The sin which man commits is automatically registered in his heart. It is registered as guilt before God or as an acknowledgment of God's anger at man's transgression, in short, as a guilty conscience. We call this process automatic because this effect of sin is beyond our control. Just as a cash register records the amount of money received, so conscience registers every sin committed as guilt before God. That is what Luther means when he says that a guilty conscience is the immediate consequence of sin.

Men may engage in wordy arguments to disprove this fact. They may resolve to forget their sin, to disregard it altogether. But there is no such remedy. The guilty conscience remains. Professor Ritschl of Goettingen and his satellites asserted that there is no such thing as the wrath of God toward man's transgression. Others averred that the guilty conscience, or the consciousness of guilt, is merely an acquired habit or prejudice. But these men succeeded in expunging neither their own guilty conscience nor that of anyone else, as we shall later learn from Ritschl's own experience.

Rationalists at all times have maintained that, although God does not favor sin, yet He cannot be so angry at sin as to condemn man for all eternity on that account. But the rationalists have never quieted a single conscience with all their denials, for the consciousness of guilt cannot be argued out of existence by human reasoning.

Sectarian preachers in our country frequently speak of "the fatherhood of God" and "the brotherhood of man." They mean to say that all men may calmly lift their gaze heavenward and expect God to be a true Father to them even without the reconciliation which was effected through Christ's blood. But all such phrases are mere empty words, which cannot possibly do away with the guilty conscience. The human conscience is a scrupulous bookkeeper of man's sins. Even if nature should cease to bear witness, or if there were no Law of God revealed in Scripture, conscience would still remain active. As we hearken to its voice, this is the damning verdict that we bear: "You are guilty before God. God is angry with you."

This was Adam's experience. When he committed sin, this fact was registered upon his conscience, and instinctively he sought to hide from God. The same experience befalls all men, even Christians. The sins which we too commit arc registered upon our conscience as guilt before God. Let us thank God — if I may say this already at this point — yes, let us thank God that we know of the precious blood of Christ, the only means of appeasing the guilty conscience. Because we know of this, we do not fall asleep each night with a guilty conscience, but with the confident prayer: —

> Should I, Lord, have gone astray From Thy path this closing day, Of Thy grace let me partake. Pardon me for Jesus' sake.

The guilty conscience remains even with those who profess to be atheists. Atheists exist in name only, not in reality, as our old theologians declare. True, the conscience, the relentless oracle within the human heart, may temporarily and partially be silenced. As St. Paul says, one may "hold the truth in unrighteousness." (Romans 1:18) Nevertheless, in the end this witness breaks all the artificial bounds with which man has hemmed it in. Unless a person suddenly is snatched away in his obdurate condition, this preacher within him condemns him with a voice of thunder: "You are guilty before God. You are damned!"

For proof of this we cite examples of scoffers like Voltaire, Heine, and others. These men, who mocked and blasphemed everything holy, succeeded for a time in silencing their inner monitor, especially by living in wickedness and shame. But in the hour of death their guilty conscience asserted itself. To read the account of the shrieks of agony and despair with which Voltaire spent his dying breath is gruesome indeed. They were so terrifying that even the physicians drew back in horror. Heine, the renowned German poet, who was as godless as he was brilliant, recanted and cursed his former ungodliness when he lay dying, although it is doubtful that he died a Christian.

Even the heathen have at all times recognized this inner voice, as the Word of God testifies. In Romans 1:32) St. Paul describes the Gentiles as "knowing the righteous judgment of God, that those who practice such things [as listed in verses 28-31] are deserving of death." In Romans 2:15 (LEB) he declares that the heathen "who show the work of the law written on their hearts, their conscience bearing witness and their thoughts one after another accusing or even defending them." Heathen writers directly corroborate this testimony of Scripture. Plutarch, for example, quotes a sick heathen as wailing: "Man, let me suffer my punishment since I am cursed and abhorred of the gods and the demons!" But the heathen manifest their guilty conscience also by their actions, namely, by their efforts to conciliate God through sacrifice and worship. In order to appease their evil conscience, they subject themselves to unspeakable torment, even going so far as to sacrifice their own children and to offer up their very lives by committing suicide.

Let this suffice to show that conscience is indeed a witness to the fact that man is in need of reconciliation with God.

The Word of God

The outstanding witness to divine wrath, however, is God Himself, who in His inspired Word reveals His anger against the sinner. Indeed, Holy Writ describes God's ire as being so great that it surpasses our conception, so dreadful that, as we confess in the well-known hymn:

> My dread-filled heart is cowed with fears
> And to my jaws my tongue adheres.

Yes, God's wrath is so terrible that we should die instantly if, as Luther declares, we were to feel its entire force. Think of the revelation of divine wrath in the Deluge, in the destruction of Sodom and Gomorrah and of Jerusalem. The holy majestic God and sinful man are extreme opposites. They are greater contrasts than even fire and water. Luther states that as long as man is sinful, God can have no communion with him because divine holiness and righteousness render that impossible.

But how does this agree with the existing state of affairs here on earth? When we behold how unrighteousness prevails in the world and in the Church, we might be led to suppose that God evidently does not take sin very seriously, for otherwise He would rain fire and brimstone from heaven upon this sin-cursed earth. But let us not forget that the world still enjoys the divinely appointed season of grace. Having atoned for the sins of the whole world, Christ is now building His Church here on earth, and therefore He postpones His righteous judgment. However, we dare not think that God condones sin because He does not smite sinful mankind. This truth still prevails: "For You are not a God who takes pleasure in wickedness, Nor shall evil dwell with You." (Psalm 5:4) "The face of the LORD is against those who do evil, To cut off the remembrance of them from the earth." (Psalm 34:16) We shall do well to consider also the so-called minatory[5] chapters of Deuteronomy,

---

[5] Ed: From Latin verb *minari*: "to threaten."

chapters 27 and 28, as the expression of God's wrath against sin.

In the New Testament we find the same divine judgment. No matter whether a man sins deliberately or not, the verdict remains: "For it is written, 'Cursed is everyone who does not continue in all things which are written in the book of the law, to do them." (Galatians 3:10[6]) Our Savior declares that even an idle word will be taken into account in the Judgment. (Matthew 12:36) In addition, He impresses the fact that the curse upon sin is not limited to this earth, for He speaks of a place of eternal punishment where there shall be weeping and gnashing of teeth, (Matthew 8:12) and where "Their worm does not die, And the fire is not quenched." (Mark 9:44)

Wrath laid upon Christ

Such, then, is God's own dread revelation of His wrath against sin, as recorded in His Word. The most powerful manifestation of divine wrath, however, is the fact that God gave His only begotten Son into death and laid upon Him the iniquity and guilt of the whole world. This fact is most certainly true: We stand in dire need of reconciliation with God.

Bearing this truth in mind, let us now turn our attention to the second part of our thesis, namely, that *man is unable to effect reconciliation with God through his own efforts.*

2.

In spite of all efforts of his own man is unable to effect a reconciliation with God. The fact that man earnestly strives to become reconciled with God is evident throughout the world, even among the heathen. Paganism is not atheism, but the endeavor of man to appease an outraged God by his own works. (Cf, Apology of the Augsburg Confession, Art. III, 85 ff.; Triglot, p. 176 f.) The heathen believe in the existence of God and know His holy will and His judgment against trespassers of His Law (Romans 1:32, 2:15), and for this reason their

---

[6] Ed: See Deuteronomy 27:26 and Jeremiah 11:3.

guilty conscience accuses them. Hence, they go to great lengths in an attempt to effect a reconciliation with God. Cicero, for instance, writes: "There is no people so savage that it does not know of God and does not worship Him." Luther, too, quite frequently points out this fact.

It is true that in their attempts to reconcile God through their own efforts the heathen, just like the papists, have not always hit upon very laudable deeds. On the contrary, they quite often devise ridiculous, even childish, works. Ancient paganism already had its praying-machines. As Luther says, the old Egyptians believed that they had to worship cats and mice and to venerate garlic and onions. (St. L. Ed., II, 1829.) All this is certainly quite puerile.[7] But let us not forget that oftentimes the heathen were very serious in their attempts to reconcile God, as is shown, for instance, by the heathen deeds of penance in India. To satisfy their deities, the Hindu penitents walk for hundreds of miles in shoes spiked with sharp nails; or they look into the light of the sun until they become blind; or they let themselves be crushed under the wheels of the idol Juggernaut. We also think of the great sums of money spent in the erection of heathen temples. In China, for example, certain temples are said to have cost more than fifty million dollars.[8]

We observe similar conditions in the outward Christian Church where the Gospel has been relegated to oblivion. Certain monks like Luther took their monastic life seriously. The great Reformer did not enter the cloister to enjoy an easy life, but to appease his tormented conscience and to reconcile God by means of a "holy life" and self-torture. Life in a cloister, with all its "good works," impresses people even today, even those who are rather indifferent in matters of religion. It is natural for man to admire anyone who makes the impression of being filled with religious zeal. The world, to be sure, does not despise the religion of works; only the Gospel of the crucified Christ, the religion of grace, is to the Jews a stumbling-block and to the Greeks foolishness.

---

[7] Ed: Juvenile, childish, silly.

[8] Ed: Recall that Pieper is speaking is 1916, of 1916 dollars.

What, however, is the result of the religion of works? What docs man accomplish with his efforts to conciliate God? In every instance the result is zero. Holy Scripture teaches: "by the deeds of the law no flesh will be justified in His sight." (Romans 3:20) St. Paul summarily declares of all the heathen that they have no hope and are without God in the world (Ephesians 2:12). There are many people nowadays who hold that God must be well pleased with the worship of the heathen since He has to consider their good intentions. In other words, they think it is impossible for God to reject the worship of the heathen because of their sincerity. But Holy Writ teaches that the things which the Gentiles sacrifice they sacrifice to devils (1 Corinthians 10:20). Those people within the pale of the visible Church who endeavor to effect a reconciliation with God through their own works arc likewise doomed to failure. The verdict of Scripture is: "as many as are of the works of the law are under the curse" (Galatians 3:10). Luther's example is indeed most significant. If anyone was serious in trying to appease his conscience, it certainly was he. Yet he confesses:

> And ever deeper yet I fell.

As a matter of fact, God recognizes only one sacrifice for the sins of the world, and that is the sacrifice of Christ.

II.

Our second thesis reads: "*Through Christ's vicarious atonement God has reconciled the whole world unto Himself.*"

1.

In this thesis we assert that a complete reconciliation with God has been effected. True, this is a reconciliation of which no man ever has or ever could have conceived. Even the great leaders of men, "the princes of this world," did not know it, as St. Paul informs us (1 Corinthians 2:8). We learn of it only through God's revealed Word.

What is the nature of this reconciliation? God had His eternal, only-begotten Son to become man, and through His obedience and suffering God reconciled the whole world unto Himself. This fact is clearly attested in Scripture. Indeed, this truth is the sum and substance of the entire Bible. In 2 Corinthias 5:19-20 we read:

> God was in Christ reconciling the world to Himself, not imputing their trespasses to them, and has committed to us the word of reconciliation. Now then, we are ambassadors for Christ, as though God were pleading through us: we implore you on Christ's behalf, be reconciled to God. For He made Him who knew no sin to be sin for us, that we might become the righteousness of God in Him.

Let us ponder upon the meaning of these words.

"God was in Christ reconciling the world to Himself." God, not man, is the One who acts. Man did not reconcile God, but God reconciled all men unto Himself without any overture on their part, yes, even without their knowledge. On the contrary, because men stood in need of atonement and yet could not secure it, God Himself, in His divine love and compassion toward us lost and miserable creatures, undertook and accomplished that reconciliation. But how did God effect it? By a most unique plan, namely: "God was in Christ, reconciling the world unto Himself." That is to say, God effected the reconciliation of the world to Himself through Christ. Scripture describes this method of reconciliation in detail. God sent His Son into the world to become incarnate through the Virgin Mary. Christ fulfilled the Law which God had given to man and paid the penalty which man had deserved on account of his transgression of that Law. It was in this miraculous way that God reconciled the world unto Himself, as we are told Galatians 4:4-5, Romans 5:10, and Galatians 3:13.

But wherein does reconciliation consist? In other words, what does reconciliation involve? God's reconciliation of the world does not mean that men have changed their attitude toward God, as these words (2 Corinthians 5:19) have erroneously been explained. For men, ignorant of God's reconciliation, could never change their attitude toward Him.

No, the reconciliation of the world consists in this, that God "in Christ," or for Christ's sake, changed His own sentiment toward man. St. Paul writes: "Not imputing their trespasses to them." Sin rendered man guilty and thus subject to God's displeasure. Despite all his own efforts he could never have placated the divine wrath. However, for Christ's sake God does not impute man's trespasses unto him. That is to say, He forgives him his sin and regards him as sinless. Indeed, God has erased the record of man's sins from His book. In His divine heart grace has taken the place of wrath.

This reconciliation, moreover, is *complete* and *perfect*. We read: "Not imputing their trespasses unto them." Everything that constitutes sin: our transgression of the divine Law, our alienation from God, our unlawful thoughts, desires, and impulses, our evil words, our wicked deeds, — all these God did not impute to the world, that is, to men. He acted as though these sins had never been committed. He canceled them from His accounts. The papists run counter to Scripture when teaching that Christ made satisfaction only for original sin but did not pay the penalty of actual sin.

Reconciliation is complete and perfect also in another respect. St. Paul says: "Not imputing their trespasses *to them*." "To them," means "to the whole world," "to all mankind." Reconciliation is complete so far as God's *disposition* is concerned. In God's heart the forgiveness of sins has been substituted for the imputation of sins. However, reconciliation is complete also with regard to its *external scope*, for it embraces the whole world. The doctrine of Calvinism that God reconciled only a part of mankind unto Himself is contrary to Scripture. We have no right whatsoever to limit the concept *world* and to interpret it in the sense of *the elect*. In addition, St. John emphatically declares: "He Himself is the propitiation for our sins, and not for ours only but also for the whole world." (1 John 2:2)

However, there is another important thought that must not be overlooked. Man's reconciliation with God is an accomplished fact; it is finished. "God was in Christ, reconciling the world to Himself." These words refer to the time when the Son of God sojourned here upon earth. Nearly nineteen centuries ago, when Christ suffered and died, God reconciled the world to Himself. When God raised Christ from the dead, He absolved the world from its guilt and sin and declared that He was no longer at odds with the sinful race of man. St. Paul thus places the death and resurrection of Christ in juxtaposition: "Who was delivered for our offenses and was raised again for our justification." [Romans 4:25]

Again, God has not kept secret the marvelous fact that He has reconciled the world unto Himself. He is not concealing it, as it were, in His own mind. On the contrary, God publishes this reconciliation throughout the world by means of the "Word of Reconciliation," the holy Gospel. This truth is expressed in the words: "and has committed to us the word of reconciliation," that is, the reconciliation which has once been accomplished, and not any reconciliation which men must effect in the future when they become converted, through repentance and faith. The message of God's complete reconciliation we designate with the Scriptural term Gospel, or glad tidings. In Acts 20:24 St. Paul calls it "the Gospel of the grace of God," and in Ephesians 6:15 "the Gospel of peace." The preachers of the Gospel therefore are thus described in Romans 10:15: "How beautiful are the feet of those who preach the gospel of peace, Who bring glad tidings of good things!" And on the first Christmas night the angels sang: "On earth peace." (Luke 2:14)

Alas, not only the papists, but also most nominal Protestants in our day grossly pervert the Word of Reconciliation. They explain the matter as though men must still complete their reconciliation through repentance and faith. In opposition to this, Scripture teaches that God is reconciled to the world and the world is reconciled to God even before there is any change within man, before bis conversion, before his repentance and faith.

It is true, the Christian Church must also declare God's wrath against the sins of men by preaching the Law, "for by the Law is the knowledge of sin." (Romans 3:20) But the real message which the Christian

Church must proclaim to the world is the glad tidings that through Christ the wrath of God toward sin has been entirely appeased. This fact the Christian Church must make known to the world, urging and exhorting all men to believe it, as the apostle goes on to say: "Now then, we are ambassadors for Christ, as though God were pleading through us: we implore you on Christ's behalf, be reconciled to God." These words leave no room at all for the teaching that men must atone for their sins and pay their debts through their own efforts. St. Paul states this expressly in his concluding words: "For He made Him who knew no sin to be sin for us, that we might become the righteousness of God in Him."

The glorious fact that the whole world has been reconciled to God through Christ is furthermore taught in all the passages of Scripture in which we are told that Christ offered Himself as an expiatory sacrifice for all mankind. In Ephesians 5:2 we read: "Christ also has loved us and given Himself for us, an offering and a sacrifice to God for a sweet-smelling aroma." According to Hebrews 7:27 Christ has offered Himself for the sins of the people; but "this He did once for all when He offered up Himself." The same truth is emphasized Hebrews 9:12 where we read: "With His own blood He entered the Most Holy Place once for all, having obtained eternal redemption." These passages in Hebrews differentiate between Christ and the priests of the Old Testament. In view of the fact that the Old Testament priests were themselves sinners, they had to offer up the sacrificial animals which the Levitical code prescribed. Christ, however, is distinguished from the priests of the Old Testament in that He presents to God an offering not of animals but of Himself, by His own blood, as the perfect sacrifice — yes, the sacrifice for the sins of the whole world. All this is summed up in the testimony of John the Baptist: "Behold! The Lamb of God who takes away the sin of the world!" (John 1:29)

This, then, constitutes the stupendous fact of the reconciliation of the whole world through Christ. On the basis of this fact everyone in the world — and that includes all of us — can and must be sure that he has been fully reconciled to God through Christ. Much falsehood indeed is rampant in the world, but the most despicable lie of all is the denial of our reconciliation to God through the blood of Christ. It is certainly bad enough that Satan has caused us to fall into sin and has thus provoked God to pronounce His sentence of condemnation on us. Let us by no means do Satan the additional favor of believing the delusion that we are not reconciled to God through Christ.

At this juncture we must be on our guard especially against the countless objections of the papists, who are much concerned not to have anyone believe that he is reconciled unto God through Christ, for that would put them completely out of business. Man's faith in his perfect reconciliation with God through Christ, or in the grace of God for Christ's sake, they brand an impertinence, basing their contention on the following arguments.

a) "Since your name is not recorded in the Bible, you need a special revelation from God before you may firmly believe that you are reconciled to Him." To this we reply: This necessary divine revelation we have in Scripture, namely, in the term *world*; and this revelation is much more reliable and certain than if my name were recorded in the Bible. If my name were mentioned in the Bible, I would have to select my own name from many others, and since many persons bear the identical name, I could not be sure after all whether I were meant or someone else bearing that same name. With reference to John 1:29, Luther remarks: "You are a part of the world, hence you are reconciled unto God; for Christ is the Lamb of God who takes away the sin of the world."

b) Furthermore, the papists raise this objection: "You cannot be sure of your reconciliation since you do not know whether your contrition is adequate." To this we answer: Where in Scripture is it written that God forgives sin on account of man's contrition? God is reconciled unto us through Christ even before we become contrite. True, contrition must precede faith, but our sins are forgiven not on account of our contrition, but on account of Christ's perfect merits.

Whatever the papists teach with respect to the necessity of confessing to the priest and of works of satisfaction which the priest must prescribe is contrary to God's Word and has been concocted in order to promote their hierarchical system, to tyrannize their people, and to dishonor the Savior. The perfect atonement for sin which the world needs has been accomplished once and for all by Christ.

2.

A further description of the divine method of the atonement. To describe the work of Christ whereby the world was reconciled to God, the Christian Church has adopted also the expression "vicarious satisfaction" (*satisfactio vicaria*). We also find the expression in Luther's writings, for instance, in his "Christian Questions," where he answers the question: "Why should we remember and proclaim His death?" as follows: "That we may learn to believe that no creature *could make satisfaction for our sins.* Only Christ, true God and man, could do that." [9] Luther then asks: "What was it that moved Him to die *and make satisfaction for your sin?*"[10]

Today this "vicarious satisfaction" is vehemently opposed in many circles. To be sure, the expression itself is not found in Scripture, yet the truth which it designates is truly Scriptural. The meaning of the term is that Christ in man's place performed unto God, who was angry at man's sins, that service by which His wrath toward mankind was changed into grace. This doctrine is clearly taught in Holy Writ. On the basis of the Word of God we must hold:

a) God possesses the attribute of inviolable holiness and righteousness, in accordance with which He demands perfect agreement with His Law on the part of all men in general and of each individual in particular and in accordance with which He is so enraged with all transgressors that He casts them away forever from His presence, that is, consigns them to eternal damnation. God has prescribed the bounds within

---

[9] Ed: Small Catechism, Christian Questions and Their Answers, Question 16.

[10] Ed: Small Catechism, Chrisian Questions and Their Answers, Question 17.

which all His creatures are to be active. The sun, moon, and stars do not follow any course of their own choice, but that which God has ordained. When a planet is hurtled from its orbit, it is instantly annihilated.

Now, man is a peculiar creature of God; that is to say, he is a rational creature, a moral being, with a distinct personality. Man has the capacity for thoughts and words as well as for actions. Accordingly, God has given him a specific Law, which he must observe. Man is not permitted to think, speak, and act as he pleases. On the contrary, God has prescribed what the proper attitude of man's heart toward his Maker should be and how he should gage his thoughts, words, and actions. Christ sums up the demands of the Law when He declares: "You shall love the Lord your God with all your heart, with all your soul, and with all your mind ... and your neighbor as yourself." (Matthew 22:37, 40)

If a person fails to do this, the results are dreadful indeed. If a star is hurled from its orbit and destroyed, that, after all, is a mishap which is comparatively small. For on the Day of Judgment the whole earth will be dissolved. But man has been created for eternity, and if he is hurled from his course, that is, if he does not keep God's Law, he indeed continues to live on, but as an eternal castaway, banished forever from the presence of God, and that implies a condition of the most excruciating torment.

Only in communion with God, his Creator, is man truly blessed. If he is removed from God's gracious presence, he is alienated from that element of life in which he belongs, just as a fish that is drawn out of the water and cast upon the shore writhes in convulsions and soon expires. In Galatians 3:10, the Holy Spirit speaking through Paul impresses upon our minds the dreadful edict: "Cursed is everyone who does not continue in all things which are written in the book of the law, to do them."

Consequently, since all men are transgressors of the divine Law, they are in a most unhappy predicament. They are children of wrath

(Ephesians 2:3) and are "guilty before God" (Romas 3:19). This appalling situation, as we have already seen, endures to eternity. In Mark 9:46 Christ speaks of the worm that does not die of the fire that is not quenched. In Matthew 8:12 He pictures to us the "outer darkness" where "there will be weeping and gnashing of teeth." Truly, the Son of God Himself in this manner portrays the demanding and the punitive holiness and righteousness of God. What, then, shall become of us? Is the whole race of men consequently to perish? No, indeed! God has provided salvation for man, and this He has done in a manner which never has and never could have entered the mind of any man. That is the second idea which is conveyed by the term vicarious atonement.

b) But how was this salvation prepared? It was not that God simply canceled the demands of His Law and His verdict of condemnation. No, indeed! Salvation was wrought in this way: God appointed His own incarnate Son to be our Substitute before His bar of justice. Christ did what we should have done and suffered what we should have suffered. This fact is brought out in many passages of the Bible, such as: "God sent forth His Son, born of a woman, born under the law" (Galatians 4:4-5); "Christ has redeemed us from the curse of the law, having become a curse for us" (Galatians 3:13); "Christ died for our sins" (1 Corinthians 15:3); "One died for all" (2 Corinthias 5:14); and "Christ also suffered once for sins, the just for the unjust" (1 Peter 3:18).

Oh, what a precious Savior we have! Compare Him with other so-called founders of religions which dupe poor mortals, just as they always have duped them. All such religious teachers — Confucius, Buddha, Mohammed, the Pope, the Unitarians, and all other proponents of work-righteousness — place a burden upon men, inasmuch as they instruct them to propitiate God through their own efforts, which is a burden so staggering that neither they nor anyone else can bear it.

Christ, however, is a Savior of a different sort. He imposes not even the slightest burden upon men. He demands of the sinner not even the most trivial work by which he must gain salvation; on the contrary, He relieved man of the entire burden and placed it upon His own shoulders. During the 33 years of His sojourn on earth He placed Himself under the divine Law which had been given to man in order that He might fulfil it in man's place. The full weight of divine wrath, the entire penalty which man had incurred by his transgression of the Law, He assumed in order to pay it by His own suffering and death.

c) Now the whole world has been reconciled to God through this fact that Christ by His obedience and His Passion became man's Substitute. The demands of divine justice and holiness have been satisfied so that God no longer imputes unto men their trespasses. God's verdict of condemnation has been repealed. On the basis of Christ's work He declares men righteous, just as though they had fulfilled the entire Law and had never transgressed a single commandment. And in order that forgiveness of sins may be bestowed upon all men, He has ordained that the Gospel be published throughout the world. To this end also He instituted Holy Baptism which works forgiveness of sins. (Acts 2:38) This, too, is the purpose of the Lord's Supper. For by partaking of our Savior's body and blood we receive His assurance that our debt has been paid. This is the express teaching of God's inspired Word: "Through one Man's righteous act the free gift came to all men, resulting in justification of life" (Romans 5:18); "we were reconciled to God through the death of His Son" (Romans 5:10); and "Who was delivered for our offenses and was raised again for our justification" (Romans 4:25).

This, then, is the Scriptural doctrine of the atonement through the vicarious satisfaction of Christ. The expression "vicarious satisfaction" as used by Luther and our theologians is indeed firmly grounded upon God's Word.

3.

Human Criticism of the Divine Method of the Atonement. — The subject which we shall now discuss is unspeakably tragic. In fact, it is the most sorrowful chapter in the history of mankind. Men need reconciliation with God, but they cannot effect it through their own efforts. Moved by His grace and compassion, God has reconciled the world to Himself through the obedience and Passion of His Son. But men are not satisfied with this method of reconciliation. They find much to criticize in the divine plan of atonement. They brand it as superfluous, as unworthy of God, as inconsistent, as totally unjust, as inadequate or inexpedient, as too external or too juridical.

This is a horrid, blasphemous, yea, crazy criticism; and yet it has been advanced at all times and is being offered to this very day, and not only by such professed Unitarians as Dr. Charles Eliot, the late president of Harvard University, but also by so-called positive (conservative) theologians, yes, even by some within nominally Lutheran circles. Some time ago the *Independent* wrote:

> The great majority of Christian teachers have abandoned this doctrine [that is, the Biblical doctrine of the atonement]. There is now growing up a generation of Christians which has never heard that Christ's death was an expiatory offering. Christianity does not demand that we regard the death of Christ as a means of reconciling the Father; for His love does not need to be aroused or stimulated. No propitiatory sacrifice is necessary. God is well able to grant forgiveness out of the store of His love.

(Cf. *Lehre und Wehre*, 1916, p. 181.) That is the position not only of the church bodies which expressly class themselves as Unitarian. In a recent discussion about the statistics of the various church denominations in the United States a certain Unitarian remarked: "Don't believe that we number only half a million members. We have our members in other Protestant bodies." This, alas, is only too true. It is likely that the majority of Congregationalist, Baptist, Episcopalian, and even Presbyterian ministers are at heart Unitarians and therefore reject the doctrine of the reconciliation through Christ's atonement. They hold that Christianity does not consist in faith in the crucified Christ but in man's efforts to keep the divine Law. This explains why the Episcopalians, who at present are holding their sessions in St. Louis, are for the most part lodge members. They have the same religion as the lodge which believes that men can safely reject the crucified Christ as their only Savior and reconcile God through their own merits. And let us not suppose that our own members are not also being infected by this venomous spirit!

In order that we may not be misled, let us consider the chief objections which are advanced against the atonement through Christ's vicarious satisfaction and then judge them according to Scripture.

The first objection is that Christ's obedience and Passion were *unnecessary* since God, as the supreme Judge, can forgive sins and be gracious to men without Christ's atonement by virtue of His divine and sovereign will. To this we reply that it is useless and foolish, indeed altogether absurd, to argue about what God *can* do after He has revealed to us in His Word what He wants to do and actually does. Now, God declares in His Word that He forgives sins "through the redemption which is in Christ Jesus" (Romans 3:24); that we were reconciled to God by the death of His Son (Romans 5:10); that we "were redeemed ... with the precious blood of Christ" (1 Peter 1:18-19); that Christ is the "one Mediator between God and men, the Man Christ Jesus, who gave Himself a ransom for all" (1 Timothy 2:6); and that "Christ has redeemed us from the curse of the law, having become a curse for us" (Galatians 3:13). These passages once and for all dispose of the question as to whether God can be gracious to men without Christ's atonement. "It is not an open question, but a closed question," since God directs all sinners to Christ.

God is a gracious Father to everyone who accepts his appointed Savior in true faith. On the other hand, God will have nothing to do with anyone who does not believe in the crucified Christ as his Savior. "Whoever denies the Son does not have the Father either." (1 John 2:23) Luther declares very bluntly, but by no means too bluntly: "Since God will grant it [namely, the forgiveness of sins and eternal salvation] through the humanity of Christ [that is, for the sake of Christ's obedience and Passion], who are you, arrogant and ungrateful devil, that dare to ask why God does not do it differently instead of in this way? Do you want to dictate to Him and prescribe to Him the mode of procedure to follow in this matter? You ought to leap for joy because He does it at all, no matter in what way, just as long as you obtain it." (St. L. Ed., XX, 882 f.)

All who want to reject Christ's expiatory sacrifice are outside the pale of the Christian Church, for their faith is like that of the Turks, Jews, and heathen. Luther writes in this regard:

> I have said repeatedly that faith in God alone is not sufficient, but that the cost — the vicarious satisfaction must also be considered. The Turk and the Jew also believe in God, but without the means and the cost. But what is the cost? This the Gospel shows us. … Christ there teaches us that we are not lost, but have eternal life, that is, that God so loved us that for our sakes He went to the greatest of all costs. He offered up His only, dearly beloved Son, subjecting Him to our misery, to death and hell, and making Him drink this cup of bitterness to its dregs. (St. L. Ed., XI, 1085.)

That is the way of salvation. Chemnitz writes: "Outside of Christ there is no grace and mercy of God toward us sinners, for grace without Christ must not and cannot be conceived." (Harm. Ev., c. 28, p. 152.) This truth we must always bear in mind in our combat with lodgery. The lodge has many sinful features, but its chief crime is the rejection of Christ as the only Savior of sinners. Since the lodge teaches that every man may be saved in his own way, or by his own beliefs, no Christian congregation dare make any compromise with lodgery. So far as the lodge is a religion, it officially proclaims: "Men may be saved without Christ."

The second objection to the doctrine of Christ's vicarious satisfaction is that it is a conception unworthy of God to picture Him as being so angry with sinners that He can be reconciled only through the substitutionary suffering and death of His Son. To this our answer is: It certainly is ridiculous, absurd, and blasphemous arrogance if we presume to determine just what is worthy or unworthy of God. Whatever is worthy or unworthy of God can be learned only from God's revealed Word. But God's express revelation in His Word is that He is angry with all sinners. "The wrath of God is revealed from heaven against all ungodliness and unrighteousness of men." (Romans 1:18) "Cursed is everyone who does not continue in all things which are written in the book of the law, to do them." (Galatians 2:10) Again, God's revealed Word tells us: "we were reconciled to God through the death of His Son." (Romans 5:10) "Christ has redeemed us from the curse of the law, having become a curse for us." (Galatians 3:13) These are truly worthy conceptions of God. In His Word, God presents to us these two truths: 1. He is angry at the sin of man; 2. He is reconciled to all sinners through the blood of His Son. God be praised that we possess these two conceptions of Him!

The third objection is that God has revealed His *love* toward men by sending His Son and, in particular, by giving His Son into death. "God so loved the world that He gave His only begotten Son." (John 3:16) "God demonstrates His own love toward us, in that while we were still sinners, Christ died for us." (Romans 5:8) For this reason, so men claim, we cannot speak of the appeasing of God's wrath through the death of His Son. Our rejoinder is: According to Scripture the sending of Christ into the world and His death on the cross reveal both facts — God's love as well as His wrath. When Scripture declares that while we were still enemies of God, we were reconciled to Him by the death of His Son (Romans 5:9), it means that through Christ's death the wrath of God toward guilty mankind has been appeased. But this same fact also manifested God's love, for it was His great love that moved Him to satisfy His righteousness through the death of His Son, which was impossible for us to accomplish. "In this is love, not that we loved God, but that He loved us and sent His Son to be the propitiation for our sins." (1 John 4:10)

A fourth objection against the doctrine of the divine atonement is: It certainly would be unjust on God's part to impose the curse and punishment of guilty mankind upon the innocent Christ. In reply let us say: Whatever God does is just. But what God did in this case He tells us plainly in His Word. It is this twofold fact: In the first place, God imputed to Christ our guilt, that is, the guilt of all men. "He made Him who knew no sin to be sin for us." (2 Corinthians 5:21) In the second place, God made the innocent Christ suffer for us guilty men. "Christ also suffered once for sins, the just for the unjust." (1 Peter 3:18) In view of these two facts we need have no compunction as to the justice of God's conduct in this matter, and we rightly condemn human reason, which always is prone to measure the almighty God according to its own standards.

At this place a word of warning may not be amiss with respect to the rational arguments on behalf of the justice of God's procedure. We admit that also in civil life the concept of vicariousness is not unknown. Even ancient teachers cited a number of examples of vicarious suffering as, for instance, that of Codrus, the last king of Athens, who in his war with the Spartans committed suicide in order to save his people; also the case of the two Decii, father and son, two Roman consuls, who voluntarily suffered death in order to save their fatherland; finally, the example of Zaleucus, the lawgiver of the Locrians in Southern Italy who, in order to spare his son from torture, permitted his own eye to be gouged out. All these illustrations, however, must not be used to prove the justice of the divine procedure in the punishment of Christ as our Substitute. Our only incontrovertible proof is this: "It is written."

Human reason will constantly raise new objections when Christ's vicarious suffering is subjected to its criticism. That is also true with regard to the contention that Christ died willingly in man's place. Even some of our old dogmaticians put too much emphasis on this argument. It is true, Christ did not become man's Substitute by coercion but by His own free will. This fact Holy Scripture attests very emphatically. (John 10:17, Ephesians 5:2) But whenever this argument is advanced, Unitarians will at once object to this, saying that we would denounce any human judge as unjust if he would declare an innocent volunteer guilty in place of a condemned criminal and accordingly punish him with death. Before the bar of human justice we permit substitution in the payment of financial debt, but never in cases of moral debt. Hence, only if we establish the justice of God's procedure in substituting Christ in our stead on the basis of God's Word exclusively do we rest our doctrine upon a firm foundation. Let us thank God that we may do this. Instead of accusing God of injustice, we should reverently adore and extol His great love, according to which He spared not His own innocent Son in order to save us guilty sinners. Let us remember, especially in this connection, that a Christian must base his faith solely and entirely upon God's Word.

A fifth objection to the doctrine of Christ's vicarious satisfaction is that Christ did not actually suffer what men should have suffered, so that it is impossible to speak of a vicarious atonement. Professor Luthardt thus says that in the matter of Christ's satisfaction we dare not speak of a "mutual settlement" (*gegenseitige Abrechnung*). Professor Frank of Erlangen holds that it was an aberration (*Verirrung*) on the part of the old theologians to teach that Christ endured the punishment which men should have suffered. To this we reply: According to Holy Scripture Christ performed and suffered exactly what man should have performed and suffered. Thus, Christ fulfilled the Law which had been given to man. (Galatians 4:4-5) Moreover, in Galatians 3:10 God's curse is pronounced upon all who do not keep the Law, but in Galatians 3:13 we are told: Christ "become a curse for us." Hence, according to God's computation the accounts balance perfectly.

Some have added another objection, namely, that Christ did not suffer eternally, but only for a time, as we are told in 1 Peter 3:18, "Christ also suffered once for sins,' and in Romans 6:9, "Christ ... dies no more." The objection is voiced that even if Christ had suffered 33 years, those 33 years would not be equivalent to eternity. This we must admit. But Scripture, in balancing the account, takes into consideration another factor — the sublime person of the Sufferer. The blood of Christ is the blood of God's Son (1 John 1:7), yes, God's own blood (Acts 20:28). If the Son of God suffers and is forsaken by God, even though for only a short time, that indeed amounts to as much as if all mankind had suffered throughout eternity, yea, to far more. The account thus balances perfectly according to the divine reckoning. God regards the divine person of the Sufferer. This is expressed very beautifully in one of our German Communion hymns, in which the poet says that because of this fact one drop of Jesus' blood would have sufficed to cleanse the whole world from sin.

A sixth objection of those who do not believe in Christ's vicarious atonement is that it is too juridical and not sufficiently ethical or moral to regard God as reconciled through Christ's vicarious satisfaction. This view is sponsored even by the positive wing of modern theologians. When Professor von Hofmann of Erlangen urged this objection to the Christian doctrine of the atonement and denied the vicarious suffering of Christ, Theodosius Harnack quite aptly replied:

> If this fact is to be held against it [namely, the doctrine of the atonement as taught in the Lutheran Confessions], that the concept of satisfaction involves a juridical view of the reconciliation of the world, this charge, so far as it is tenable, falls back upon Scripture. ... The doctrinal presentation of our Symbols can be abolished only after the concepts of the righteousness and holiness of God, of the Law and of conscience, of guilt, punishment and judgment, of the Mediator, the ransom price and the imputation have been deleted from Scripture." (The Confession of the Lutheran Church concerning Reconciliation," etc. Erlangen, 1857, p. 139.)

The point is well taken. According to Holy Scripture the reconciliation of the world was effected in a thoroughly juridical manner. Juridical is its very presupposition, namely, the demands of the divine Law upon man, "You shall love the Lord your God" (Matthew 22:37), and the curse of the Law upon all transgressors (Galatians 3:10). Juridical is the subjection of Christ under the Law which God gave to man, because so far as His own person was concerned, Christ was the Lord of the Law. (Matthew 12:8) Juridical is the imputation of our guilt and punishment to Christ, because Christ knew no sin (1 Corinthians 5:21). Juridical also is the infliction of the punishment; for the Just suffered for the unjust (1 Peter 3:18). God be praised that thus far everything has been accomplished in a juridical way, for now the juridical process continues. Now God in a purely juridical manner does not impute to men their trespasses (2 Corinthians 5:19), but declares them righteous (Romans 5:18, 4:25), and so in a purely juridical manner we are justified before God without the deeds of the Law (Romans 3:28). Whoever rejects the purely "juridical" character of the atonement and justification and mingles into our reconciliation with God the "ethical" character, that is, human morality or human self-improvement, subverts the whole Christian faith and prevents man from becoming reconciled to God. This truth will be developed at greater length in our third thesis.

4.

All Criticism of the Reconciliation Effected by Christ Comes to Nothing. If a man criticizes God, he may be sure beyond all shadow of a doubt that he, the critic, is a downright fool. Also the criticism of the heavenly doctrine of the atonement proves itself utter folly so far as the effects of its substitutes are concerned. All substitutes for the redemption effected by Christ are really futile because they cannot appease a single conscience.

The consciousness of guilt in the heart of man is an awful reality. It is a writ of condemnation inscribed by God Himself into man's heart and supported by the whole force of His holiness and righteousness. "Be holy, for I am holy." (1 Peter 1:16) The consciousness of guilt which sinful man feels owes its origin to the power of divine holiness and righteousness. It is not dependent on man's will, although since the Fall the conscience of man is beclouded so that only on the Day of Judgment the consciousness of guilt will be complete. (Romans 2:16) Nevertheless, the finger of God has written the verdict "Guilty" upon the heart of man already in this life. It will remain there until God Himself blots it out by faith in the blood of Christ. God must remove His sentence of condemnation from our conscience by replacing it with

His decree of justification through faith in Christ. We confess in a familiar hymn:

> If at last death's awful hour
> Every knowledge from me hides,
> Let my comfort be the power
> Of this truth which e'er abides:
> Jesus' suffering, cross, and pain
> Shall my knowledge true remain.

Let us prove by a few examples that all criticism of the atonement, together with all its substitutions, do indeed come to nothing. Men who throughout their lives denied and combated the vicarious satisfaction of Christ finally in the hour of death when their conscience was aroused and God held out to them His loving arms, sought refuge solely in the blood of Christ, that is, in Christ's vicarious atonement.

Hugo Grotius, the well-known Arminian († 1645), who throughout his life denied the doctrine that Christ satisfied divine justice in man's place and regarded Christ's death merely as a public example to deter men from sin (Governmental Theory), died in the Lutheran faith under the pastoral care of the Lutheran minister John Quistorp the Elder (†1648) comforted by the Scriptural doctrine of the atonement. Horace Bushnell († 1876), a proponent of the Moral Influence Theory, passed away with this confession on his lips: "O Lord Jesus, I trust for mercy in the shed blood that Thou didst offer on Calvary." In his dying moments Albrecht Ritschl († 1889), who during his lifetime had criticized the beautiful Lenten hymn of Paul Gerhardt "O Bleeding Head and Wounded" as unworthy of God, requested bis son to read to him the last two stanzas of this hymn, which in their English version read as follows:

> My Savior, then be near me
> When death is at my door,
> And let your presence cheer me;
> Forsake me nevermore!
> When soul and body languish,

Oh, leave me not alone,
But take away my anguish
By virtue of your own!

Lord, be my consolation,
My shield when I must die;
Remind me of your passion
When my last hour draws nigh,
My eyes will then behold you,
Upon your cross will dwell;
My heart will then enfold you.
Who dies I faith dies well!

Duke George of Saxony († 1539), a rabid enemy of the Reformation and a bitter foe of Luther, was known to speak of the "Wittenberg heresy pit." But in his dying confession he declared: "Oh, help me, dear Savior, Jesus Christ! Have mercy on me and save me through Thy bitter suffering and death!" All this goes to show that whatever is substituted for the vicarious satisfaction is utterly futile. Only this comforting knowledge is of practical value:

Christ's precious blood and righteousness
My glory are, my beauteous dress;
So clothed, before my God I'll stand
When I shall reach the heavenly land.

Nothing else can console. In the end everything else only drives the sinner to despair. In vain do all human works and all human arguments strive to appease the wrath of God. We are reconciled to God only through what Christ did and suffered in our stead.

III.

Our last thesis reads: "*Man on bis part becomes a partaker of God's reconciliation if he believes the divine message of the atonement effected by Christ.*"

1.

Faith Is Necessary. — According to the divine order of salvation, faith in the atonement which Christ has secured is indeed necessary in order that we personally may share in the divine reconciliation. God has completely reconciled the world unto Himself. Every debt is paid. Nothing remains charged to our account. But God has ordained that all persons must receive the message of the grace of God in Christ Jesus by faith. Even in our own time the claim is put forth that, since the world has been reconciled unto God through Christ, it is permissible to teach that God will accept those heathen who have lived virtuously even though they did not believe the Gospel.

In our own time Professor von Hofmann of Erlangen has expressed this opinion. In the sixteenth century it was propounded by Zwingli. Some even aver that Luther championed this view, although the great Reformer had this to say on the matter:

> Zwingli recently wrote that Numa Pompilius, Hector, Scipio, and Hercules will rejoice with Peter, Paul, and the other saints in the paradise of eternal salvation. But this is nothing else than a public confession on his part that neither faith nor Christianity is of any value. For if Scipio and Numa Pompilius, those idolatrous men, have been saved, why did Christ have to suffer and die, or why is it necessary that Christians should be baptized or that Christ should be preached so emphatically and that persons should be directed alone to Him? So deeply do the enthusiasts fall if they neglect and surrender the Word, become ignorant of the faith, and bold, and proclaim the same error that was taught by the Papacy: If man does what he can, he will be saved by his efforts. (St. L. Ed., II, 1828.)

The reconciliation which was effected by Christ is indeed objective, that is to say, God has reconciled all men to Himself and hence in His heart has absolved every single sinner of all his guilt. To use an expression current in the business world: God has reconciled the world to Himself one hundred per cent. Whoever does not take his stand upon this truth does not understand the Christian doctrine. Indeed, he does not know that a man is justified by faith, without the deeds of the Law. For Christ's sake all wrath has been banished from the heart of God, as the angels testified on the first Christmas night in their song: "On earth peace, good will toward men."

Our pastors are messengers of peace. Their message is the proclamation of the grace of God, of grace without qualifications, of grace pure and overflowing. However, after the apostle has made the statement, "God was in Christ reconciling the world to Himself, not 4 imputing their trespasses to them," he adds, "and has committed to us the word of reconciliation." [2 Corinthians 5:19] God thus ordained that His work of reconciliation should be proclaimed to the world by the Church and that it should be accepted by men in true faith. Whoever does not believe this message abides under the wrath of God. Only those who believe the Gospel are partakers of salvation. In Mark 16:15-16 we read not only, "Preach the Gospel to every creature," but also: "He who believes and is baptized will be saved."

2.

Faith Alone Is Necessary. Faith in the atonement which has been effected by Christ and is proclaimed in the Gospel is necessary to salvation; but faith alone and nothing else — no work of man. The reconciliation of the whole world with God was consummated almost nineteen hundred years ago, and it was effected through the suffering and death of the Savior as our Substitute. This reconciliation God makes known to us in the "Word of Reconciliation," or the Gospel, in order that we may receive and believe it. Hence, we on our part are in possession of this reconciliation as soon as the first spark of faith is kindled in our hearts. In the Gospel, in Baptism, and in the Lord's Supper, God on His part extends to us His hand of peace. But on our part faith is the hand with which we grasp God's hand of peace. In other words, faith in our hearts is the amen to the promise of the Gospel. We thus partake of the reconciliation effected by Christ through faith and through nothing else than faith — by faith alone (*sola fide*). All those who teach that works on the part of man are necessary for reconciliation teach contrary to Scripture, despoil Christ of His glory as the only Savior and the sole Sin-offering of the world, and do everything in their power to prevent men from being reconciled. In Romans 3:28 we read: "We conclude that a man is justified by faith apart from the deeds of the Law;" and in Romans 4:5, "But to him who does not work but believes on Him who justifies the ungodly, his faith is accounted for righteousness." Hence these errorists wrest from Christ His glory as the only Savior, for according to 1 John 2:2 Christ alone and no one else is the Propitiation for the sins of the whole world. Moreover, they prevent men from becoming reconciled, for Scripture teaches, "You have become estranged from Christ, you who attempt to be justified by law; you have fallen from grace." Galatians 5:4-5).

Our Confessions also bear witness to this truth. For example: "Faith reconciles and justifies before God the moment we apprehend the promise by faith." (Apology, Art. Ill; *Triglot*, p. 213.) Thus, the Augsburg Confession, too, expounds the doctrine of Scripture:

> Our works cannot reconcile God or merit forgiveness of sins, grace, and justification, but we obtain this only by faith, when we believe that we are received into favor for Christ's sake, who alone has been set forth as the Mediator and Propitiation, 1 Tim. 2, 5, in order that the Father may be reconciled through Him. Whoever therefore trusts that by works be merits grace despises the merit and grace of Christ and seeks a way to God without Christ, by human strength. (Augsb. Conf., Art. XX; *Triglot*, p. 53 f.)

The Augsburg Confession calls this doctrine of faith "the chief article of the Christian religion." In the Church of Rome this fundamental article is not only denied, but even anathematized. (Cf. *Decrees of the Council of Trent*, sixth session.) However, this chief article is being denied quite generally today also within the Protestant Church and the papists glory in this. The *Catholic Encyclopedia*, a recent work, to which Catholic theologians from all over the world have contributed, waxes jubilant over the assertion that only the "Missourians" and the "Saxon Free Church" maintain "the strict orthodoxy of the Old Lutherans." (Cf. Joseph Pohle, in *Cath. Encycl.*, VIII, 576.)

Regretfully we concede that the Catholics are correct with regard to those who today by the ignorant world are considered the representatives of Protestantism. Even the so-called "positive theologians" deny the truth that we become reconciled to God by faith alone. Professor Kirn in Leipzig, the successor of Luthardt, propounds the so-called Guarantee Theory (*Buergschaftstheorie*), according to which Christ's work of reconciliation means simply this, that Christ thereby guaranteed to His heavenly Father that men will amend their ways and conduct their lives in obedience to the divine Law.

Nevertheless Dr. Joseph Pohle, the Catholic theologian, is not quite accurate when he states that only the Missouri Synod and the Saxon Free Church believe and teach justification solely by faith, faith in the reconciliation effected by Christ. This truth is being taught and believed also outside the Missouri Synod and the Saxon Free Church. All true Christians, even those in heterodox church bodies, accept the doctrine of reconciliation through Christ. Whoever possesses this faith is a Christian; and vice versa, whoever has not this faith is not a Christian. Even in the Church of Rome, Luther reminds us, there are true Christians who, although they outwardly take part in the service of the Mass, nevertheless put their trust alone in Christ's merit. Also, many sectarian preachers still proclaim the crucified Christ, and not a few of their hearers, thanks to the gracious operation of the Holy Spirit, put their trust in Him.

From the war zone in Europe reports come to us that very many army chaplains deny Christ, the Savior of sinners. But laymen in the army, both soldiers and officers, bear witness to the atonement through Christ's blood. For the sake of illustration permit me to quote an example. A certain Dr. Asmussen of the Queen of Flensburg Regiment was mortally wounded, along with many of his comrades, as they assaulted a steep escarpment behind which the French were securely intrenched. Although bleeding from many wounds, he crept from one dying soldier to another and, his New Testament in hand, reminded them once more of Him who died for all. In this way God provides for the proclamation and acceptance of His Word even in those religious circles where infidelity prevails.

Have we such faith, that faith which relies solely on the divine mercy which Christ has merited for us? There are people who believe that they have this faith. Yet their so-called faith is not wrought by the Holy Ghost, but is pure fiction. On the other hand, there are those who really possess true faith implanted in their hearts by the Holy Ghost, and yet they constantly torment themselves with the fear that they have not yet come to faith. Even the most earnest Christians in their trials are afflicted with such misgivings. Think of Luther. He tells us that, harassed by terrors of conscience, he hurried from his cell to confess his sins to the father superior in order that he might be absolved by him. Also, the founders of our Synod, Walther, Sihler, and others, endured severe trials with regard to their state of grace. In fact, no Christian will be entirely spared such hours.

Since this matter is of such great practical importance, Luther, our Lutheran Confessions, and our Lutheran dogmaticians were continually bent on describing the marks of both a fictitious and of the true faith, the work of God in man. They were impelled to do this also by the fact that the papists defined faith as a mere knowledge of the history of Christ and stamped a sinner's sincere trust in the forgiveness of sins merited by Christ, that is, in the atonement of Christ, as "presumption" (*praesumptio*). (Cf. *Decrees of the Council of Trent*, sixth session.) The Roman theologians declared faith to be merely an act of the intellect and not at all of the will. Indeed, they went so far as to assert that faith, considered as an act of the will, is a monstrosity and a chimera (*monstrum et chimaera*).

Against this error our Lutheran Confessions and all our old Lutheran teachers from Luther down to Hollaz contended that true faith, which is wrought by the Holy Ghost, is not merely a matter of the intellect, but also of the heart and will. In other words, faith consists in this, that the heart puts its trust in Christ, that the heart and will of man desire, yea, yearn for the grace secured by Christ, the atonement effected by Christ and proffered in the Word of Reconciliation. This truth Luther emphasizes in all his writings when he describes the true faith wrought by the Holy Spirit. Unremittingly does He inveigh against the papistical delusion that faith is not the inward yearning or craving for grace, but a cold calculation of the intellect or a quiescent quality (*otiosa qualitas*) in man.

Among other things he writes, "That faith which man himself fabricates (*fides acquisita*) stands like a sluggard with his arms akimbo and says: "That is none of my business." But true faith eagerly seizes with outstretched arms the Son of God who was given for him and declares, "My Beloved is mine, and I am His." That is the faith which alone justifies us, without the Law and works, through the tender mercies of God offered in Christ Jesus." (*Opp. v. a.* IV, 379 sq.) In the same strain the Apology says, "That is faith which wishes those things that are offered in the promise." (Art. III, 191; *Triglot*, p. 207) Again, "Likewise faith ... exists in repentance; that is, it is conceived in the terrors of conscience which feels the wrath of God against our sins and seeks the remission of sins and to be freed from sin." (Art. III, 21; *Triglot*, p. 161.)

Chemnitz states that in pointing out the nature of justifying faith, we must inquire into two facts: in the first place, what its object is (namely, the promise of the Gospel); then, how and in what manner justifying faith deals with its object in order that it may justify. The second question he answers thus:

> Justifying faith deals with its object not merely by cold calculation nor by a general and superficial assent, but in such a way that it acknowledges, considers, desires, seeks, apprehends, accepts and embraces, and so appropriates to the individual believer, Christ with all His merits and through Christ, by virtue of the promise, God's mercy, which

forgives all sins. (Cf. *Examen, De Fide Iustificante,* p. 161.)

He furthermore teaches:

> In this transaction there are two hands. The one is the
> hand of God, with which He offers us reconciliation; the
> other is our own hand, which receives what God proffers."
> (*Examen, De Sacr. Eff. et Usu,* p. m. 20.)

Quenstedt distinguishes between a theoretical apprehension of Christ,
which is an act of the intellect, and a practical apprehension of Christ,
which is an act of the will. The first characterizes the "faith of the head,"
which is found also in unbelievers; the second constitutes the essence
of true justifying faith, which the Holy Ghost creates. (*Syst.,* II, 1339.)

To sum up the matter: Faith originates and exists only amid the terrors
of conscience; that is to say, faith is found only in those persons who
confess that they are guilty of God's eternal condemnation. The terrors
of conscience are always the background of true faith. Of course, these
pangs of conscience manifest themselves in different ways. One man is
outwardly overwhelmed with remorse. Another exhibits little emotion,
although inwardly he is really broken-hearted. But as soon as the
message of reconciliation awakens in the contrite heart even a mere
longing for the grace which Christ has secured, true faith has been
kindled in it. The very desire to be saved through Christ in itself
constitutes faith. For this reason our Lutheran Confessions declare that
it is exceedingly comforting to know that even a small spark of longing
for divine grace and eternal salvation is the beginning of true godliness
and that we need only to pray God to strengthen and preserve this faith
unto the end. (Formula of Concord, Thor. Deck, II, 14; *Triglot,* p. 885.)
Carnal security excludes the possibility of true faith. But wherever the
divine Law has humbled the heart and the Gospel has engendered a
longing for that grace which Christ has merited, there true faith exists.

Sad to say, the doctrine of salvation by faith in the atonement effected
by Christ is often shamefully abused so that sanctification and good
works are grossly neglected. But this neglect is caused by man's refusal

to believe in the reconciliation which Christ has made. The world is full of falsehood and slander, for it is inhabited by liars and slanderers. It likes to lie and to be lied about. The truth of this statement we experience everywhere; in all spheres of activity; in our social, commercial, political, and international life. We observe it even in times of peace, and especially during this World War. But all these lies are the merest trifles in comparison with that deception and defamation which says that faith in Christ's reconciliation hampers sanctification and good works.

As a matter of fact, true faith is by no means a barrier to sanctification and good works. On the contrary, it is their only source. It is the only means by which a person can live a holy and God-pleasing life. God assures us in His Word that the covenant of the Law was ineffectual so far as sanctification and good works are concerned, and that He therefore determined to establish with His people a new covenant, namely, the covenant of grace. (Jeremiah 31:31ff) Sanctification and good works flow only and altogether from faith. Whatever man docs without and prior to faith is damnable in the eyes of God. (Galatians 3:10, 5:4) God's verdict is: "Whatsoever is not of faith is sin." (Romans 14:23) To the Romans St. Paul writes: "Sin shall not have dominion over you." Why not? "For you are not under the Law, but under grace." The effect of the Law upon men's hearts is either despair or hypocrisy. In Romans 8:7 the apostle says that the Law makes mobile everything that is sinful in man. He writes: "But sin, taking occasion by the commandment, produced in me all manner of concupiscence." Those who deny the sola fide forfeit not only justification but also sanctification and good works.

Of course, we are willing to concede that the grace of God in Christ has always been used for a cloak of maliciousness. That was the case already in the ancient Apostolic Church. It was rather evident again at the time of the Reformation, for Luther complains that conditions in this respect were indeed shocking. Now that the Gospel in its purity was being preached, the people became so miserly that they could not salary a single Christian minister where formerly they had supported ten false prophets. Luther often reproved this ingratitude most severely.

But the doctrine of free grace is being abused even in our own time. Many of our church members, instead of showing their gratitude for God's grace by being diligent in good works, are lazy and indifferent, and still they comfort themselves with God's grace. That is a satanic delusion. True faith exists only amid the terrors of conscience. It is found only in hearts which repent before God in sackcloth and ashes, but through the gracious operation of the Holy Spirit have apprehended divine grace and now rejoice at the good fortune which has come to them through the atonement of Christ. Such persons are in possession of both sanctification and good works. However, where these are wanting, the fault does not lie with the doctrine of divine grace. On the contrary, it is due to man's refusal to believe the doctrine of grace. In that case a man believes only in his business or in his farm. Others, again, who still have faith are led by the deception of the devil and their flesh to commit the great folly of relegating the redemption of Christ to the background. They hold no family worship, nor do they regularly attend church. This dreadful abuse of God's grace we certainly must combat.

There is another thought, however, that we must also bear in mind: The pastor and bis congregation, inasmuch as they must pass judgment upon either the faith or the unbelief of the individual member, do not judge according to the faith in the heart, for faith is something that only God can see, not the pastor or the congregation. But they must insist that all who profess to have faith furnish proof of their faith by sanctification and good works. Indeed, all Christians always remain blunderers in sanctification and good works, but this they readily acknowledge, and with repentant hearts they not only promise to make amends, but actually strive to do so. Isn't it true that often the pastor and the congregation are to be blamed for the fault we are speaking of, inasmuch as they forget to insist that all who profess to be Christians must also prove their faith by works?

3.

How does a person come to faith in the Gospel of reconciliation? Faith in the atonement of Christ is a plant which does not grow in the soil of natural man's heart, but God Himself implants it by means of His almighty power and grace. This is the clear testimony of Scripture, which says, "The natural man does not receive the things of the Spirit of God." (1 Corinthians 2:14) Moreover, "No one can come to Me unless the Father who sent Me draws him." (John 6:44) And again:

> That you may know ... the exceeding greatness of His power toward us who believe, according to the working of His mighty power which He worked in Christ when He raised Him from the dead and seated Him at His right hand in the heavenly places. (Ephesians 1:18-20)

The case is this: By nature man can perform many outward deeds, yes, great and difficult works, the object of which is to conciliate God. For as the Apology declares, it is the nature of all men to believe that they can and must satisfy God by their own works. In accordance with this fact we find all men by nature quite willing to become reconciled to God by their own deeds. Men scourge themselves, starve themselves, impoverish themselves, cast themselves into the fire, take their own lives, and sacrifice their children to Moloch, all this because they believe that they are able to propitiate God. But there is one thing which man cannot do by nature: he cannot believe in the atonement which Christ has effected. This lies beyond his power. It is something he neither understands nor desires. (1 Corinthians 2:14) Luther therefore says: "Faith is as great a work as though God would recreate heaven and earth."

This being the case, how does a man come to faith in the Gospel of the crucified Christ? The Gospel has a remarkable power. It creates recognition for itself among men. That is to say, it produces the very faith which it demands. St. Paul writes: "Faith comes by hearing," (Romans 10:17), and by that he means the hearing of the Gospel.[11]

---

[11] Ed: "Faith comes by hearing, and hearing by the word of God." Romans 10:17.

There is indeed a great difference between the Law and the Gospel. The Law is powerless to assert itself in man. It makes sin active but does not destroy it. If a pastor should preach nothing but Law for half a century, during all those fifty years he would not succeed in inducing a single soul to keep the Law, even by only a half or a tenth part. The Law produces not the fulfilling of the divine commandments, but only the knowledge of sin. (Romans 3:20)

But the case is quite different with regard to the Gospel. The Gospel, unlike the Law, asserts itself and works the very faith which it demands. For this reason we rightly distinguish between the conferring and the effecting power of the Gospel. The Gospel does not only offer divine grace to us, but it at the same time produces faith in that divine grace. In other words, it calls men to faith. Holy Scripture explains this fact very clearly. Wherever the Gospel is preached, there the Holy Spirit operates through the Word. In fact, that is the Holy Spirit's only mission on earth until the Day of Judgment. Christ says of the Holy Spirit: "He will glorify Me." (John 16:14) That this is true we learn from St. Paul's experience at Corinth, where he preached Christ Crucified. He tells the Corinthians:

> I determined not to know anything among you except Jesus Christ and Him crucified. I was with you in weakness, in fear, and in much trembling. And my speech and my preaching were not with persuasive words of human wisdom, but in demonstration of the Spirit and of power, that your faith should not be in the wisdom of men but in the power of God. (1 Corinthians 2:2-5)

Two great factors must at all times be the theme of our preaching: the Law, which decrees that all the world is guilty before God (Roman 3:19), and the Gospel, which assures us that God has reconciled the whole world unto Himself. The success of this preaching we may well leave to the Holy Spirit, as Moody once said: "Give the Gospel a chance. The Gospel takes care of itself." The pity is that we do not go to church every Sunday, for that is the place where all Christians belong on the holy-day. It is a sorry fact that there are still Christian homes without a family altar. How can faith thrive when, as Luther says, the Gospel is hid under a bushel?

4.

The Task of the Christian Church in the World. The Gospel of reconciliation is the message which the Church must proclaim to the world. It is only in order that it may hear this message that the world still stands.

The message which the Christian Church must present to the world is not the message that there is a God, for this even the heathen know. (Romans 1:19) Nor is it the message that God has created and preserves this world, for also this truth is known to the heathen. (Romans 1:20) Nor is it the message that God demands morality of men, that He insists on their doing good, and that He punishes all evil with death and damnation, for the heathen are aware of this fact also. (Romans 1:32, 2:14) Nor is it the message that Christ is true God and man, a fact which even the devils know. (Matthew 8:29) No, the message of the Gospel is the glad tidings of the blessed fruits of Christ's work, of the atonement which Christ, true God and man, has effected, of the forgiveness of sins, of the grace of God which is in Christ Jesus.

Indeed, that is the message which we must preach to the world, and the reason why the world exists to this day is that we may preach this Gospel. The whole history of the human race is centered in the atonement of men with God through Christ. We divide the time of the world into the periods before and after Christ. The four thousand years before Christ were granted to the world in view of the reconciliation which was to follow in the fulness of time. The nineteen hundred and sixteen years after Christ were granted to the world on account of the reconciliation which was effected nineteen hundred and sixteen years ago. [12]

---

[12] Ed: Pieper was speaking to a conference in 1916.

God has committed unto us the Word which proclaims to the world the reconciliation which has been accomplished. That Word is to be spread abroad. "This gospel of the kingdom will be preached in all the world as a witness to all the nations, and then the end will come." (Matthew 24:14) The world which is standing to this day is merely the scaffold for the edifice of the Christian Church. The fact that there are states, cities, and countries is only to serve the purpose of preaching the Gospel. The sun, moon, and stars shine only for the sake of the Gospel. Everything that takes place in heaven and on earth occurs not for its own sake, but only in the interest of the Gospel. All things, even this war,[13] must serve the preaching of the Gospel, so that men may be brought to a knowledge of sin and salvation.

That is the clear teaching of Holy Scripture. That, too, is the correct worldview, yes, the Christian worldview. For this reason we ought not to harbor any regrets as to the humble position which we occupy in the world. Even though the world regards us Christians as insignificant, we are in reality the center of the universe. Heaven and earth, wind and weather, all things are governed in the interest of the Church, for "all things work together for good to those who love God." (Romans 8:28)

Let us, then, use the time during which God still permits the world to continue for the propagation of the Gospel and the true Christian faith. Let us all be diligent in our capacity as spiritual priests, as St. Peter exhorts us:

> You are a chosen generation, a royal priesthood, a holy nation, His own special people, that you may proclaim the praises of Him who called you out of darkness into His marvelous light. (1 Peter 2:9)

As spiritual priests let us proclaim the atonement of Christ to our children, our households, our neighbors, and all those with whom God brings us into contact in our daily life. Let us be faithful, too, in training Christian teachers and pastors in order that the precious blood of

---

[13] Ed: World War I or the Great War.

Christ may bear abundant fruit as a result of their witness in church and school. Let us be zealous also in giving of our earthly possessions for the preaching of the Gospel in the world. Cursed be every form of avarice which hinders us in this work! But blessed be now and forever every service which we consecrate to our Savior in His kingdom.

Chapter Three

The High Priestly Office of Christ[1]

Outline

The grace that Christ proclaims as a prophet, he has acquired as a priest. This close connection between the prophetic and high priestly offices must be kept in mind from the outset. The high priestly office provides the content for the prophetic office. If Christ in his high priestly office only brought about a quasi-reconciliation of man with God, then the prophetic office also has only a quasi-reconciliation to proclaim. If, on the other hand, Christ brought about a real, perfect, objective reconciliation of all people with God through his vicarious life and suffering, then the Gospel is now a message of grace for all people, which they only have to accept by faith in order to come into possession of the grace acquired by Christ. It is said, for example, that the Socinians, rationalists, etc., by their denial of the vicarious satisfaction of Christ, leave the prophetic office of Christ standing. But this is not

---

[1] Franz Pieper, "*Das hohepriesterliche Amt Christi*" in *Christliche Dogmatik* (St. Louis: Concordia Publishing House, 1917), II.404-461, trans. T. R. Halvorson, eds. Neil Carlson and Marcus J. Baikie (2024).

quite accurate. With the denial of the high priestly office, the prophetic office in the biblical sense also falls away. In his prophetic office, Christ is then no longer the giver of grace to a world of sinners under the curse of the Law, but merely a moral preacher who teaches and encourages people to earn salvation through their own efforts to be virtuous. So much depends on the correct understanding of Christ's high priestly work!

So what does the high priestly work of Christ consist of?

The high priestly office of Christ in the state of humiliation.

Christ, whom the Scriptures of the Old and New Testaments expressly call "priest",[2] reconciled all humanity to God in his state of humiliation. 2 Corinthians 5:19: "God was in Christ reconciling (καταλλάσσων) the world to Himself." But Scripture not only reports the fact of reconciliation, but above all also describes the manner of reconciliation (*modus reconciliationis*) or the means by which reconciliation is brought about (*medium reconciliationis*). Christ reconciled man with God by offering himself (*seipsum*) to God as an atoning [or propitiatory] sacrifice. John 17:19: "For their sakes I sanctify Myself;"[3] 1 Timothy 2:6: "Who gave Himself a ransom for all." 1 John 2:2: "He Himself is the propitiation (ἱλασμός) for our sins, and not for ours only but also for the whole world." This, according to Scripture, is the difference between the exemplary priestly work in the Old Testament and the unique priestly work of Christ in the New Testament: *In Veteris Testamenti sacrificiis offerebantur victimae a sacerdotibus distinctae, Christus semetipsum sacrificavit.* (Baier.) [In the sacrifices of the Old

---

[2] Cf. Ps. 110, 4: כֹּהֵן לְעוֹלָם; Zech. 6. 13: כֹהֵן עַל-כִּסְאוֹ and accordingly in the New Testament ἱερεύς, ἀρχιερεύς, ἱερεύς μέγας etc., Hebrews 5:6, 8:4, 10:11, 2:17, 3:1, 4:14, 5:16.

[3] Meyer: "ἁγιάζω ἐμαυτόν — Christ solemnly consecrates Himself to God in offering Himself through His death to God; ἁγιάζω is substantially the same as προσφέρω σοι θυσίαν (I bring Thee a sacrifice). It is the same as הקדיש, the solemn word for offering a sacrifice in the Old Testament (Deuteronomy 15:19 ff.). — Christ is both priest and sacrifice at the same time."

Testament, victims distinct from the priests were offered, while Christ sacrificed himself.] In the New Testament, Christ is both priest and sacrifice, Hebrews 7:27: ὃς οὐκ ἔχει καθ’ ἡμέραν ἀνάγκην, ὥσπερ οἱ ἀρχιερεῖς, πρότερον ὑπὲρ τῶν ἰδίων ἁμαρτιῶν θυσίας ἀναφέρειν, ἔπειτα τῶν τοῦ λαοῦ· τοῦτο γὰρ ἐποίησεν ἐφάπαξ ἑαυτὸν ἀνενέγκας. [Who does not need daily, as those high priests, to offer up sacrifices, first for His own sins and then for the people's, for this He did once for all when He offered up Himself.] This self-sacrifice of Christ includes a twofold aspect according to the scripture: Christ gave himself for us in his holy life (*obedientia activa*), Hebrews 9:14: "who through the eternal Spirit offered Himself without spot to God" (ἑαυτὸν προσήνεγκεν ἄμωμον τῷ Θεῷ;[4] Hebrews 7:26 etc., and in his suffering and death (*obedientia passiva*), Ephesians 5:2: Christ "gave Himself for us, an offering and a sacrifice to God" (θυσία, sacrifice). Through this high priestly work accomplished by Christ on earth, God has now been reconciled with man once and for all, that is, the grace of God has been given to man, Hebrews 9:12: διά τον ἰδιον αἱματος εισήλ’&εν εφάπαξ εις τα αγια, αἰωνίαν λντρωσιν ενράμενος [with His own blood He entered the Most Holy Place once for all, having obtained eternal redemption]. This is what Scripture teaches about the fact and the means of the reconciliation of the world through Christ's self-sacrifice. The details will be explained later.

But the following must be added to this immediately: If men are reconciled to God through the sacrifice offered by Christ, or, what is the same, if the guilt of sin of men is blotted out before God, then through this sacrifice men are also redeemed from all the terrible consequences of the guilt of sin, from death, from the power of the devil, from the dominion of sin, etc.. This effect of reconciliation brought about by Christ is described in detail in Scripture. The power of death has been abolished by Christ, 2 Timothy 1:10: Christ "has

---

[4] One must not allow the term "sinlessness" to be flattened [or, trivialized]. Sinlessness is obedience to the divine Law.

abolished death and brought life and immortality to light."[5] The power of the devil, which he had over mankind due to God's judgment, has been destroyed. Hebrews 2:14: "Inasmuch then as the children have partaken of flesh and blood, He Himself likewise shared in the same, that through death He might destroy him who had the power of death, that is, the devil."[6] Men are redeemed from the dominion of sin through Christ's atoning sacrifice, Titus 2:14: "Who gave Himself for us, that He might redeem us from all lawlessness and purify for Himself His own special people, zealous for good works."[7] All this is to be diligently inculcated on the basis of Scripture, so that it may be recognized that through Christ we are redeemed from all evil, but in such a way that the redemption of the guilt of sin by Christ's sacrifice once offered always remains in the foreground and is taught as the cause and ground of redemption from death, from the devil, from the dominion of sin, etc. Because our guilt of sin has been redeemed before God, therefore we are also redeemed from death, etc.[8]

The vicarious satisfaction.

(Satisfactio vicaria. Vicarious Satisfaction.)

An ecclesiastical expression for the high priestly work of Christ in the state of humiliation is "vicarious satisfaction." The meaning of this

---

[5] The *locus classicus* of the overcoming and abolition of death by Christ, 1 Corinthians 15.

[6] Christ's atoning death [is] the judgment of the devil and the expulsion from the kingdom; νύν ο αρχών τον κόσμου τούτου εκβληθήσεται εξω, John 12:31, 14:30, 16:11; Colossians 2:15.

[7] 1 Peter 1:18-19, 2:24; especially also Romans 7:1-6.

[8] Th. Harnack says quite correctly against von Hofmann: "Salvation has its center and focus not in the abolition of death, but in the abolition of the divine judgment of punishment and human guilt, which are the cause and the power, the actual deadliness of death. Therefore, as our confession also teaches in accordance with Scripture, the abolition of the state of guilt objectively precedes the abolition of the reign of death." (*The Lutheran Church's Confession of Reconciliation*, etc. By D. G. Thomasius, with an epilogue by D. Th. Harnack. Erl. 1857, p. 138 f.)

expression is that Christ vicariously (in the place of men) rendered to God, who was angry at the sins of men, that which transformed God's wrath against men into grace towards men. The expression is not found in Scripture. But the thing designated by the expression is nothing other than the doctrine of Scripture concerning the redemption that took place through Christ. Just as in the [ecclesiastical term] ὁμοούσιος [one in being, one in essence] the teaching of Scripture on the true deity of the Son of God is briefly expressed [as being of one substance with the Father], so in the expression "vicarious satisfaction" we have a summary of what Scripture teaches about redemption through Christ in contrast to false doctrine.

The expression "*satisfactio vicaria*" expresses the following truths clearly revealed in Scripture:

I. There is in God an immutable justice towards men, according to which he demands from men perfect conformity with his law given to man (*institia vindicativa,punativa*) and, in the case of non-conformity, he is so angry with men to the extent that he pronounces upon them the sentence of eternal damnation (*institia legislatoria, normativa*). Christ expresses the *iustitia legislatoria* in Matthew 22:39-40: "You shall love your Lord God with all your heart; you shall love your neighbor as yourself." The *iustitia vindicativa* in the case of transgression is testified to in Galatians 3:10: "Cursed be everyone who does not continue in all things which are written in the book of the law to do them." Christ expresses the fact that this curse extends into eternity in Mark 9:48: in "hellfire, where 'Their worm does not die, And the fire is not quenched.'"

In order to combat *satisfactio vicaria*, the modern theologians push aside the biblical doctrine of *iuatitia legislatoria* and its consequence, *iustitia vindicativa*, by claiming "that punitive justice refers more to world government in the sense of providence, and leniency more to the economy of salvation." God's justice should not have a "private law" character [applicable to individuals]."[9] These are anti-biblical expressions. According to Scripture, the legislative and punitive justice of God does not merely refer to world government in general, but is so eminently "private law" [applicable to individuals] that it refers to every human individual both with regard to the demand and with regard to the imposition of punishment and curse: "You shall love God, your Lord", and: "Cursed be everyone who does not abide in all that is written!" In this relationship of law-giving and punishing justice to every individual of the human race is the further judgment of Scripture that all people, because they do not meet the requirement of God's Law, nor can they meet it (Romans 8:7), are sinners, guilty before God and actually under the wrath of God or the curse of the Law. Romans 3:9-18: Jews and Gentiles are under sin; Romans 3:19: the whole world is guilty before God (ὑπόδικος); Romans 5:10: men are enemies (εχθροί), hated by God, subject to his wrath;[10] Ephesians 2:3: children of wrath by nature, τέκνα φύσει οργής.

II. God has placed Christ and Christ has placed Himself in the place of men under both the obligation and under the penalty of the divine Law given to men. Christ's fulfillment of the Law given to men in the place of men is attested in Galatians 4:4-5: "God sent forth His Son, born of a woman, born under the law (γενόμενον ὑπό νόμον), to redeem those who were under the law."[11] Christ's vicarious suffering of the punishment which men incurred through their failure to fulfill the Law is attested in Galatians 3:13: "Christ has redeemed (ἐξηγόρασεν) us from the curse of the law, having become a curse for us;" 2 Corinthians 5:14: "One died for all;" 1 Peter 3:18: "Christ also suffered once for sins, the just for the unjust." The idea that Christ came under the obligation and punishment of the Law only "for the benefit" of men but not "in

---

[9] Cf. the remarks of Nitzsch, *Ev. Dogmatik* 3, p. 468.

[10] Meyer, Philippi. Also Luthardt z. St.: "Εχθροί οντες, not active (as e.g. Beck and Ritschl [say]), but passive: to whom God was enemy, who were under God's wrath."

[11] A restriction of νόμος to the Israelite ceremonial law is not in the text.

the place" of men (*loco hominum*) is a rationalistic-dogmatic reinterpretation of the cited and other scriptural statements.[12]

III. Scripture also clearly expresses that through Christ's vicarious action and suffering, God's wrath against men, or what is the same thing, God's judgment of condemnation over men is now completely lifted. Romans 5:18: "Through one Man's (namely Christ's) righteous act (δικαίωμα, v. 19: υπακοή [obedience]) the free gift came to all men, resulting in justification of life." Romans 5:10: "While we were still enemies of God" (εχθροί, passive: *Deo invisi*), "we were reconciled to God through the death of His Son." Luthardt rightly comments on the latter passage: "It is about a change of position on the part of God [or, on God's side]." That the reconciliation of the world which has taken place through Christ is a change of heart, not on the part of man, but

---

[12] Rather, it should be said: therefore "for our good", because "in our place". Kliefoth rightly wrote against von Hofmann: "This whole long interrogation of apostolic statements does nothing other than pursue the υπέρ ('died for us, given to us' etc.) and wants to make us understand that it must everywhere be translated not 'instead of us', but 'for our good'. Of course it can be translated "for our good" everywhere, because since it was for our good that the Lord died in our place, "for our good" everywhere also fits into the context. Hofmann is not telling us anything new, for the old rationalists have already told us so many times; the only question is how the Lord's death was for our good, and whether it was not for our good precisely because was done in our place." (*Der Schriftbeweis des D. v. Hofmann*. Schwerin 1859, p. 482 f.) That αντί also has the meaning "in place of", "instead of", should not be denied in view of such places as passages like Matthew 20:28 and 1 Corinthians 11:15: Meyer rightly comments on Matthew 20:8 (giving his life denotes substitution. That which is given as a ransom takes the place (instead) of those who are ransomed with it. The λυτρον is an ἀντίλυτρον (1 Timothy 2:6), ἀντάλλαγμα (Matthew 16:26)." Also υπέρ has the meaning 'instead of' in places like 2 Corinthians 5:14: εις υπέρ πάντων, 1 Peter 3:18: δίκαιος υπερ ἀδικων. Steiger aptly remarks on the latter passage: "The sharp juxtaposition of these two predicates leaves no one who has a sense of language in doubt for a moment that by υπέρ a change of person is expressed, that the apostle's meaning is that we are the unrighteous who deserve suffering through our sins, that Christ deserved none and yet took it over, namely by suffering what sinners should have suffered, that is, instead of them and thus for their good." Luthardt makes an unnecessary and unscriptural concession when he remarks (*Dogmatik*, p. 246): "Substitution is not directly expressed, but underlies the whole view and exposition."

on the part of God, is expressly stated in 2 Corinthians 5:19, where the κόσμον καταλλάσσων ἑαντῴ [reconciling the world to himself] is defined by μη λογιζόμένος αυτοῖς τά παραπτώματα αυτών [not imputing their trespasses to them]. The reconciliation of men with God was accomplished by the fact that God, in his heart (*in foro divino*), did not impute sins to men, but forgave them, that is, he brought the wrath over the sins of men to an end, not through his absolute power, but through the interposition [or, intervention] of Christ as a mediator (μεσίτης Qεου καί ἀνQρώπων), especially of the work [or, doings or actions] and sufferings of Christ (*di'* ενός παραπτώματος, διά τής υπακοής του ενός - διά τον θανάτου του υιου αυτου, εις υπερ πάντων ἀπέ'Qανεν). This is the teaching of Scripture on the reconciliation of the world, which came about through the incarnate Son of God. And this is what we also hold against the modern deniers of vicarious satisfaction. This doctrine is not a "theory" as Luthardt calls it (*Dogm.*, p. 266), but a doctrine which Christians of all times have believed, even before the emergence of the expressions *satisfactio* and *satisfactio vicaria*, and which is therefore also confessed [or, proclaimed] by the Christian church in its hymns. Not only is "the underlying idea" correct, as is often expressed today, but the thing itself is completely correct, that is, in accordance with Scripture. Luthardt's objection "that what Christ did and suffered does not fully coincide in the sense of mutual reckoning with what we would have to do and suffer" is based on the modern-theological abandonment of the Scriptural principle. If anything is clear on the basis of Scripture, it is clear that the redemption through Christ was accomplished "in the sense of mutual reckoning." Scripture presents the "mutual reckoning" in all its factors. Christ interceded for the world, for all men, with what he did and suffered. The reckoning is therefore perfectly extensive. Through Christ's actions and suffering, the world has actually been reconciled with God, that is, God's wrath against the world has been lifted, μη λογιζόμενος αυτοῖς τά παραπτώματα αυτών [not imputing their trespasses on them]. The reckoning is therefore also perfectly intensive. Finally, God himself has settled the account in the sense of a complete "mutual reckoning" by raising Christ from the dead. For just as Christ was given up for our sins, so He was also raised διά τήν δικαίωσιν ημών [for our justification]. According to the divine account revealed in Holy Scripture, what Christ has done and suffered is a complete "mutual reckoning" between God and the sinful human world.

As far as Luther's and the dogmatists' doctrine of vicarious satisfaction is concerned, the statements already mentioned in the section "Grace in Christ" (p. 19 ff.) belong here. Luther declares it to be a characteristic of paganism [or, heathenism] if someone would think that God is "without cost" — and by this he means Christ's vicarious satisfaction — merciful to man. All the concepts that belong to vicarious satisfaction are expressed by Luther, for example in his explanations of John 3:16-21 (St. L. XI, 1084 ff.), John 1:29 (VII, 1716 ff.), Galatians 3:13 (IX, 367 ff.). Luther's writings against the Antinomians also belong here (XX, 1610 ff.), just as all opponents of vicarious satisfaction are caught up [or, trapped or imprisoned] in antinomianism.

Objective and subjective reconciliation.

According to Scripture, there is an objective reconciliation, that is, a reconciliation of all people with God that was brought about by Christ 1900 years ago. Reconciliation is there; it exists before all human action and apart from it [or, independently of human actions]. It is *fait accompli* [an accomplished fact] like the creation of the world. Romans 5:10: "We were reconciled to God through the death of His Son;" so at that time, when Christ died, our reconciliation with God came about. Just as Christ's death occurred in the past, so did the accomplishment of our reconciliation. 2 Corinthians 5:19: "God was in Christ reconciling (meaning when Christ lived and died on earth) the world to Himself" The Greek word καταλλάσσειν, used in Romans 5:10 and 2 Corinthians 5:19, refers – and this must be emphasized again and again – not to a change of heart on the part of men, but to an occurrence in the heart of God. At that time, when Christ offered his atoning sacrifice, God let go of his wrath against men. This is not our explanation, but that of the apostle, when he adds to the words: "God was in Christ reconciling the world to himself" μη λογιζόμενος αυτοϊς τά παραπτώματα αυτών, not imputing their sins to them, that is, even then [or, already] forgiving the sin of the whole world in his heart, justifying the whole world. For, according to the language of Scripture (Romans 4:6-8), "not imputing sin" is as much as "forgiving sin" and "justifying" sinners. According to Scripture, the fact of Christ's resurrection from the dead is also an actual absolution or objective justification of the whole world of sinners, as seen in Romans 4:25: ἠγέρϋQη διά την δικαίωσιν ἡμῶν. [13] This is how clearly Scripture testifies to the objective reconciliation of all people with God, brought about once and for all through Christ![14] The gospel is the message of

---

[13] See the detailed explanation on page 380 and note 893 [references are to the 1917 German edition].

[14] Meyer is right in his explanation of 2 Corinthians 5:18-19: "Men were afflicted with God's holy wrath on account of their unredeemed sin, εχQροι Qεου. Romans 5:10, *Deo invisi*; but because God caused Christ . . . to die, He brought about the redemption of their sins, whereby God's wrath ceased. The same thought is contained in Romans 5:10, only in passive expression The reconciliation of all men was effected objectively by Christ's death." *The Report of the Southern District of the Synod of Missouri, etc.*, 1883, p. 20 ff., deals with this subject in detail. There it says: "Through the work of Christ a perfect reconciliation of God with man has been achieved. The work which Christ, as the 'mediator' (1 Timothy 2:5) between God and men, accomplished was pleasing to God, as it is said of Christ in Ephesians 5:2, that he 'gave himself for us as an offering and sacrifice, a sweet savor to God.' Just as God in grace made Christ, 'who knew no sin, to be sin' for men (2 Corinthians 5:21), that is, imputed to Christ the sins of men as his own, so He also regarded the atonement made by Christ as if it had been made by men themselves. The Holy Spirit writes through St. Paul in 2 Corinthians 5:14: 'We judge thus: that if One died for all, then all died.'. Through Christ's suffering and death, the sins of all people have been atoned for as completely as if all thousands of millions of people had themselves suffered eternal punishment in hell. The result is now: God is completely reconciled with all people and with every single one of them. No human being needs to do or suffer anything in order to be reconciled with God and to attain righteousness and salvation. Holy Scripture expressly testifies to this. In 2 Corinthians 5:19 we read: 'God was in Christ, reconciling the world to himself,' that is, 1900 years ago, when Christ fulfilled the Law for mankind and endured the punishment for mankind's transgression of the Law, God was reconciling mankind to himself. We

this objective, accomplished reconciliation, which is why it is called [in] 2 Corinthians 5:19 ὁ λόγος τῆς καταλλαγῆς (the word of reconciliation). And hence it comes about that people are now reconciled to God for their part or subjectively through nothing other than faith (*sola fide*). To put it another way: we are now reconciled to God through faith because reconciliation through Christ's satisfaction is already present and is proclaimed and offered in the Gospel. Paul calls for faith in the objectively existing reconciliation in 2 Corinthians 5.20 with the words: katallaghte τω Qεω, and he confesses Romans 5:11 in the name of all Christians, that through Christ "now" – that is, when we become believers and are justified – "we have received reconciliation".[15] In accordance with Scripture, the Lutheran confession also emphasizes the truth that there is only one way of man's subjective reconciliation with God: that of faith in the reconciliation or forgiveness of sins acquired by Christ. The Apology states: "Faith reconciles and makes us righteous before God, if and when we receive

---

need to grasp the simple, clear words here and let them sink in. We know what it means to be reconciled with someone. We say of someone that he is reconciled with another when he has let go from his heart all the anger he once harbored against the other person for whatever reason. In the same way, God, for the sake of Christ's work, has let go all wrath against those people with whom He was angry because of their sins. This is expressed in the words: 'God reconciled the world to himself.' In Christ, God now relates to people as if they had never offended him with sins, as if there had never been any division between God and man. Here the so-called objective justification is clearly taught; for if God is reconciled with men through Christ, He no longer has anything against them, He has absolved them of their sins in his heart, He regards them as righteous for the sake of Christ Thus, according to Scripture, there is a reconciliation of God with men and a justification of them through faith. The circumstances of Christ's death also point to this: Christ's cry: "It is finished!"; the darkness until the ninth hour, when Christ died, [and then] at the ninth hour the sun broke forth again as an image of the sun of grace, which rose again for us through Christ's death; and the tearing of the veil in the temple, for by this miraculous process God actually declared that every sinner now has free access to him."

[15] Correctly Philippi on Romans 5:11: "The καταλλαγή is present; we receive it by faith, so that καταλλαγήν λαμβάνειν == dikaiousQai; cf. 2 Corinthians 5:21: καταλλάγητε τω Qεου."

the promise by faith." "*Sic igitur reconciliamur Patri et accipimus remissionem peccatorum, quando erigimur fiducia promissae misericordiae propter Christum* (Therefore we are reconciled to the Father and receive the forgiveness of sins when we are lifted up with confidence in the promised mercy because of Christ.)." "Fides nos Deo reconciliat (Faith reconciles us with God) ", namely *quia accipit remissionem peccatorum* (because he receives the remission of sins).[16]

The preservation of objective reconciliation is of decisive importance for the whole of Christian doctrine. What is left out here cannot be made up later. If it is established that humanity is completely reconciled with God through Christ's actions and suffering, then there is no longer any room for the heresy, which has appeared in many forms, that men themselves must still achieve their own reconciliation with God in whole or in part. The ground has been removed from all rationalistic, Roman, and modern theological doctrines of works.[17] The objective reconciliation of all people with God brought about by Christ compels the correct understanding of the Gospel and of faith. The Gospel can now be nothing other than the proclamation and presentation of the forgiveness of sins acquired by Christ,[18] and saving faith can now be nothing other than the mere acceptance of the forgiveness of sins

---

[16] Apol. M., P. 144; 101, § 81; 108, § 114; 119, § 61.

[17] Thus Luther argues against the Papist doctrine of works simply with Christ's perfect work. He writes: "There is the article which the children pray: I believe in Jesus Christ, crucified, dead, etc. No one has died for our sins except Jesus Christ, the Son of God. Only Jesus, the Son of God. Again I say: Jesus alone, the Son of God, has redeemed us from sins; this is certainly true and the whole Scripture; and if all devils and the world should be torn asunder and burst, then it is [still] true. But if it is He alone who takes away sin, we cannot do it with our own works." (E. A. 25, 76.)

[18] Luther on Luke 24:46, 47: "Secondly, forgiveness of sins should also be preached in his [Christ's] name; this is nothing else than that the Gospel should be preached, which proclaims to all the world that in Christ all the sin of the world has been swallowed up, and that He therefore went into death to take away sin from us, and rose again that He might devour and destroy it." (XI, 693.)

acquired by Christ.[19] The attempted reinterpretation of saving faith by old and new false teachers as a human achievement, good human behavior, etc., is immediately recognized as heresy in the light of the objective reconciliation brought about by Christ.[20] On the other hand, if the Scriptural doctrine of complete reconciliation through Christ's substitutionary satisfaction is not recognized or abandoned, then the rationalistic, Roman, Arminian, modern theological doctrine of works follows quite automatically [or, quite naturally or inevitably]. If Christ has either not sufficed for men at all, or only partially, it remains for man to do what Christ failed to do. Then only the quantity and the outward form of works-righteousness are in question. The Gospel is then not ὁ λόγος τῆς καταλλαγῆς, 2 Corinthians 5:18, ο λόγος τῆς χάριτος, Acts 20:32, etc., but sinks down to an instruction as to how men themselves can completely appease God through more or less their own doing. The gospel thus *eo ipso* becomes law. According with that, faith is not the simple acceptance of the reconciliation brought about by Christ, but the human achievement by which man places himself in God's favor.

---

[19] Luther: "Therefore the Gospel does not include works, for it is not a law, but faith alone; for it is purely a promise and offer of divine grace. Whoever therefore believes in it receives grace," etc. (XI, 84.) Furthermore: "Faith holds out its hands and its sack and only receives benefit. For just as God, the giver, gives such things through his love, so we are the recipients through faith, which does nothing but receive such gifts. For it is not of our doing and cannot be earned by our work; it is already given and offered; only that you open your mouth, or rather your heart, and keep still and be filled, Ps 81:11." (XI, 1103 p.)

[20] Walther reminds us that the opposition to absolution also has its reason in the fact that one does not recognize the perfect redemption of the whole world of sinners through Christ. He writes (*Pastorale*, p. 157): "Whoever, of course, does not believe that Christ has already redeemed the whole world completely, and that therefore the good news of the Gospel is nothing other than an absolution to be brought to the whole world, based on that redemption which has already taken place, and which, in order to bear its blessed fruit, requires nothing but faith in it or, in a word, acceptance . . . who, of course, will never be able to convince himself of the preciousness of private confession and absolution."

Thus dogmatics, which has to present the Christian doctrine in its context revealed in Holy Scripture, must first of all [or, above all, or first and foremost] present the objective and perfect reconciliation established by Christ, and hold it against all distortion [or, perversion] and weakening. The doctrine immediately loses its Christian character and becomes a pagan doctrine of works as soon as the perfect reconciliation of all men through Christ's vicarious satisfaction is abandoned. Moreover, the whole doctrine immediately becomes practically useless, since no conscience that has been properly affected by God's Law can find peace until it is founded in faith solely on the reconciliation brought about by Christ and proclaimed in the Gospel.

The objections against vicarious satisfaction.

In discussing these objections, we come to the saddest chapter in all of human history. People cannot reconcile themselves with God. Out of love for mankind[21] God has taken reconciliation into his own hands,[22] in such a way that He did not spare even his own Son, but gave him in place of man under the obligation and curse of the Law given to man. People should be able to say, according to Romans 5, that they have been justified by the blood of Christ (δικαιωQέντες εν τω αϊματι αυτου), that they have been reconciled to God by the blood of his Son (κατηλλάγημεν τω Qεου διά του θανάτου του υιου αυτου). Yes, through Jesus Christ, through whom they have received the atonement [or, reconciliation], they should be able to boast of God himself [or, glory in God Himself] as their now gracious God, and in the hope of the glory of God (καυχώμενοι εν τω Qεώ — κανχώμεQα επ' ἐλπίδι της δόξης του Qεου). But instead, people have criticized and continue to criticize the divine method of reconciliation as unnecessary, as unworthy of God, as contradictory and unjust, as not covering the

---

[21] Romans 5:8: sunisthsi την εαυτόν αγάπην είς ημάς ό Qεός.

[22] Because reconciliation is not effected by men but by God, 2 Corinthians 5:19 does not say: εαυτόν καταλλάσσων τω κόσμω but rather: κόσμον καταλλάσσων εαντω, as is evident from v. 18: δε πάντα, εκ του Qεου του καταλλάξαντος ημας κτλ.

matter at all, as too juridical [or, too connected with the law], etc. The human objections to the reconciliation brought about by Christ's vicarious satisfaction had to be discussed in the doctrine of grace, when it was a matter of describing saving grace as grace in Christ or for Christ's sake.[23] The following points are repeated here and elaborated further.

I. It has been said that God can forgive sin by virtue of his power without any satisfaction made by Christ for man.[24]

Answer: It is useless and foolish to argue about what God can do by virtue of his power, since God has declared in Scripture that he forgives sin only on the basis of the satisfaction made by Christ for sinners διά τής ἀπολυτρώσεως τής εν Χριστώ Ιησού, Romans 3:24. Cf. Luther's blunt rejection of the folly of those who philosophize [or, speculate] about what God could do when Scripture clearly states what God actually does and wants to do.[25] The contention that ἀπολυτρωσις, Romans 3:24 etc., denotes liberation [or, deliverance] in general (as the Socinians and their like-minded colleagues, including von Hofmann, have objected), and not redemption by the payment of a ransom, disregards the fact that Scripture expressly and explicitly names this ransom, namely, Christ himself, 1 Timothy 2:6; Christ's life, Matthew 20:28; and Christ's blood, 1 Peter 1:18.[26]

---

[23] S. 17-21.

[24] So Socinians etc. Note 45.

[25] Note 56.

[26] Note 46. Meyer on Rom. 3:24: With ἀπολυτρωσις the special term redemption by ransom (Eph. 1:7, 1 Cor. 6:20, Gal. 3:13) is not to be converted into a general deliverance; for the λυτρον or ἀντίλυτρον (Matt. 20:28, 1 Timothy 2:6) which Christ rendered . . . was his blood, which was the expiatory sacrificial blood. Indeed, ἀπολυτρωσις can express the general concept of deliverance, that is, in the Christian sense, messianic salvation (Romans 8:23); but where it speaks of the effect of Jesus' death, as here and Ephesians 1:7 etc., the atoning sacrificial blood is meant as the purchase price (against Ritschl), as is clear from Matthew 20:28, 1 Corinthians 6:20, 7:23; Galatians 3:13 etc. The same reasoning by Quenstedt, *Syst.* II, 653 ff.

II. It is said that it is an unworthy conception of God to portray him as so angry with sinful man that he could only be reconciled through Christ's vicarious suffering and death.[27]

Answer: Man can only learn what is a worthy or unworthy conception of God from God's revelation, that is, from Holy Scripture. According to Holy Scripture, however, God is angry with sinful man according to his righteousness, Romans 1:18: "The wrath of God is revealed from heaven against all ungodliness and unrighteousness of men;" Galatians 3:10: "Cursed be everyone who does not continue in all things which are written in the book of the law, to do them;" Romans 5:10: εχΘροϊ οντες.[28] That God is angry with men because of their sins, every man also feels in his conscience; all philosophical speculation about the impossibility, irrationality etc. of God's wrath cannot calm [or, sooth] the conscience. The wrath of God against man's sin is also evident in the fact of death that comes upon man, Hebrews 2:15. But that this actual wrath of God against the sin of men came upon Christ, was broken in Christ and through him was transformed into grace, is clearly taught in Galatians 3:13: "Christ has redeemed us from the curse of the law, by becoming a curse (κατάρα) for us."

III. It is said that the love of God is revealed in the fact that Christ died for mankind, Romans 5:8: "God demonstrates (συνίστησι) His own love toward us, in that while we were still sinners, Christ died for us:" so there can be no talk of a reconciliation of God's wrath through the death of Christ.

---

[27] This objection is found not only among the Socinians, crude rationalists, Ritschl, etc., but also among many American sectarian preachers of our time. They have become timid to tell the tender generation of our time of the wrath of God upon the sinful human race.

[28] Meyer on Romans 5:10 (εχΘροί).- "It is not to be understood actively — we were God's enemies — for Christ's death did not extinguish the enmity of men against God. Only the passive explanation is correct: enemies of God, that is, those against whom the holy οργή of God is directed because of sin, θεοστυγέϊς Romans 1:30; τέκνα οργής, Ephesians 2:3." Cf. note 50.

Answer: According to Scripture, both the love and the wrath of God are revealed in the death of Christ. This is especially evident in this passage, Romans 5:8-11: ExQrou ontes (= *Deo invisi*, under God's wrath) κατηλλάγημεν τω θεω. Love moves God to reconcile us to himself through the death of his Son, that is, to satisfy his penal justice. According to Scripture, God's will to love does not exclude the reconciliation with God's justice, but rather includes it.[29]

IV. It is said that to suppose that the innocent Christ was punished in the place of guilty men is manifest injustice.

Answer: What God does is just. Now the Scriptures expressly testify:

a. that God imputed the guilt of men to the innocent Christ, Isaiah 53:6; 2 Corinthians 5:21; John 1:29; Psalm 69:6, etc.

b. that God actually caused the innocent Christ to suffer in the place of guilty man, 1 Peter 3:18: "Christ also suffered once for sins, the just for the unjust (δίκαιος ὑπερ ἀδικων). Galatians 3:13: "Christ has redeemed us from the curse of the law, having become a curse for us."

Thus, we can be completely reassured about the justice of the trial. In the face of the fact clearly attested in Scripture, all human criticism based on injustice must remain silent. Incidentally, there is also no lack of examples in the area of natural opinion where a person stands up or intercedes for others and an entire people with his acts and suffering (Codrus, Decius, Zaleukus, etc.). But such examples should not be used to prove the justice of the divine procedure in the penal suffering of Christ to human reason. The only conclusive proof is: "It is written." When the vicarious penal suffering of Christ is subjected to human reason, it will always raise new objections again and again. This is also true with regard to reason that Christ suffered voluntarily and therefore

---

[29] So correctly Meyer. Luthardt also: "With whom God was hostile, who were under the οργή of God — in spite of the αγάπη, v. 8 — κατηλλάγημεν — καταλλαγέντες, passive: 'He will let go of anger.'" Calov's explanation of how both *caritas* (love) and *ira Dei* (the wrath of God) are manifested in the atoning death of Christ, *Socinism. proflig.*, p. 503. 392 *sqq.*

his vicarious suffering of punishment does not involve any injustice. It is true: Christ was not forced or compelled but voluntarily stepped into the place of guilty man, John 10:17, 18; Ephesians 5:2; John 18:4-11. But immediately human reason is ready with the objection that we would declare any earthly judge unjust who, in the place of a criminal condemned to death, would declare guilty and punish with death an innocent man who voluntarily offered himself. It is therefore safest to simply appeal to the revealed will of God for the justice of divine action, since God reconciled the world to himself through Christ's vicarious satisfaction.[30]

V. It is said that Christ did not in fact suffer what all men should suffer, namely eternal punishment in hell; thus the concept of vicarious penal suffering falls away. As we have already seen, Luthardt also lacks the courage to stand up for the biblical and church teaching. He believes that Christ's satisfaction should not be understood "in the sense of mutual reckoning." Frank, as quoted by Luthardt, even describes it as an "aberration" "if Christ was made to suffer the punishment that fallen man would have had to endure as an unredeemed person."[31]

But, it must be said that Scripture clearly and unequivocally teaches that Christ suffered exactly the punishment that was supposed to befall men because of their sins. People are under the curse of God because of their sins, according to Galatians 3:10: "Cursed be everyone who does not continue in all things which are written in the book of the law, to do them." And this curse has fallen upon Christ not in part, but in its entirety, when the Scriptures go on to say, "Christ has redeemed us from the curse of the law, having become a curse for us," v. 13. The objection that Christ's suffering was only temporary while the suffering

---

[30] Cf. *Lehre und Wehre* 1883, pp. 354-356. Philippi, too, (*Glaubenslehre*, IV, 2, 24 ff.) makes too much effort to obtain from human reason a favorable judgment of vicarious satisfaction. Therefore, the criticism of Nitzsch - Horst Stephan (*Ev. Dogm.* 1912, p. 587 ff.) is not entirely unjustified.

[31] Luthardt, *Dogmatik*, p. 255.

that was to befall men was eternal also does not negate the vicarious satisfaction. In describing the value of Christ's suffering, Scripture deliberately and explicitly emphasizes that Christ's suffering was the suffering of the Son of God, 1 John 1:7: "The blood of Jesus Christ His Son cleanses us from all sins;" Acts 20:28: "the church of God which He purchased with His own blood." The doctrine of the "orthodox theologians" that the temporary suffering of Christ, as the suffering of the Son of God, was worth as much as the eternal suffering of all men, is not a dogmatic construction, but a doctrine of the Scriptures.[32] In Christ's suffering, there are truly "corresponding punishments." The "reckoning" is quite accurate, even "arithmetically" accurate, if one accepts God's judgment, as is only right. It is the theologians, burdened with their own wisdom and measuring divine things according to their own yardstick, who object to the adequate character of Christ's satisfaction.

VI. It has been said and is still being said, especially in our time, that this whole view, according to which God reconciled mankind to himself through Christ's vicarious satisfaction, is too "juridical" and not "ethical" enough.

Answer: This cannot be changed if we want to remain true to Scripture. According to Scripture, the process of world reconciliation is inherently juridical in all its aspects. God's Law is decidedly juridical in that it requires perfect obedience from men, Matthew 22:37 ff. The curse of the Law, which is pronounced on transgressors of the Law, is also unadulteratedly juridical, Galatians 3:10. The subordination of Christ to the Law given to man is purely juridical, Galatians 4:4, 5, because Christ for himself was [or, stood] above the Law, Matthew 12:8. The divine transfer of human guilt and punishment to Christ is purely juridical, because God made him who knew no sin of his own person

---

[32] Dorscheus (in Baier III, 87): *Quod apud homines aeternum fuisset, ipsa maiestate et excellentia personae [Christi] compensatum est.* (What would have been eternal among men was compensated by the very majesty and excellence of the person [of Christ].)

to be sin for us, 2 Corinthians 5:21. The execution of punishment on Christ is purely juridical, because Christ personally did not deserve punishment, but in him the righteous suffered for the unrighteous, 1 Peter 3:18. Purely juridical, or an unadulterated *actus forensis*, is the divine act according to which God, when He reconciled the world to himself, did not impute men's sins to them, μη λογιζόμενος αυτόϊς τά παραπτώματα αυτών [not imputing their trespasses to them], 2 Corinthians 5:19,[33] and according to which, through the righteousness of the one Christ, there came to the justification of life for all men, Romans 5:18. Therefore, "the word of reconciliation" (ὁ λόγος τής καταλλαγής, 2 Corinthians 5:19) is also of a purely juridical nature, namely of the reconciliation already accomplished by Christ, which proclaims grace or divine forgiveness of sins to all nations (Luke 24:47) and awaits only acceptance by faith. It is due to the purely juridical character of the Gospel, which proclaims grace or forgiveness of sins, that the Gospel works faith in man (ἡ πίοτις εξ ακοής, Rom. 10:17), and that man is subjectively justified before God by faith (*sola fide*), without any righteousness of his own (μή εχων εμήν δικαιοσύνην την έκ νόμου [not having the righteousness of the law], Philippians 3:9). Scripture further teaches us that all human ethics, which the opponents of the juridical concept of world reconciliation are so concerned about, are based on these purely juridical processes. It is only after man has become righteous in a purely juridical way, that is, through faith in the God who justifies the ungodly (επί τον δικαιούντα τον ἀσεβή, Rom. 4, 5), does he love God and his neighbor and thus begin to fulfill God's Law. All those who want to transform the purely "juridical" character of reconciliation and justification "ethically" both make justification impossible (οσοι γάρ εξ έργων νόμου είσίν, υπό κατάραν εισίν, Galatians 3:10) and remove the foundation of sanctification (αμαρτία γάρ υμών ου κυριεύσει· ού γάρ έστε υπό νόμον, ἀλλ' υπό χάριν [For sin shall not have dominion over you, for you are not under law but under

---

[33] Meyer: "This is the changed judicial relationship into which God has entered and stands towards the sins of men."

grace] Romans 6:14). So, we are faced with the result that all those who want to push aside the legal character of world reconciliation and its appropriation with their criticism are consciously or unconsciously engaged in the sad undertaking of eliminating the whole Christian doctrine as it is revealed in Holy Scripture. When von Hofmann denied vicarious satisfaction and polemicized against its "juridical" character, Theodosius Harnack wrote quite correctly: ""If [the doctrine of reconciliation of the Lutheran confession] could be reproached for allowing the concept of satisfaction to open the door to a juridical view of world reconciliation, then this reproach falls back on Scriptures. . . . The confession of our symbols, therefore, can only be removed after the concepts of God's righteousness, justice, and holiness, of law and conscience, of guilt, of punishment and judgment, of mediator, of ransom, and of imputation have first been removed from Scripture."[34] All polemics against the "juridical view" of world reconciliation cease as soon as this process is judged according to Scripture.

History of the doctrine of vicarious satisfaction.

Over time, vicarious satisfaction sometimes has been denied altogether, sometimes restricted, and sometimes mutilated.

All deniers of the divinity of Christ from apostolic times (1 John 4:2 ff.; 1:1 ff.; 5:20; John 1:1 ff.) down to our own time deny the *satisfactio vicaria* [Ritschl, A. Harnack] This is quite consistent. Every mere human being needs his righteousness for himself. If Christ were a mere man, he too would need his righteousness for himself no matter how "absolutely," "essentially," "uniquely" or in any other way under the "influence" of God. [Contrasted with that], the weight of deity [in Christ] belongs to vicarious satisfaction according to Scripture (Galatians 4:4, 5; Romans 5:10; 1 John 1:7). All deniers of the deity of Christ attribute to the life and suffering of Christ only the meaning that men are thereby stimulated to their own efforts for virtue and in this

---

[34] *The Confession of the Lutheran Church on Reconciliation*, etc. Erl. 1857, p. 139 f.

way reconcile themselves with God.

Abelard († 1142) also belongs to the deniers of vicarious satisfaction. Abelard deserves special mention because he set an example [or, became exemplary] in his denial of the doctrine of Scripture. According to Abelard, the Son of God did not come in the flesh to satisfy God's justice [or, righteousness], but rather to give men the supreme proof of divine love through teaching and example (especially by his death) and thus to awaken in them love in return. Through love for God awakened in this way, people are then reconciled with God and become righteous and justified. Abelard calls the teaching that God is reconciled with the world through the blood of the innocent Christ "cruel and unjust."[35] Abelard's doctrine of a revelation of God's love through Christ without

---

[35] Abelard says in his interpretation of the Epistle to the Romans: *Nobis videtur quod in hoc justificati sumus in sanguine Christi et Deo reconciliati, quod per hanc singularem gratiam nobis exhibitam, quod filius suus nostram susceperit naturam et in ipsa nos tam verbo quam exemplo instituendo usque ad mortem perstitit, nobis sibi amplius per amorem astrinxit, ut tanto divinae gratiae accensi beneficio, nil iam tolerare propter ipsum vera reformidet caritas ... Redemptio itaque nostra est illa summa in nobis per per passionem Christi dilectio, quae nos non solum a servitute peccati liberat sed veram nobis filiorum Dei libertatem aquirit, ut amore eius potius quam timore cuncta impleamus, qui n obis tantam exhibuit gratiam, qua major inveniri, ipso attestante, non potest.* (We believe that we are justified in the blood of Christ and reconciled to God, that through this singular grace shown to us, that his Son took on our nature and in it, both in word and in example, led us all the way to death, bound himself to us through love, so that inflamed by such a great benefit of divine grace, true charity now fears nothing for his sake... Our redemption is therefore that highest love of Christ in us through his passion, which not only frees us from the bondage of sin but acquires for us the true freedom of the sons of God, so that we may fulfill all things with his love rather than fear, who has shown us such great grace that, as he himself testifies, greater cannot be found.) Against vicarious satisfaction he says: *Quam crudele at iniquum videtur, ut sanguinem innocentis in pretium aliquod quis requisierit aut ullo modo ei placuerit innocentem interfici, nedum Deus tam acceptam filii sui mortem habuerit, ut per ipsam universo reconciliatus sit mundo?* (How cruel and unjust it seems that someone would seek the blood of the innocent as payment or in any way be pleased with the killing of the innocent, let alone that God would have the death of his own Son so acceptable that through it the whole world would be reconciled.) (In Schmid, *Dogmengesch.*, 4th ed., pp. 259, 258.)

vicarious satisfaction of Christ is closely followed in our time by Albrecht Ritschl († 1889).[36] Ritschl teaches: In God there is no wrath over the sin of men. So there is no need for vicarious satisfaction on the part of Christ. The purpose of Christ's actions and sufferings is to reveal God's fatherly disposition to men and thereby teach and convince men that they need not fear God because of their sins. When people have come to this conviction, then their reconciliation is accomplished. The objective reconciliation is here completely converted into a subjective one. Böhl aptly characterizes Ritschl's doctrine of reconciliation as follows: "At Ritschl's hand, we find ourselves in the pleasant position of no longer knowing God's wrath."[37] Böhl calls Ritschl "*Socinus redivivus*" [Socinus revived, or, recycled].[38]

To the class of those who limit the vicarious satisfaction of Christ belong all those who deny the intrinsic and infinite value of Christ's satisfaction by teaching that Christ's actions and sufferings were not in themselves (*ex interna sua perfectione*) a perfect ransom for the sins of men, but were only accepted by God for that purpose (*per liberam Dei acceptationem, per gratuitam Dei acceptationem* [By the free acceptance of God, by the gratuitous acceptance of God]). [acceptilation theory] This was the case among the scholastics, especially the Scotists. Anselm († 1109), however, taught in his work

---

[36] Nitzsch-Stephan, *Dogm.*, p. 566.

[37] *Dogmatik*, p. 412; Strong *(Syst. Theol.*, p. 734): "Ritschl regards the sense of guilt as an illusion which it is the part of Christ to dispel."

[38] Ritschl characterizes his entire doctrine when he says, explaining the title of his main work "Christian Doctrine of Justification and Reconciliation:" "However, the order of the two terms is unusual. One expects to see them listed in the reverse order, reconciliation and justification, by thinking of the reconciliation of God through Christ, and accordingly of the justification of sins through Him. The title of Justification and Reconciliation is meant to show that the correct presentation of the matter is linear which excludes the assumption of a change in God's disposition from wrath to grace through Christ." (1,2.) Cf. the detailed exposition and assessment of Ritschl's doctrine by L. Fürbringer in "*Lehre und Wehre*" 1894, pp. 218 ff.; 1895, p. 97 ff.

Cur Deus homo with all clarity and decisiveness that Christ, the God-man, by giving his life to divine justice for the sin of men, which sin was a violation of the divine majesty and therefore incurred an infinite debt, had made complete satisfaction.[39] Duns Scotus († 1308), on the other hand, taught that Christ's merit had only a finite value and had been accepted by God for an infinite one according to the freedom of the divine omnipotent will.[40] This is not only the case with the Scotists proper, but also other theologians who are regarded as Thomistic, such as Durandus († 1333). Of course, Thomas himself († 1274) had already laid the foundation for this acceptance theory, despite his "*satisfactio superabundas*", when he taught that God, because he is the Most High,

---

[39] *Vides igitur quomodo vitae haec* (namely the God-Man) *vincat omnia peccata, si pro illis detur.* II,14. (You see then how this life (namely the God-Man) overcomes all sins, if it is given for them.) And just before that: *Anselm: Cogita etiam, quia peccata tantum sunt odibilia, quantum sunt mala; et vita ista tantum amabilis est, quantum est bona. Unde sequitur; quia via vita ista plus est amabilis quam sint peccata odibilia. Boso: Non possum hoc non intelligere. Anselmus: Putasne tantum bonum tam amabile posse sufficere ad solvendum, quod debetur pro peccatis totius mundi? Boso: Imo plus potest in infinitum.* (Think also, because sins are only hated as much as they are evil; and this life is only lovable as much as it is good. Therefore it follows; because this life is more lovable than sins are hateful. Boso: I cannot fail to understand this. Anselmus: Do you think that such a great and lovable good can be enough to fully pay what is owed for the sins of the whole world? Boso: indeed, it can do infinitely more.) Anselm's denial of *obedientia activa* will be discussed later in the treatment of Christ's *obedientia activa*.

[40] Duns Scotus says (cited III, 19): *Quod attinet ad meriti sufficientiam, fuit profecto illud finitum, quia causa eius finita fuit, videlicet voluntas naturae assumtae et summa gloria illi collatga. Non enim Christus quatenus Deus meruit, sed in quantum homo. Proinde si exquiras, quantum valuerit Christi meritum secundum suffientiam, valuit procul dubio quantum fuit a Deo acceptatum. Siquidem divina acceptatio est potissima causa et ratio omnis meriti.* (In Schmid, *op. cit.*, 1st ed., p. 103.). (As for the sufficiency of merit, it was definitely finite, because its cause was finite, namely the will of the assumed nature and the highest glory conferred upon it. For Christ did not merit as God, but as man. Therefore, if you inquire how much Christ's merit was worth in terms of sufficiency, it doubtless was worth as much as it was accepted by God. Indeed, divine acceptance is the most powerful cause and reason for all merit.)

can forgive sin even without satisfaction.[41] The theory of acceptance[42] was later espoused again by the Arminians.[43] Calvin also is thrown back to the acceptance theory by his false doctrine of predestination. For Calvin allows Christ's merit, as the merit of a man, to acquire sufficient value only through predestination.[44] The Romans limit the vicarious

---

[41] Note 45: H. Schmidt in *RE.* 2 XVI, 383.

[42] Usually called the theory of acceptilation by the old teachers.

[43] Limborch polemicizes against the *satisfactio plenaria* thus: *Satisfactio Christi dicitur, qua pro nobis poenas omnes luit peccatis nostris debitas, asque perferendo et exhauriendo divinae justitiae satisfecit. Verum illa sententia nullum habet in Scriptura fundamentum. Mors Christi vocatur sacrificium pro peccato; atqui sacrificia non sunt solutiones debitorum neque plenariae pro peccatis satisfactiones; sed illis peractis conceditur gratuita paccati remissio. (Theol. christ.* III, 21,6). (The satisfaction of Christ is said to be that by which He paid all the penalties owed by our sins for us, and by enduring and exhausting [them], He satisfied the divine justice. However, this opinion has no foundation in Scripture. The death of Christ is called a sacrifice for sin; but sacrifices are not payments of debts nor complete satisfactions for sins; but after they are offered, free remission of sin is granted.) Christ´s sacrifice suffices: *primo, respectu voluntatis divinae, quae ad generis humani liberationem nihil ultra requisivit, sed in unica hac victima acquievit.* (22,5). (First, respecting the divine will, which required nothing more for the liberation of the human race, but was content with this one victim.)

[44] The quote in context *Inst.* II, 17, § 1: *Equidem fateor, si quis simpliciter et per se Christum opponere vellet iudicio Dei, non fore merito locum, quia non reperietur in homine* (Calvin nestorianizes here the same as Scotus) *dignitas, quae possit Deum promereri. [...] Quum ergo de Christi merito agitur, non statuitur in eo principium, sed conscendimus ad Dei ordinationem, quae prima causa est, quia mero beneplacito mediatorem statuit, qui nobis salutem acquireret. . . . Nam Christus nonnisi ex Dei beneplacito quidquam mereri potuit. Sed quia ad hoc destinatus erat, ut iram Dei sacrificio suo placaret suaque obedientia deleret transgressiones nostras, in summa, quando ex sola Dei gratia (quae hunc nobis constituit salutis modum) dependet meritum Christi, non minus apte quam illa humanis omnibus iustitiis opponitur.* (In fact, I admit that if someone wanted to compare Christ simply and by himself against the judgment of God, He would not be worthy in that place, because no dignity can be found in man (Calvin Nestorianizes here the same as Scotus) which can earn God's favor. ... For Christ could earn nothing except by the good pleasure of God. But because He was destined for this, to appease God's wrath with his sacrifice and to blot out our

satisfaction of Christ in many ways. They claim that men themselves must atone [or, expiate] the temporal punishment for sins committed after Baptism either in this life or in purgatory. They therefore deny that Christ's merit covers the entire guilt of man's sins. Furthermore, what they do leave standing of Christ's merit is only meant to benefit men on the basis of their own improvement [or, correction] and sanctification. In this way, they actually render the entire merit of Christ useless for the sinner. Furthermore, in the Roman sacrifice of the Mass, in which the body and blood of Christ supposedly must be and are continually and perpetually offered to God in an unbloody manner, is a denial of the once-offered perfect sacrifice of Christ. The excuse that the sacrifice of the Mass is a means of appropriating the full sacrifice of Christ is not valid, since the fruit of Christ's sacrifice is distributed through the Gospel and the Sacraments, and received by men through faith. It is true that the Romans do speak of a "surplus merit" of Christ (*satisfactio superabundans*). But they entrust this "surplus merit" to the Pope, who distributes it to the people under the conditions he sets. The Papists also place the merits of Mary and the saints alongside the merits of Christ in such a way that "the saints free us from the temporal punishments of sins, even from the punishments of purgatory."[45] This is how the *satisfactio Christi vicaria* is denied by

---

transgressions by his obedience, in conclusion, when the merit of Christ depends solely on God's grace (which has established this way of salvation for us), the merit of Christ is no less apt than all human justice is opposed to it.) On the other hand, it should be said: It is true that God did not force but in his free mercy gave Christ to the world as their Savior; but to deduce from this that Christ's merit has no value in itself, but only obtains value through God's pleasure or ordinance, is conjecture and incompatible with Scripture. Where the Bible says that we are purified by Christ's blood, the blood of the Son of God, from all our sins (1 John 1:7, Acts 20:28, and others), it ascribes infinite value to Christ's blood.

[45] Thus Bellarmin. Cf. Quenstedt, *Systema* II, 661 Quenstedt replies briefly and aptly: *Solus (Christus) ita nos redemit, ut castigatio sit super ipsum, et nos pacem habeamus, Isaiah 53:5. Ergo etiam redemit nos a poenis peccatorum nostrorum temporalibus. Nisi*

the papal church in many ways. The Papacy is and remains the great antichristian institution [or, antichrist institution] through which Christ's vicarious satisfaction is dismissed and mocked under an outwardly Christian guise [or, trapping or paraphernalia].

Hugo Grotius' theory also has spread in America. According to Grotius († 1645), God punished the innocent Christ in the place of guilty men, not to satisfy [or, do justice to] his holiness, but to make Christ an example of punishment, thus upholding the authority of the law before men and deterring them from sin.[46] This theory is known here under the name "Governmental Theory" and has been especially embraced by "New England Theology".[47] While this theory still maintains a faint

---

enim et hae essent per Christum solutae et sublatae, nondum pacem haberemus cum Deo. Quidquid enim iustificatis hominibus immittitur afflictionis , id non amplius est maledictio et τιμωρία, sed castigatio et paterna δοκιμασία. (He alone (Christ) redeems us in such a way that the punishment is upon him, and we have peace, Isaiah 53:5. Therefore, He also redeemed us from the temporal punishments of our sins. For if these were not also removed and taken away through Christ, we would not yet have peace with God. For whatever affliction is inflicted upon justified men, it is no longer a curse and punishment, but rather correction and paternal testing.) Moreover, it is well known that in Roman practice, the distinction between temporal and eternal punishments often completely disappears, and the forgiveness of sins is founded solely on the merits and intercession of the saints.

[46] Grotius says: Deus ... cruciatibus et morte Christi uti voluit, ad statuendum exemplum grave adversus culpas immensas nostrum omnium, quibus Christus erat conjunctissimus natura, regno, vadimonio. (De satisfactione IV, §18) (God ... wanted to use the sufferings and death of Christ to set a serious example against the immense sins of all of us, with whom Christ was most closely connected by nature, kingdom, and pledge [or, as a surety]. To this before: Poenas infligere et a poenis aliquem liberare ... non est nisi rectoris qua talis promo et per se: ut, puta, in familia partris; in republica regis, in universo Dei. (II, 1.) (To inflict punishments and to free someone from punishments . . . is nothing other than the prerogative of a ruler as such and inherently: as, for example, in a father's household; in a king's kingdom, in the universe of God. (II, 1.)

[47] Hopkins, the younger Edwards, E.A. Park von Andover, among others. Hugo Grotius' "Regentenmaßregel" is also found to a large extent in the German

semblance of a satisfaction rendered by Christ — Grotius himself retains the term *satisfactio* — others have gone on to deny any satisfaction rendered to divine justice and to place the essence of reconciliation merely in the moral influence that Christ's teachings and example exert on people (moral power view of atonement, moral-influence theory).[48] Christ's teaching and example are variously defined by different people, for example: Christ, as the representative of mankind, confessed and repented fully of mankind's sins[49] and thereby made God inclined to forgive mankind's sins if people follow Christ in confession of sin and repentance.[50] It is unnecessary to further delineate the deviations from Christian doctrine of reconciliation in detail. As with the doctrine of Christ's person, as division into only two parts is appropriate. There are only two essentially different doctrines of the

---

supranaturalists Stäudlin, Flatt, Reinhard, etc. Even Storr does not avoid it. He calls the "appeasement of God's wrath" through Christ's life and suffering a "false delusion." "Rather, it was intended to support" (by the punishment of sin against Christ) "the very true opinion of the holiness of the Law, which is highly beneficial not only to men, but also to the purest and most intelligent minds." (*Lehrbuch d. christl. Dogmatics*, ed. Flatt. 1803, § 91, note 9.)

[48] So especially Horace Bushnell († 1876) in *Vicarious Sacrifice*. Bushnell says: "His [Christ's] work terminates, not in the release of penalties by due compensation, but in the transformation of character, and the rescue, in that manner, of guilty men from the retributive causations provoked by their sins." (In Hodge, *Syst Theol.*, II, 568.) Bushnell, however, admits that his "moral view" of reconciliation has no effect on men unless it is clothed in the "altar expressions," that is, representing Christ as a sacrifice for our sin. Hodge therefore says of Bushnell: "Toward the end of his book, however, he virtually takes it all back." In a later work, *Forgiveness and Law*, Bushnell says that God cannot forgive sin without "making cost to himself" [or, without it costing himself something]. Therefore, God makes it cost Himself the suffering of His Son. But not in the sense that his justice demands satisfaction, but in the way that a person can only truly forgive his offender from the heart when he has sacrificed himself for him. A critic of Bushnell rightly said at the time that he theologized as if "God were made in the image of man."

[49] Christ is the great Penitent (Macleod Campbell). Cf. Strong, *Syst. Theol.* p. 734.

[50] Cf. my detailed exposition and refutation of this doctrine in "*Lehre und Wehre,*" 1883, pp. 349 *et seq.* (against D. Graves in the *Baptist Quarterly Review*).

person of Christ. If one teaches the *unio peronalis*, that is, the union of God and man into one person, then one teaches Christianity. The doctrinal formations, so numerous and varied, by which the *unio personalis* is denied, all belong to an unbiblical and unchristian class.[51] In the same way, in the doctrine of Christ's atoning work [or, work of reconciliation] a twofold division must be observed: either objective reconciliation is taught or it is not taught. As soon as it becomes apparent that the objective reconciliation of all men through Christ's vicarious life, suffering and death is denied, the foundation of Christian doctrine is abandoned [or, forsaken]. You can then shape your view of reconciliation and name it whatever you want, but in some way or another, what Christ alone has accomplished will always be attributed in whole or in part to the actions of men. That ends salvation by grace for Christ's sake, through faith, with Christ's honor as savior. The certainty and assurance of grace and salvation are lost once and for all!

Further description of modern theories of reconciliation.

Looking at the current state of affairs, it can unfortunately be rightly said[52] that even the "conservative theology of the present," including that which calls itself Lutheran, has not returned to the "old Protestant church doctrine" of vicarious satisfaction (*satisfactio vicaria*), that is, to the teaching of Holy Scripture.[53] "None of the newer dogmatists," Kirn reports, "thinks of the transfer of punishment in the full sense, including the feeling of guilt, onto the person of the Redeemer.[54] [In their view Christ suffered], either the world's judgment [or, hatred] or the sentence of the law" (as if the law were not an expression of God's demanding and punishing justice) "or the evil inflicted on mankind for

---

[51] Cf. note 250.

[52] Nitzsch-Stephan, *Ev. Dogmatik* 3, p. 588 ff.

[53] S. 407 ff.

[54] On the fact of Christ's feeling of guilt, see p. 370 ff.

the sake of sin, is carried out on him."[55]

Positive and middle-partisan [or, mediating] theologians do concede: "Numerous representatives of" (modern) "New Testament scholarship today admit a juridical [or, legal] interpretation of the death of Jesus and a penal substitution in Paul."[56] In particular, Holtzmann has shown that the apostle Paul quite obviously teaches vicarious satisfaction ("satisfactorily performed by the Son of God", "a satisfaction made to divine justice"), and that the "modern-positive theology", which denies this, is guilty of "the violent reinterpretation and elimination" of the Pauline statements.[57] Holtzmann also appealed to the scientific sense of honor of modern positive theologians by reminding them: "The freedom of religious thought does not arise from a violent reinterpretation of a matter leading to its elimination, but only from acknowledging its existence historically and understanding [or, appraising] it as extant in history." Vicarious satisfaction, Holtzmann says, is "the nerve of all Pauline thoughts of atonement" and forms the basis for "the justification of sinners", that is, for the doctrine of justification. Holtzmann has also pointed out that scriptural statements such as Galatian 3:13; Colossians 2:14-15; Romans 3:25, 26; 2 Corinthians 5:21 were understood and interpreted more correctly by the older orthodoxy than by modern positive theology.[58] But modern "positive" theology has not allowed itself to be dissuaded from its opposition to substitutionary atonement. On the contrary, it devotes all its strength to rejecting *satisfactio vicaria* as an allegedly too "juridical" and too little "religiously moral" view of Christ's work of

---

[55] *RE.*3 XX, 573.

[56] Nitzsch-Stephan, *op. cit.* p. 601, note.

[57] *Neutestamentliche Theologie* II, 105 ff.

[58] Holtzmann, *op. cit.,* offers one of the best brief presentations of the Christian doctrine of reconciliation, which he calls the Pauline doctrine. It is only necessary to disregard a few caricatures which he has included, because he does not regard the apostle Paul as an apostle of Jesus Christ, in whom Christ himself speaks (2 Cor. 13:3), but as a representative of "later Judaism."

reconciliation, by continuing to reinterpret scriptural statements, by caricaturing scriptural and church doctrine, and by making extensive and abundant use of unclear, partly learned [or, scholarly or erudite], partly pious-sounding phraseology. There will be more to say about this later. At the same time, this theology also declares itself willing to pay the necessary price for the rejection of vicarious satisfaction. The price is the abandonment of the Christian doctrine of justification. For the situation necessarily unfolds [or, turns out] in this way: If man has not been completely reconciled to God by Christ's vicarious satisfaction, then there is no λόγος τῆς καχαλλαγής (2 Corinthians 5:19) or λόγος τῆς χάριτος (Acts 20:32), through whose faithful acceptance man in his turn is (subjectively) reconciled to God, but man must complete his reconciliation with God and bring it to a decisive conclusion through his own "religious-moral" goodness, renewal and sanctification. Thus Kirn explicitly summarizes the positive outcome of the fight against *satisfactio vicaria*: "We are pointedly reminded to include the transformation of humanity in the concept of the work of reconciliation."[59] That is to say, we are advised to strip Christian doctrine of its Christian character and convert it into a Roman-Pagan doctrine of virtue or works.

This is true of all the theories of reconciliation that are opposed to *satisfactio vicaria* in our time. This is clearly evident in the so-called "declaratory" theory,[60] according to which there should be no wrath of God at all against the sin of men, and God declares His love to men without any satisfaction from Christ. Proponents of this theory, such as Ritschl and Adolf Harnack, place the essence of Christianity entirely in the human morality inspired by Christ. Other modern theories also push towards the same non-Christian standpoint, seeking to "supplement" and "deepen" the "orthodox" doctrine of vicarious

---

[59] *RE.*3 XX, 574; likewise *Ev. Dogmatik* 3, p. 118.

[60] Kirn, *Dogmatik*, p. 115: "Declaratory theories, which declare the divine forgiveness of sins to be possible even without mediatorial action and therefore leave only a prophetic office of Christ."

satisfaction by making the "transformation of humanity," "implantation into Christ," human renewal, and sanctification factors in Christ's work of reconciliation [or, atoning work]. Similarly, in these theories, the justification or forgiveness of sins ultimately depends on [or, comes to stand decisively one] human sanctification and actions, thereby tearing out the heart of Christianity. Let us now look at some modern' surrogates for the *satisfactio vicaria*.

Hofmann, and those who follow his way, replace the vicarious satisfaction of Christ with the establishment of a new holy humanity in the person of Christ.[61] With regard to this surrogate, it must be said that, of course, a new humanity was established in Christ's person. After all, Christ was the only sinless man since the Fall. This new sinless humanity in the person of Christ was also a necessary prerequisite for the reconciliation to be accomplished through Christ. We had to have such a high priest, who would be "holy, innocent, undefiled, separated from sinners" (Hebrews 7:26). But it was not by what Christ was in his person, but by what this unique person did and suffered for the good and in the place of mankind, that men were reconciled to God. The high priest not only had to be "holy" etc., but also had to offer himself to God as a sacrifice (θυσία) for men (Ephesians 5:2), through his own blood (διά τοῦ ἰδίου αἵματος) he had to enter into the holy place (Hebrews 9, 12).Through the death (τω θανάτω) of his Son we have been reconciled to God, redeemed by the precious blood (αἵματι) of Christ as an innocent and undefiled lamb (1 Peter 1, 19), redeemed by his obedience under the law given to men (Galatians 4, 4. 5). This scriptural teaching, according to which reconciliation came about through Christ's substitutionary action and suffering, is completely set aside by Hofmann with his positing of a new humanity in the person of Christ. Therefore, according to Hofmann, the forgiveness of sins or

---

[61] Hofmann, *Schutzschriften*, 2. Stück, p. 102 ff. - Nitzsch-Stephan, p. 562 ff.; Baier-Walther III, 117; Kirn, *RE.3* XX, 569 f.; H. Schmidt, *RE.2* XVI, 393 f.; Dorner, *Glaubenslehre* 2 II, 586 ff.; Thomasius and Th. Harnack, *Das Bekenntnis der luth. K. von der Versöhnung* (Erl., 1857).

justification does not take place (or, is not accomplished or does not occur] by through faith insofar as faith takes hold of (or, seizes) the forgiveness of sins acquired by Christ and offered in the Gospel, but through faith, insofar as it brings about the incorporation [or, inclusion or implantation] into the new humanity. Dorner correctly says of Hofmann's theory: "At bottom, sanctification is the principle upon which we have reconciliation."[62] Meyer remarks against Hofmann's

---

[62] *Glaubenslehre* II, 587. We have said elsewhere (*Christi Werk*, 1898, p. 39s.) about the effect of Hofmann's doctrine of reconciliation on the doctrine of justification: According to Hofmann, the immediate content of the Gospel and thus also the immediate object of faith is not the forgiveness of sins acquired by Christ, but a piece of history, namely this, that Christ held on to his fellowship [or, communion] with God until the end and thereby established in his person the beginning of a new, holy humanity. The guilt of sin and the forgiveness of sins immediately completely fade into the background here. Of course, this also changes the nature of justifying and saving faith: it is not the acceptance of the forgiveness of sins brought to light by Christ, but the fact that man allows himself to be told of the restoration and perfection of humanity through "the archetypal goal of the world" (Christ). The forgiveness of sins only comes to light here on the basis of the transfer to the new community of life established by Christ, it is not the direct object of faith; moreover, Hofmann's doctrine of reconciliation is also based on a view of sin that is contrary to Scripture. According to Hofmann, sin is not both an offense against God and thus guilt before God, but rather a loss of oneself in the physical world and thus captivity under an evil. Thus, when it comes to redemption, Hofmann is not concerned with the removal of the judgment of guilt and punishment, but rather with overcoming the power of sin. He therefore does not need a Savior who experiences God's wrath and punishment in the place of mankind and lifts the divine judgment of guilt and punishment against mankind, but rather, in accordance with his doctrine of sin, he constructs a redeemer who breaks the power of sin in his person by proving himself even under the greatest consequences of sin and setting the beginning of a new, holy humanity, and thereby directing the flow of humanity back to God. The affinity of Hofmann's theology with the theology of Menken and Schleiermacher cannot be denied: its essence consists in "the mystical substitution of subjective redemption instead of objective reconciliation." Hase remarks against the modern deviations from the church's doctrine of reconciliation: "The deepest feeling of sinfulness alongside the highest trust in God's infinite mercy is expressed in the church's doctrine. The newer objections are mostly based on the superficial concept of sin; those who do not consider the greatness of their guilt can

doctrine of reconciliation: 2 Corinthians 5:18-21 contains the very opposite of Hofmann's assertion that reconciliation did not happen [or, take place or occur] through Christ but rather in Christ, insofar as in his person a new relationship of humanity to God was restored." "No, the death of Jesus worked as ἱλαστήριον (Romans 3:25; Galatians 3:13), therefore as God's holy enmity (Romans 11:28), erasing the ὀργή θεου, so that He now did not impute to men their sins (2 Corinthians 5:19), and in this way, namely, *actu forensi* [in a forensic act, in a judicial procedure], reconciled them with himself (v. 21), faith alone being the subjective condition of appropriation on the part of man. Gratitude, new courage, holy life, etc." (also the *unio mystica* or the implantation in the body of Christ) "are *consequens* of reconciliation appropriated by faith, not part of it." And Kliefoth wrote against Hofmann: "Like that poor naturalist who searched through heaven and earth, but could not find only God, so von Hofmann searches the whole of Holy Scripture, but he cannot find in it the understanding of the simple word of faith: 'given and shed for the forgiveness of my sins. Hofmann's theory goes against "the core and heart not only of our church doctrine, but of Christianity in general".[63]

The same applies to the theory that has been called the "surety" or "guarantee theory" and is put forward, for example, by Nitzsch-Stephan[64] in the following words: Indirectly, reconciliation itself is based on the success of the mediator of salvation in gaining disciples and thereby overcoming the dominion of sin; for by guaranteeing to

---

easily argue against the Reconciler, but those who are conscious of the impossibility of redeeming themselves from evil through their own strength will gratefully accept the merit of the divine Reconciler." (Hutterus *red.* 6, p. 251.)

[63] *Der Schriftbeweis v. Hofmanns*, p. 472.

[64] *Ev. Dogmatik* 3, p. 597. Kirn holds the same theory, *Dogmatik*, p. 118. Likewise, everything Schleiermacher says about reconciliation comes down to this, *Der christl. Gl.* II, § 125. Hofmann's doctrine also has the same sense. With the deniers of *satisfactio vicaria*, we are basically always dealing with the same thing. Only the expressions change.

the Father the success of this and safeguarding godly life in a church of the dominion of God to be founded by him, he procures the necessary atonement. But reconciliation consists rather in this guarantee, [before and] not in the moral-religious transformation itself." This theory, too, is the exact opposite of the doctrine of Scripture. Of course, in the work of Christ we have a "surety," and that is the only guarantee or "assurance of godly life." The "orthodox" theologians expressed it like this: *Lex praescribit, evangelinm inscribet* [the law prescribes, the gospel inscribes]. Although the law demands "godly living," sanctification, and keeping God's commandments, it does not bring about or achieve this. Rather, only the gospel of the forgiveness of sins for the sake of Christ does this. In order to write his law in people's hearts, God abolished the covenant of the law and replaced it with the covenant of forgiveness of sins, as Jeremiah 31:31 ff. attests. And Paul teaches: "Sin shall not have dominion over you, for you are not under the law, but under grace" and: "now having been set free from sin, and having become slaves of God, you have your fruit to holiness", Romans 6:14, 22. Only those who belong to Christ crucify their flesh with its lusts and desires, Galatians 5.24; only they are zealous for good works, Titus 2:15. But this effect of Christ's work of redemption on men, this "godly life", has nothing in the least to do with the reconciliation of the world. The reconciliation of the world was neither entirely nor partially achieved through the "guarantee" by the "mediator of salvation," but rather completely and entirely through the fact that the mediator of salvation himself met the divine demand and paid the debt fully and completely, calculated in "arithmetic and juridical" terms, and for this received a receipt from God in his resurrection from the dead, a receipt made out and issued in the name of man. For Christ was given over to death for our sins and also raised from the dead for our justification (εἰς δικαίωσιν ἡμῶν), Romans 4:25. God now publishes the paid and receipted bill to the world through the Gospel. The Gospel calls forth faith on the part of men through the working of the Holy Spirit (John 16:14) (ἡ πίστις εξ ακοής, Romans 10:17), and hence it is that a man is justified *sola fide* before God with the exclusion of works (χωρὶς ἔργων νόμου), apart from "the transformation of mankind." Faith is now counted [or, reckoned] by God as righteousness, not insofar as it guarantees or vouches for a "godly life" — which, of course, it also does, and indeed alone — but insofar as it believes the paid and receipted bill, namely believes that God raised him (the "mediator of salvation") from the dead (ἤγειρεν εκ νεκρῶν), Romans 10, 9 and, in view of the nature of man, not the "transformed" but "the ungodly (τόν ασεβή) is justified" (Rom. 4, 5). The "surety" or "guarantee theory", which allows the reconciliation of people to be "indirectly based" on the successful acquisition of discipleship by the mediator of salvation, on the defeat of the dominion of sin, i.e. on sanctification and works, is in direct contradiction to Christian teaching. Meyer correctly says concerning Romans 3, 24: "Deliverance from the principle of sin [from its dominion] is not the essence of απόλυτρωσις [redemption] itself, but its consequence through the Spirit, when it is appropriated by faith. Every view that does not attribute redemption and forgiveness of sins to the real atonement through the death of Christ, but subjectively to the new life [that is] guaranteed and effected by his death (Schleiermacher, Nitzsch, Hofmann), is contrary to the New Testament, a confusion [or, mixture, mingling] of justification and sanctification."

Since Professor Ihmels (Leipzig) is widely regarded as the most conservative representative of modern Lutheranism, it seems appropriate to say a few words about Ihmels' position in particular. In Nitzsch-Stephan we find the judgment about Ihmels that he "has not yet offered a more precise realization of his thoughts." But if, as it seems, the immediately following words are also intended to refer to Ihmels: "In such a general and empirical attitude, the difference from Ritschl's theology only marginally stands out," then it is necessary to limit this judgment. While for Ritschl's position it is essential to understand the anger of God and consequently also human conscience of guilt as erroneous human imagination, Ihmels says that the human conscience of guilt is not an imagination, but corresponds to "an objective reality in God."[65] Based on what Ihmels says in his "Central Questions" about the work of Christ,[66] we would judge that Ihmels also here, as in the doctrine of the Person of Christ,[67] makes serious attempts to return to the Scripture and Church doctrine. But there, as here, and here as there, it is impossible for him to achieve the desired goal because he has abandoned the Scriptural principle in his theology. Because he does not regard Scripture as God's word *per se*[68] and therefore does not stand on the word of Scripture but, in contrast to it, stands on the "impression of reality and the "experience,"[69] he repeatedly slips back into the sea of subjectivism, especially into the waters of Schleiermacher, Hofmann and Ritschl, in all his efforts to return to the doctrine of Scripture. Ihmels' position is, as in the doctrine of Christ's person, also in the doctrine of Christ's work, a vacillating and therefore necessarily contradictory one. On the one hand, he contains pretty much the entire catalog of sayings that only make sense if, like Ritschl and the old rationalists, one denies God's demanding and judging justice, God's wrath and reconciliation through Christ's work. This includes his speeches against the "juridical" view and all "legal categories" in the work of Christ, the rejection of the "material understanding of the death of Jesus", in particular the rejection of the idea "as if Christ had suffered what lost humanity would otherwise have had to suffer without him." And "to speak of God changing his mind in the work of Christ," he explains, is "not just clumsy, but misleading."

---

[65] *Zentralfragen*, p. 130 f.: "Is man's sense of guilt only an imagination? Does it correspond to an objective reality in God? Would God call back the sinner who wants to flee from him and assure him that the flight from his holiness is nothing but an illusion, that he is not angry with man at all? Or is our God, as Scripture says, necessarily a consuming fire towards sin? Must the holy God exclude sin and therefore the sinner from himself? The answer of conscience is not doubtful; it can only agree with the testimony of Scripture in all things."

[66] *Zentralfragen*, 5th Lecture, pp. 104-133.

[67] p. 122 ff.

[68] *Zentralfragen*, p. 68 ff.

[69] A. a. O., p. 89 f.

On the other hand, however, he speaks in such a way that the rejected concepts, juridical conception, etc., are nevertheless reintroduced. Of man he says that in his conscience he experiences God's judgment on his sin, and that the human consciousness of guilt is not merely imagination, but corresponds to an objective reality in God (i.e. God's demanding and punishing justice). And of Christ he says that Christ in his person stood under God's judgment over the sin of mankind, indeed that in the death of Christ "the proof of the judicial justice of God, which the sin of mankind demanded, came about" (p. 125). In this way, Ihmels restores the rejected "juridical" conception and the "legal categories." And as for the "change of God's mind in the work of Christ" (p. 122), which is so vigorously rejected, he essentially restitutes this again in occasional statements. He explains that the passage in Corinthians ("God reconciled the world to himself") does not refer to a change in the world's attitude, but to God. "In principle, Paul links reconciliation to the historical work of Christ in the sense of a change in God's relationship, attitude, and behavior towards the world." Ihmels is only talking here about a change in the relationship or position of God. But he goes on to point out correctly that a change in God's attitude towards men cannot be separated from a change in God's mind. He says: "Certainly, there in that passage from the Corinthians there is at first only a new relationship between God and men;[70] But if this new relationship involves a change in God's attitude toward mankind, is it possible to make a distinction between the position and mind of God? Wouldn't that necessarily amount in some way to assuming an untruthfulness in God? And if the relationship with humanity determined by the wrath of God comes to an end there, does this not necessarily imply a change of attitude?" And positively he says:

---

[70] This is decidedly not the case. The καταλλάσσων does not denote a relationship, but an action, and the immediately following μη λογιζόμχνος αυτοῖς τα παραπτώματα αυτών also denotes an action: God did not impute man's sin to him, that is, he justified man and forgave him his sins (Rom. 4:6-8) == objective justification of the whole world of sinners.

"Thus it is the eternal love of God which, in the historical work of Christ, transforms the relationship determined by holy wrath (including the mind of God) "to humanity into a relationship" (including attitude) "of being reconciled." If this alleged "change of God's mind" towards humanity in the work of Christ is contrasted with the rejected "change of God's mind in the work of Christ," it is evident that it is highly possible for Ihmels to say yes and no in the same respect to the same thing.[71] Psychologically, however, this yes and no position

---

[71] The "change of God's mind" through the atoning work [or, work of reconciliation] of Christ has embarrassed many theologians. Ihmels says: "The expression would necessarily give the impression that reconciliation is forced upon God; and even more embarrassing is the impression that the word must give, as if God were subject to a change of mood. Ihmels' first reason is based on an incorrect presentation of Scripture and church doctrine. One cannot really come up with the idea that reconciliation was "forced" from God on the basis of the doctrine of Scripture and the Church, because according to the doctrine of Scripture and the Church, God has not been determined from without, but by His own love, to let go of his wrath against the τέκνα οργής by way of vicarious satisfaction. So John 3:16; Romans 5:8; 1 John 4:9-10. Concerning the αμνός του Qεου, John 1:29, Luther remarks that the Lamb of God is "the sacrifice which God Himself has ordained for the sin of the world." Ihmels' second reason is a direct criticism of the Holy Spirit's speech in Scripture. The Holy Scripture certainly testifies to the "eternal immutability" of God (Psalm 102:25-28), and it definitely must be maintained. But because we human beings, owing to the finiteness of our power of comprehension, cannot encompass the "eternal immutability" of God, but rather all our thoughts necessarily move in time and space, Scripture itself guides us to think of things before and after one another in the unchanging God. On the basis of Scripture, we must think of God's wrath against man not before but after man's sin, and we must let the forgiveness of sins follow the reconciliation through Christ in our thoughts (in puncto rationis). Scripture consistently speaks of the beginning and cessation of both the wrath and the grace of God. This is done in divine condescension to our human comprehension. And if we humans do not want to engage with these ideas presented by God himself, with reference to God's "eternal immutability", then we are evading God's revelation in Scripture, which is calculated for our powers of comprehension, and we are going astray. The theologians of old worked through the "problem" of God's eternity and immutability on the one hand and "God's entry into history" on the other very precisely on the basis of Scripture. They summarized the result as follows: In Deo non dantur causae formaliter causantes (that is God in his unchangeable majesty,

can be explained by a twofold desired goal. On the one hand, Ihmels wants to remain in harmony with the modern theology inaugurated by Schleiermacher, which wants to stand on the impression of reality and experience instead of on the word of Scripture. On the other hand, however, he also feels the need to strive for harmony with the statements of Scripture and to "classify" what has been experienced under historical "impressions" with the testimony of Scripture. The result is that neither of the two principles really comes into its own. The false principle triumphed in Ihmels at the point where it is a question of applying Christ's atoning work to the faith and justification of man. Here the truth of Scripture is completely set aside. According to the Scriptures, as is well known, faith in Christ arises and exists only through the word of Christ. God has expressed the fact that in Christ he reconciled men to himself and did not impute their sins to them, that is, justified men, in the λόγος τῆς καταλλαγῆς, in the word about accomplished reconciliation. This word now resounds in the world at God's command so that people believe it and are reconciled to God through faith. This faith arises through nothing other than the Word itself, as Paul testifies in Romans 10:17: ἡ πίστις εξ ακοής, and Christ

---

incomprehensible to us); *dantur tamen causae virtualiter sive in puncto rationis* (conceptually) *causantes* (that is God as he presents himself to human understanding in Scripture). Cf. Baier, *Kompendium* II, 33; Joh. P. Reusch, *Annotationes*, p. 175 sqq. Therefore, on the one hand, we must hold on the basis of Scripture that the counsel of the reconciliation of the world through Christ belongs to immutable eternity, and on the other hand, Scripture instructs us to think of a change of God's mind, or of a transformation of his wrath into grace, which was accomplished by Christ's actions and sufferings in the fullness of time 1900 years ago. In condescension to our human comprehension, Scripture presents the matter in this way: At that time, when the Righteous suffered and died for the unrighteous, we were reconciled to God by the death of his Son. At that time, when Christ was put under the Law of God given to man and fulfilled it in man's place, the justification of life for all men came about through the righteousness of One. At that time, when God reconciled the world to Himself through Christ, He (God) did not impute sin to the world of men, that is, He allowed grace to take the place of wrath against the world of men "in his forum" [or, "in his court"].

says in John 17:20 that all believers will believe in him through the apostles' word (διά του λόγου αυτών). However, Ihmels opposes the development of faith in Christ through the word of Christ alone. He says: "The faith of the first disciples did not arise in this way. Rather, it grew out of the impression of reality under which the disciples stood every day. Even today, only that is real faith in Christ which is imposed on man by his" (Christ's) "appearance itself. It cannot be said seriously enough that if Jesus really is the one the Church confesses him to be, he himself must also be able to convince people of this reality through his reality." These are very strange words. There is no question as to whether Christ would be able to convince us of his "reality", or even of God's reconciliation, through his appearance or through powerful historical impressions (the latter are probably meant here by Christ's "appearance"). When Luther comes to this point, he would say: Who would want to set a goal for God's ability? Christ could probably make all people believe in him at twelve o'clock at night and in an instant through historical, physical and other "impressions". But it is not a question of what Christ is "able" to do, but what he wants to do, and which way he has chosen to make people believe in him. And there he says that all will believe in him through the word of the apostles, and that those who abide in his word (έν τώ λόγω τw έμw) will know the truth. No one has ever "experienced" reconciliation with God in any other way and no one will experience it until the Last Day other than through faith in the word of the accomplished reconciliation that has taken place. Everything that is said about a direct or immediate [without the mediate word] "experience" of Christ before and apart from the word of Christ is enthusiasm. It is the enthusiasm of which the Schmalkaldic Articles rightly say: *est omnium haeresium et papatus et Mahometismi origo, vis, vita et potentia. Quare in hoc nobis est constanter perseverandum, quod Deus non velit nobiscum aliter agere, nisi per vocale verbum et sacramenta, et quidquid sine verbo et sacramentis iactatur ut spiritus, sit ipse diabolus* ("It [enthusiasm] is the origin, power, life, and strength of all heresy, especially of that of the Papacy and Mahomet. Therefore we ought and must constantly maintain this point, that God does not wish to deal with us otherwise than through the spoken Word and the Sacraments. Whatsoever is extolled as Spirit without the Word and Sacraments is the devil himself."). (III, 8.) Insofar as someone like Ihmels fights for the origin of faith in Christ without the word of Christ, he has not only partially, but completely forgotten what Scripture teaches about reconciliation through Christ, about the message of reconciliation, the Gospel, about faith, and about justification. With a faith that is based on experienced "impressions" rather than on the Word of the Gospel alone, justification and sanctification are fundamentally and in principle mixed.

But even in this sad state of affairs in modern theology, we would like to remind you again of the fact that not all those who publicly teach unchristian things in their own person and in their hearts. The fact is that all old and new theories of atonement which deny the "juridical" reconciliation of the whole world of sinners achieved by Christ's vicarious satisfaction, are in practice completely useless. They all have the characteristic that they cannot bring a conscience struck by the law of God peace [or, to rest or quiet the conscience or calm the conscience). Only "Christ's blood and righteousness", that is, Christ's *satisfactio vicaria,* can do this. When Ritschl teaches and preaches for fifty years that God is merciful to man without Christ's vicarious satisfaction, he does not bring anyone to faith, because the Holy Spirit does not occupy himself with convincing people of untruths, but only glorifies [or transfigures] Christ, that is, Christ the crucified, Christ in his vicarious satisfaction, in the hearts of men (ἐκεινος - τό πνεύμα τῆς ἀληΘείας - ἐμε δοξάσει, John 16:13-14). The Holy Spirt is just as reticent (or, behaves just as resistantly or behaves just as stubbornly) with regard to the more "positive" theories by which some want to "supplement" and "deepen" the "orthodox" doctrine of vicarious satisfaction in such a way that "the transformation of humanity" (human renewal, sanctification, implantation into the person of Christ, in the body of Christ, in the Church, etc.) is also included in the "accomplished work of salvation" of Christ and thought of as "constitutive of his value before God."[72] All of these theories do not put consciences at rest either, because they do not base consciences solely on Christ's work, but rather decisively on man's own actions and man's "religious-moral" constitution. For this reason, the theological teacher who carries in his heart the faith wrought by the Holy Spirit through the Gospel, or who comes to this faith before the end of his life, leaves his "completion" and "deepening" of the "orthodox" doctrine of reconciliation at the study table and bases himself in his heart and before God on the *satisfactio vicaria* alone. Ihmels can also serve as an example here. After he has honestly and – as he notices – in vain struggled with the "religious-moral" improvement of vicarious satisfaction, he concludes with the assurance that he only wanted to ensure what is expressed in the old Passion song: "You have borne all our sins, otherwise we would have to despair." In these words of the Passion Song, however, nothing more and nothing less is expressed than the "juridically" conceived *satisfactio vicaria* that Ihmels theoretically rejected. The consciousness of guilt in the human heart is a terrible reality. It is an indictment written in the heart, behind which stands the full force and weight of divine justice and holiness: You shall be holy, for I am holy; cursed be every one who does not abide in what is written in the book of the law, to do them!"[73] The writing of guilt cannot be erased by any human thought operations and efforts. Just as the Rocky Mountains and the Himalayas have their existence through divine omnipotence, so the consciousness of guilt in the human heart has its existence through the force of divine justice in its demanding and condemning activity. The sense of guilt only recedes when the word of the written and torn up indictment (χειρόγραφον) [or, handwriting of guilt] nailed to the cross by Christ comes to man and the Holy Spirit works faith in this word and thus places the divine judgment of pardon in the human heart in place of the divine judgment

---

[72] Kirn, *Dogmatik*, p. 118.

[73] This includes Luther's powerful *Disputations Against the Antinomians*, St. L. XX, 1628 ff.

of condemnation. To declare the sentence of condemnation in the conscience to be imaginary, or at least to want to do away with it by calling for the transformation of humanity, the implantation in Christ, the renewal and sanctification, is theological childishness, self-deception and worldly trickery.

With regard to the practical uselessness of all theories of reconciliation that somehow contradict the scriptural doctrine of *satisfactio vicaria*, Strong gives these historical reports (Syst. Theol.., p. 739 sq.): "It is interesting to note that some of the greatest advocates of the Moral Influence theory have reverted to the older faith when they came to die. In his dying moments, as L. W. Munhall tells us, Horace Bushnell said: 'I fear what I have written and said upon the moral idea of the atonement is misleading, and will do great harm'; and, as he thought of it further, he cried: 'O Lord Jesus, I trust for mercy only in the shed blood that Thou didst offer on Calvary!' Schleiermacher, on his deathbed, assembled his family and a few friends, and himself administered the Lord's Supper. After praying and blessing the bread, and after pronouncing the words: 'This is My body, broken for you,' he added: 'This is our foundation!' As he started to bless the cup, he cried: 'Quick, quick, bring the cup! I am so happy!' Then he sank quietly back and was no more. (See *Life of Rothe*, by Nippold, 2, 53. 54.) Ritschl, in his *History of Pietism* (2, 65), had severely criticized Paul Gerhardt's hymn: 'O Haupt voll Blut und Wunden' [literally, 'O Head Full of Blood and Wounds,' know] as O Sacred Head Now Wounded] as describing physical suffering; but he begged his son to repeat the two last verses of that hymn: 'O Sacred Head How Wounded!' when he came to die. And in general, the convicted sinner finds peace most quickly and surely when he is pointed to the Redeemer, who died on the cross, and endured the penalty of sin in his stead." Grotius also did not die holding to his "regency rule" [i.e, governmental theory] that is, not to Christ as an example of punishment and deterrence,[74] but to

---

[74] Note 1016.

Christ as his reconciler with God. He died under the pastoral care of the Lutheran theologian Johann Quistorp.[75]

But the fact that the Holy Spirit, in his great faithfulness, is able to keep

---

[75] 1045 Johann Quistorp sen., † 1648. — Trench, in his *Notes on the Parables of Our Lord* on Luke 18:9–14, has an interesting account of this: "Grotius, returning in 1645 from Sweden to Holland, where he proposed to pass the evening of his days, was wrecked on the coast of Pomerania. He made his way with difficulty to Rostock, where mortal illness, brought on by the hardships and dangers he had undergone, acting on a body already infirm, overtook him. Being made aware of his danger, he summoned Quistorp, a high Lutheran theologian, not unknown in the history of the Lutheran Church, to his side. I will leave to this latter to tell the remainder of the story in his own words: 'I drew nigh, and found the sick man almost in his last agony. I spoke to him, and told him that nothing would have pleased me more than to have met him in health and held conversation with him. To this he replied, "God has willed it thus." I then proceeded to admonish him to prepare himself for his blessed journey, to acknowledge himself a sinner, and to grieve for his misdeeds, and as in my talk I touched upon the publican who confessed himself a sinner, and prayed that God would have mercy upon him, he made answer, "I am that publican." I then went on, and committed him unto Christ, besides whom there is no salvation, and he rejoined, "All my hope is placed in Christ alone." With a clear voice I then recited in German that German prayer which begins: "*Herr Jesu Christ, wahrer Mensch,*" etc.; and folding his hands, he followed me under his breath. When I had ended, I asked if he had understood me. He replied, "I understood well." I then went on to recite from the Word of God such things as are wont to be recalled to the memories of those on the point of death, and asked if he understood me. He replied, "I hear your voice, but find it hard to understand the words." When he had said this, he fell into complete silence, and a little while afterwards gave up the ghost. When one thinks of all which must have divided Grotius, the Arminian, and Quistorp, the Lutheran, each, too, a foremost leader in his own camp, it is deeply interesting to note how in that supreme moment everything which kept them apart falls out of sight, alike on one side and on the other" (but so that the Arminian Grotius, who had hitherto drifted strongly in indifferentist Roman waters (Walch, *Bibl. theol.* II, 220. 353 sq.) abandons his position and takes the biblical standpoint of the Lutheran Quistorp, as Trench also reports below. "In Christ, and in His free grace as the one hope of sinners, they are at one. To this, and to this only, the one [Quistorp] points; in this, and in this only, the other [Grotius] rests. Quistorp's letter (which is not addressed to Calov, as I stated in some former editions, relying on secondhand information which betrayed me here into more than one inaccuracy, but to Elias Taddel, Professor of Theology at Rostock) is reprinted in Krabbe's *Aus dem kirchl. und wissenschaftl.* Leben Rostocks, 1863, p. 383."

teachers in their hearts from the error they present with their mouths and in writings must not prevent the Christian church from fighting such teachers with all seriousness. They are and remain dangerous enemies of the Christian Church. And this from a whole series of points of view:

1. As has been fully demonstrated, by the substitutes which they propose to replace vicarious satisfaction, they in some way or other base reconciliation with God on human action, and thus make the Christian faith, as far as their teaching is concerned, impossible. Kliefoth did not exaggerate when he explained that Hofmann's erroneous doctrine of reconciliation nullified Christianity in general. Without the perfect reconciliation of mankind with God through Christ's *satisfactio vicaria*, there is no Gospel, no faith, no justification, no regeneration and sanctification, no church, no ministry of the New Testament, no eternal life.

2. They present their false teaching as if it were scriptural doctrine. They would not be so dangerous if, like Adolf Harnack, for example, they openly confessed their opposition to Scripture.[76] Most of the more or less "positive" theologians claim to be presenting scriptural doctrine.

3. They conceal the reinterpretation and redirection of biblical truths with the appearance of deeper theological scholarship. Thus, they generally pass off the interference of human renewal in Christ's work of reconciliation, which is the complete abolition of the biblical concept of atonement (αυτός - namely Christ - εστι ιλαομος περί των αμαρτιών ημών), as a "deepened concept of atonement." The appearance of higher theological scholarship, however, is very apt to make a seductive impression on the young students.

4. They educate in logical ambiguity, for example, by instructing young students to reject any "juridical" understanding of Christ's atoning

---

[76] According to Harnack, the Apostle Paul taught "objective salvation" in a careless manner. (*Wesen des Christentums*, p. 114 f.)

work on the one hand, and to understand Christ's death as a proof of God's "judicial justice" on the other. This is a seduction of the studying youth to a disordered economy of thought that is difficult to eliminate, as experience has shown.

5. They educate to an inner untruthfulness by instructing the young students to reinterpret the words of Scripture[77] and to distort the doctrinal position of the "orthodox" theologians, thereby arousing an odium against them.[78] Kliefoth said of Hofmann at that time what is pretty much true of all modern deniers of the *satisfactio vicaria*: "If von Hofmann, where he deviates from the doctrine of the church, also said straight out that and how he deviates, then the church, which has to bear much nowadays, might also be able to bear his system. But he does not do this. He does not even stop at teaching deviantly without making his deviation noticeable, but he claims to conform to the Church's doctrine, indeed to further develop and promote it through is theology. This is an untruth that confuses the minds, especially of the younger generations irremediably; and if the theology of the Lutheran Church

---

[77] Cf. Holtzmann's criticism of modern positive theologians cited above. Grimm also says of Hofmann: *Inter eos, qui pro Gnesiolutheranis haberi volunt* (Among those who wanted to be considered Gnesiolutherans), I. Chr. K. Hofmannus (in the book *Der Schriftbeweis*), *Iesum patiendo moriendoque vicarias poenas dedisse negans earumque notionem e sacris libris exegetica arte exterminare tentans, maxime ethicam eorum, quae Christus passus est, vim et potestatem praedicavit.* (*Institutio theol. dogmaticae* 2, p. 382.) (Denying that Jesus underwent vicarious punishments by suffering and dying, and attempting to exterminate the idea of them from the sacred books by exegetical art, he preached above all the ethical force and power of those things which Christ suffered.)

[78] The doctrine of vicarious satisfaction shares in this respect the fate of the doctrines of inspiration and the person of Christ. Thus Nitzsch-Stephan states (p. 597 f.): "It was a mistake of orthodox doctrine that the basic order of the relationship between God and man was conceived in categories taken from the legal system [or, sphere] of the state." Of course, the "Orthodox" never thought of such a procedure, but, as Holtzmann reminds us, they took their teaching from the Apostle Paul. But the assertion that the Orthodox thought of the matter in "categories" that were "taken from the legal sphere of the state" must influence the young student against the "Orthodox" even though it (the assertion) is a historical falsehood.

no longer has the desire or ability to dispel these mists, then it is no longer worthy of its name, and the Lutheran Church has seen its last hour."[79]

The active obedience of Christ (obedientia Christi activa).

The vicarious satisfaction made by Christ also includes, as has already been taught above, Christ's keeping the divine law given to man in the place of man (*loco hominum*). In other words, in order to satisfy divine justice, Christ not only bore the punishment for human transgression of the law, but also, by his holy life, obeyed the divine law that men are duty-bound to obey but do not obey. Like our human guilt, so also our human duty toward God has been imputed to Christ (γενόμένος υπέρ ημών κατάρα - γενομένος υπο νόμον, ίνα τους υπό νόμον έξαγοράση, Galatians 3:13; 4:4. 5) We will now follow with a special discussion of this aspect of vicarious satisfaction, because it has been partly relegated and partly outright denied in the presentation of the doctrine of redemption. This includes: a. Anselm, when he says in *Cur Deus Homo* II, 11, that Christ's obedience in life is not part of the satisfaction made for men because Christ, like every rational creature, owed this obedience himself.[80] b. Georg Karg, General Superintendent in

---

[79] *Der Schriftbeweis von Hofmanns*, p. 559 f.

[80] Philippi, however, draws attention to the fact that in his life of faith Anselm went beyond his scholastic theory and in his meditations and prayers says, for example: "While I would not obey, you atoned for my disobedience with your obedience; I indulged, you thirsted" etc., thus expressly counting the active obedience of Christ as part of the vicarious satisfaction. Anselm's distorted presentation in *Cur Deus Homo* reads: *Anselmus: Quaerendum est nunc, cuiusmodi haec datio debebit esse. Dare namque se non poterit Deo aut aliquid de se quasi non habenti, ut suus sit, quoniam omnis creatura Dei est. Boso: Sic est. Anselmus: Sic ergo intelligenda est haec datio, quia aliquo modo ponet se ad honorem Dei aut aliquid de se, quo modo debitur non erit. Boso: Ita sequitur ex supra dictis. Anselmus: Si dicimus, quia habit seipsum ad obediendum Deo, ut perseveranter servando iustitiam subdat se ejus voluntati, non erit hoc dare, quod Deus ab illo non exigat ex debito. Omnis enim rationalis creatura debet hanc obendientiam Deo. Boso: Hoc negari nequit. Anselmus: Allo itaque modo oportet*

Ansbach († 1576), who later retracted his view in 1570;[81] c. by a part of

---

ut det seipsum Deo aut aliquid de se. Boso: Ad hoc nos impellit ratio. Anselmus: Videamus, si forte hoc sit vitam suam dare sive ponere animam suam sive tradere seipsum morti ad honorem Dei. Hoc enim ex debito Deus non exiget ab illo; quoniam namque non erit peccatum in illo, non debebit mori, ut diximus. (Anselm: We must now inquire what kind of offering this should be. For He will not be able to give himself, or something about himself, to God as if God did not have it [already], so that it might be God's own, since every creature is God's. Boso: So it is. Anselm: This offering must be understood, because in some way He will give himself, or something about himself, to the honor of God, in some way that it would not already have been due. Boso: Yes, it follows from what was said above. Anselm: Thus we say, because He commits himself to obey God, by persistently submitting himself to God's will in upholding justice, it will not be to give what God does not demand from him out of debt. For every rational creature owes this obedience to God. Boso: This cannot be denied. Anselm: Therefore it is necessary that He offer himself or something of himself to God. Boso: Reason drives us to this. Anselm: Let us see if this means to give his life, or to lay down his soul, or to surrender himself to death for the honor of God. For God does not demand this from him out of debt; for since there will be no sin in him, He will not have to die, as we have said.) In this way, Anselm clearly excludes the active obedience of Christ from vicarious satisfaction. The greatest error in Anselm's writing (*Cur Deus Homo*) is, incidentally, that it does not present the doctrine of reconciliation simply from the Holy Scriptures, but seeks to develop it in accordance with reason. The ponderous train of thought, which is so unpleasantly noticeable in this writing, is also connected with this. The teaching of the Holy Scriptures, so simple and clear, is stretched on the torture rack of theological speculation. Anselm's method is not to be held up to students of theology as a model, but rather as a cautionary tale. Nor should one overestimate the importance of Anselm's writing for the period that followed [or, for the future]. The common claim that the basic ideas of Anselm's theory were excluded from the Reformation is misleading. Luther read Anselm. He called him the "*monachissimus monachus*" ("most monastic monk"). But one should not assume a particular influence of Anselm on Luther. What is correct in Anselm's *Cur Deus Homo* could have been found closer and better in the Holy Scripture.

[81] Georg Karg (Parsimonius), a Philippist, proceeded from the proposition: "The law binds either to obedience or to punishment, not to both at the same time." The extent to which this sentence is misleading will soon be explained, but Karg concluded from this sentence: "Because Christ suffered the punishment for us, he performed obedience for himself." The immediate opposition that arose on all sides against Karg's teaching proves how clearly the truth had been recognized within the Lutheran Church that

the Reformed theologians, especially by Joh. Piscator († 1625); d. by more recent theologians who want to limit the active obedience of Christ to the fact that Christ willingly gave himself up to his "call to be a savior" and also willingly suffered what the "call to be a savior" entailed in the midst of a sinful humanity, but deny that Christ fulfilled the law given to men in the place of men.[82] The "vocational obedience" in contrast to Christ's obedience to the law given to men and in place of men has become a πρῶτον ψεῦδος [first falsehood, or first lie] of modern theology. The Book of Concord (p. 612 f.) clearly and sharply states that the *obedientia Christi activa* is an integral part of Christ's achievement of satisfaction when it says: "For since Christ is not man alone, but God and man in one undivided person, He was as little subject to the Law," (that is, obligated to keep the law, *legi subjectus*), "because He is the Lord of the Law, as He had to suffer and die as far as

---

obedientia activa was part of the satisfaction made by Christ. Karg was suspended. He traveled to Wittenberg, where he was convicted of his error, persuaded to recant and reinstated in his office. Because a recantation is a rare occurrence among high-ranking persons in the church, we are reporting it here. The recantation reads: "Having hitherto disputed with some concerning the highly important article of our holy Christian faith of the justification of the sinner before God, concerning the imputation of Christ, our only Mediator's righteousness and obedience, I have now been graciously reported and instructed by the venerable and learned gentlemen theologians and doctors at Wittenberg, that in the office of mediator his innocence and righteousness in divine and human nature cannot and should not be separated from obedience in the suffering and entire humiliation of the Son of God, our Lord and Savior Jesus Christ, because his death and sacrifice are precious and valuable to God the Father because of the worthiness, holiness, and righteousness of the Person who is God and man and innocent: I thank God, the eternal Father of our Lord Jesus Christ, together with his only-begotten Son and the Holy Spirit, and also the venerable doctors, for such a fatherly report, and I promise with all my heart before God that I will drop [or, abandon] this disputation in the future and will use and conduct common, customary discourses in accordance with God's Spirit with other Christian teachers by God's grace and help according to the agreement that was made between the aforementioned doctors and myself at Wittenberg. August 10, 1570."

[82] Cf. "*Lehre und Wehre*" 1896, p. 137; on modern "vocational obedience" Nitzsch-Stephan, p. 557 ff.

His person is concerned. For this reason, then, His obedience, not only in suffering and dying, but also in this, that He in our stead was voluntarily made under the Law, and fulfilled it by this obedience, is imputed to us for righteousness, so that, on account of this complete obedience, which He rendered His heavenly Father for us, by doing and suffering, in living and dying, God forgives our sins, regards us as godly and righteous, and eternally saves us." [Formula of Concord, Solid Declaration, III.15] There the limitation of Christ's active obedience to "the voluntary assumption of suffering" is explicitly rejected.

The doctrine of the Formula of Concord is the clear doctrine of Scripture. Galatians 4:4-5 makes two things clear: 1. That what is being spoken of here is the divine law given to men. [Christ's being] under "law" is not meant to be understood as only the "salvific will" of God. 2. That Christ was subject to this law given to man and fulfilled it for the redemption of mankind.[83] When recent theologians contrast [or,

---

[83] Philippi is certainly right when he remarks on Galatians 4:4-5: "Israel was ... subject to the statutes of the *nomos* (law) which demanded fulfillment; accordingly, the redemptive work of the Son of God is also to be regarded as a vicarious fulfillment of the law." (IV, 2, 300.) Likewise Stöckhardt: "The law under which Israel stood is the sum total of all God's demands on man, especially on Israel, everything that God wants man to do and not do. And it is precisely this law to which Christ is also subject, and He has adopted it and has taken it upon himself, thus fulfilling all of God's commandments. And it was precisely this obedience that served for our redemption." (*L. and W.* 1896, p. 137.) We also hold with most of the old theologians that Matthew 5:17 is a proof of the *obedientia Christi activa*. Interpreting τον νόμον πληρῶσαι, "fulfill the law," as limited to fulfillment "in teachings" the expression does not suffer [or, does not do justice to the expression]. It is also arbitrary to restrict the δικαίωσμα [righteousness, or righteous act] of Christ in Romans 5:18 to the mere obedient suffering of Christ. The παράπτωμα, the transgression of Adam, is contrasted here with the δικαίωσμα, the righteous deed of Christ, by which Christ, in contrast to Adam, presented himself as righteous, the obedience of Christ (the υπακοή, v. 19) without restriction. Clear and sharp Quenstedt: δικαίωσμα opponitur παράπτωματι. *Ut ergo* παράπτωμα *est* ἀνομία, *ita* δικαίωσμα *vi oppositionis est* ... ἐννομία *actio* ἔννομος *seu activa Christi obedientia.* (Δικαίωμα is opposed to παράπτωμα. Therefore, just as παράπτωμα is lawlessness, so δικαίωμα by way of opposition is lawful conduct ... the

set in opposition to each other] Christ's fulfillment of God's law and the fulfillment of God's "salvific will," this involves a blatant [or, glaring] *petitio principii* [begging the question]. It is necessary first to establish on the basis of Scripture what the "salvific will" that Christ was to carry out entails. According to Scripture, however, this salvific will is not only about obedience through suffering, but also about vicarious obedient living, about the positive fulfillment of the law in man's place. Therefore, on the basis of Scripture, regarding the righteousness of Christ's life, the following must be maintained: Christ's righteous life is not merely a model or example for us — though of course it is a model insofar as we are to follow Christ, 1 Peter 2:21. It is also not merely a prerequisite for his obedient [or, innocent] suffering — though of course it is, insofar as only the death of a perfectly Holy One has atoning power, 1 Peter 1:19 — but it is also an integral part of the work (or, accomplishment or achievement] that Christ has vicariously offered to the righteous God for the reconciliation of mankind. This is the teaching of Scripture in the passages cited, and recognizing and holding on to this is also of the greatest importance for practice, namely for the Christian life of faith, as can be seen from Luther's following explanation. After Luther has said of Christ's vicarious fulfillment of the law: "He satisfied the law, He fulfilled the law completely; for He loved God with all his heart, with all his soul, with all his strength, with all his mind, and his neighbor as himself," etc.; [Luther] continues: "Therefore, if the law comes and accuses you for not keeping it, point it to Christ and say: There is the man who did it; I cling to him who fulfilled it for me and gave me its fulfilment; so it must be silent." (E. A. 13, 61, 63.) We have also already pointed out above how Anselm's life of faith led him beyond his theoretical denial of the *obedientia Christi activa*.

It remains necessary to examine the objections that have been raised

---

action of lawful or active obedience of Christ.) Therefore, it is not enough to say, as Philippi thinks, that here only "the foundation" for the doctrine of *obedientia activa* is given.

against the active obedience of Christ as part of his vicarious satisfaction. It has been objected:

I. Christ used his active obedience for himself, since as a true man he was obligated to fulfill the law. Answer: This assertion denies the personal union (*unio personalis*) of God and man in Christ. By virtue of the personal union, human nature belongs to the person of the Son of God. But the person of the Son of God is not under the law; consequently, neither is the human nature of Christ that belongs to this person. By assuming a human nature, the Son of God did not come under the law, but rather he took this human nature out from under the law by taking it into his divine person. The fact that Christ nevertheless came under the law (γενόμενος ὑπό νόμον) was the result of a special act which, although it coincides in time with the incarnation, is nevertheless factually separated from it in Scripture. God put his Son — and he gave himself — under the law for mankind and for their redemption, Galatians 4:4, 5; Psalm 40:7-9. This is how obedience to the law (δικαίωμα, ὑπακοή, Romans 5:18-19) came about, which Christ can and will give to mankind: Even in the state of humiliation, Christ expressly declares himself to be one who stood above the law for his own person, Matthew 12:8.[84]

---

[84] Quenstedt (II, 407): The Fisher objects: *Christus ut verus homo tenebatur obedire Deo Creatori, pro se igitur activam obedientiam legi praestitit. Eodem modo Socinus L. 3. de Christo Servatore, c. 5., ait: Christum ut verum hominem iure creationis pro seipso debuisse Deo obedientiam vitae totius plenam, quapropter illa nihil nobis promeruisse. Respondeo: 1. Filius hominis est Dominus Sabbathi, Matth. 12, 8, et sie etiam totius legis. 2. Si Christus esset* ψιλός ανφρωπος; *obstrictus fuisset legi, iam vero in unitate personae est verus Deus, proinde sui ratione non fuit legi obstrictus.* Πρῶτον ψευδός *huius argumenti, adeoque erroris huius universi consistit in eo, quod actiones et passiones Christi considerantur, ac si essent tantum naturae humanae actiones et passiones; atqui persona est, quae agit et patitur. Obedientia Christi non est naturae tantum humanae actio, sed Christi* θεανῦθρώπον, *qui ut nobis natus et datus, Es. 9, 9, ita et pro nobis sub lege factus, Gal. 4, 4.* (Christ as true man was bound to obey God the Creator, therefore He rendered active obedience to the Law for himself. In the same

II Scripture ascribes the redemption of men to the shedding of the blood of Christ, that is, to *obedientia passiva*. Answer: But not exclusively! While passages like 1 Peter 1:19, Colossians 1:14, etc. emphasize [or, place in the foreground] *obedientia passiva*, there are also scripture passages in which redemption is ascribed to *obedientia activa*. Romans 5:18, 19; Psalm 40:7-9. Therefore, neither the former nor the latter passages are to be understood exclusively.[85]

---

manner, Socinus in L. 3. *de Christo Servatore*, c. 5., states: Christ as true man rightfully owed full obedience of life to God for himself, therefore He did not earn anything for us. I reply: 1. the Son of man is the Lord of the Sabbath, Matthew 12:8, and so also of the whole Law. 2. If Christ were ψιλός ανθρωπος (only a mere man), He would have been bound by the Law, but since in the unity of the person He is true God, therefore by his own nature He was not bound by the Law. The first falsehood of this argument, and therefore of the whole error, consists in this, that the actions and sufferings of Christ are considered as if they were only actions and sufferings of human nature; but it is the person who acts and suffers. The obedience of Christ is not only an action of human nature, but of the Christ-God-man, who was born and given to us, Isaiah 9:9, and is also made subject to the Law for us, Galatians 4:4).

[85] Gerhard (*De iustif.*, § 55 sqq.): *Quamvis in pluribus Scripturae dictis morti et effusioni sanguinis Christi redemptionis opus tribuatur, id tamen haudquaquam exclusive accipiendum, ac si sancta Christi vita ab opere redemptionis per hoc excludatur; sed ideo illud fieri existimandum, quia nusquam illuxit clarius, quod nos dilexit ac redemit Dominus, quam in ipsius passione, morte ac vulneribus, ut loquuntur pii veteres; et quia mors Christi est velut ultima linea ac complementum,* τέλος, *finis et perfectio, totius obedientia, sicut apostolus inquit Phil. 2, 8. Quid? Quod plane* αδύνατον *est, activam obedientiam a passiva in hoc merito separare.— Quenstedt (II, 351 sq.):* Agendo culpam, quam homo iniuste commiserat, expiavit, et patiendo poenam, quam homo iuste perpessurus erat, Christus sustulit. . . . Quia enim non tantum ab ira Dei, iusti iudicis, liberandus erat homo, sed et, ut coram Deo posset consistere, iustitia ei opus erat, quam, nisi impleta lege, consequi non poterat: ideo Christus utrumque in se suscepit et non tantum passus est pro nobis, sed et legi in omnibus satisfecit, ut haec ipsius impletio et obedientia in iustitiam nobis imputaretur. (Although in several passages of Scripture the work of redemption is attributed to the death and shedding of the blood of Christ, this is by no means to be taken exclusively, as if the holy life of Christ were thereby excluded from the work of redemption; but it should be understood that this is done because nowhere did the Lord show His love for

Through the *obedientia passiva*, divine justice had been fully satisfied. God would demand too much if he not only had Christ pay the penalty for the transgression of the law, but also demanded a positive fulfillment of the law. *Lex obligat vel ad obedientiam vel ad poenam* [The law binds one either to obedience or to punishment]. Answer: This objection, which seeks to treat the matter rationally apart from the relevant scriptural passages, does not even satisfy human reason. Even according to human law, suffering the punishment for breaking the law is still not a fulfillment of the law, *feine conformitas cum lege*. A thief who has suffered the legal penalty for his theft is not yet a person who has kept the law, that is, who has not stolen it. Much less is the suffering of the punishment for the transgression of the divine law a fulfillment of the law before God. Who will say of the damned in hell, who suffer the punishment for their transgression of the law, that they thereby fulfill the law of God, the sum [or, essence] of which is: to love God with your heart and your neighbor as yourself? The sentence: *Lex obligat vel ad obedientiam vel ad poenam* is appropriate when it is necessary to emphasize that man cannot refuse obedience to the law without penalty when considering the case before any transgression of the law has already occurred. When explaining what the law demands of fallen man, however, we should instead say: *Lex obligat et ad poenam et ad obedientiam* [The law binds both to punishment and to

---

us and redeem us more clearly than in His passion, death, and wounds, as the devout ancients say; and because the death of Christ is like the final line and completion, the τέλος, the fulfillment and perfection, of all obedience, as the apostle says in Philippians 2:8. It is quite αδύνατον (impossible) to separate active obedience from passive obedience in this (Christ's) merit. Quenstedt (II, 351 sq.): By acting, Christ atoned for the sin which man had unjustly committed, and by suffering, Christ bore the punishment which man was justly to suffer. For man had to be freed not only from the wrath of God, the just judge, but also to be able to stand before God, he needed righteousness, which he could not achieve without fulfilling the law; therefore, Christ took both upon himself and not only suffered for us, but also satisfied the Law in all things so that his fulfillment and obedience might be imputed to us as righteousness.)

obedience].[86]

IV. The doctrine that Christ fulfilled the law vicariously for all men would damage morality, since no one would then seriously strive to fulfill the law.[87] Answer: Arguing in this way, one could also deny Christ's vicarious suffering of punishment, the *obedientia passiva*, by claiming that people would no longer be afraid of hell and would not repent if they heard that Christ had already atoned for the punishment of sins.[88] The objection reveals a complete unfamiliarity with

---

[86] Questedt says (II, 407 sq.): *Lex obligat vel ad poenam vel ad obedientiam, nimirum creaturas rationales nondum in peccatum prolapsas, v.g. sanctos angelos obligat tantum ad obedientiam, non vero ad poenam. Adamum in statu innocentiae tantum obligavit ad obedientiam, non autem simul ad poenam (nisi sub conditione). Ubi enim nulla est transgressio, ibi poena locum non habet. Sed creaturas rationales in peccatum prolapsas lex obligat ad poenam et ad obedientiam; ad obedientiam, quia sunt creaturas rationales; ad poenam, quia sunt in peccatum prolapsae. Iuri obligationis ad obedientiam per lapsum nihil quidquam decessit, quin potius nova obligatio, videlicet et poenam propter peccatum sustinendam, eidem accessit. Christus legitur et Adae et nostrum omnium loco sese sistens, legem perfecte implevit et poenas peccatorum nostrorum in se recepit.* (The Law binds either to punishment or to obedience rational creatures who have not yet fallen into sin. For example, it binds the holy angels only to obedience, but not to punishment. He bound Adam in the state of innocence only to obedience, but not at the same time to punishment (except under a condition). For where there is no transgression there is no punishment. But rational creatures who have fallen into sin are bound by the Law to punishment and obedience; to obedience because they are rational creatures; to punishment because they have fallen into sin. Nothing of the obligation of the people to obedience to the Law passed away through the fall, but a new obligation, that is to say, to bear the punishment for sin, was added to them. It is read that Christ, standing in the place of Adam and all of us, completely fulfilled the Law and took upon himself the punishment for our sins.)

[87] Adolf Harnack also criticizes the apostle Paul, stating that through his teaching of "objective reconciliation" he had "concealed the seriousness of religion for entire generations." (*Wesen des Christentums*, p. 115.)

[88] Gerhard (*De iustif.*, § 63): *Argumentum petitum ex schola Samosatenianorum, qui itidem verentur, ne per doctrinam de satisfactione Christi frigescat studium bonorum operum.* (The argument is taken from the school of the Samosatenians, who also fear that through the doctrine of Christ's satisfaction, the zeal for good works may grow cold.)

Christianity, the "experience", according to Romans 6:1 ff: Οἵτινες ἀπεQάνομεν τη αμαρτία, πώς ετι ζήσομεν εν αντη (How shall we who died to sin live any longer in it)?

The accusation made by more recent theologians against the old theologians, that the latter mechanically juxtaposed or tore apart the *obedientia* *activa* and *passiva*, is one of the common misrepresentations of the teaching of the old theologians.[89]

The sacrifice of Christ and the atoning sacrifices of the Old Testament.

Scripture explicitly states that the Atonements of the Old Testament were types of Christ's sacrifice. Hebrews 10:1 says of the annual and daily atonement sacrifices of the Old Testament: "The law has the shadow" (σκιάν = shadow outline, image) "of the good things to come, not the very image of the things themselves" (οὐκ αυτην την εικόνα των πραγμάτων = not the very image of things). The following verses leave no doubt as to what is meant here by "shadow" and "image". Verses 1b-14 explain that the real atonement for sin is not effected by the Old Testament sacrifices, but only by Christ's self-sacrifice. Verse 4: "It is impossible to take away sins with the blood of oxen and goats." Likewise verse 11. On the other hand, the taking away of sins "was accomplished once by the sacrifice of the body of Christ," verse 10. Likewise verses 12 and 14. The Old Testament sacrifices were therefore, according to Scripture, only foreshadowings of the sacrifice of Christ. In them the objective atonement for sins was not carried out, but they pointed to the objective atonement to be carried out by Christ's sacrifice. The Old Testament sacrifices have been appropriately called "prophetic acts", that is, just as the reconciliation of people through Christ is prophesied in many Old Testament Scriptures, the same

---

[89] Cf. above Gerhard (*De iustif.*, § 55): *Quid? Quod, plane αδύνατον est, activam obedientiam a passiva in hoc merito separare.* (What? That it is clearly impossible to separate active obedience from passive obedience in this merit.) So especially also Quenstedt II, 407.

prophecy is present in the act by which animals were offered as atoning sacrifices at God's command. The essential difference between these sacrifices and the sacrificial cult of the Gentiles lies in the exemplary [or, typical], prophesying character of the Old Testament sacrifices. The pagans ascribed real atoning power to their sacrifices; the sacrifices in Israel had their significance in that they were a prophecy of Christ's sacrifice. There are seemingly contradictory statements in Scripture regarding the power of the Old Testament atonement. While Hebrews 10:4 says, "It is impossible that the blood of bulls and goats should take away sins," we read Genesis 17:11, etc.: "I have given it" (namely, the blood of animals) to you upon the altar to make atonement for your souls; for it is the blood that makes atonement for the soul." The harmony of these statements is obvious. The blood of the sacrificial animals did not atone, namely not in itself; but it atoned typically, that is, it prefigured the atoning sacrifice of Christ to the Israelites and therefore offered them, as a means of grace ordained by God, the atonement to be brought about by Christ. Thus, the believing Israelite obtained forgiveness of sins through the proper use of the Old Testament atonement.[90]

---

[90] Kromayer (*Theol. pos.-pol.* I, 775): Φαινομένη *contradictio inter Mosen et apostolum facile tollitur; cum enim Mosen Lev. 17, 11 inquit:* "Sanguis hircorum expiat peccata", *Paulus [?] Hebr. 10, 4 inquit:* "Sanguis hircorum non expiat peccata": *non expiat in se, sed typice, quatenus Christi sacrificium* Ιλαοτικόν *pro peccatis mundi adumbrat.* (The apparent contradiction between Moses and the apostle is easily resolved; when Moses says in Leviticus 17:11: "The blood of goats atones for sins", Paul in Hebrews 10:4 says: "The blood of goats does not atone for sins": it does not atone in itself, but in a typological way, inasmuch as it foreshadows Christ's sacrificial offering for the sins of the world.) Quenstedt on the *duplex usus* of the Old Testament sacrifices: *legalis* (remembrance of sins) and *evangelicus* (prefiguring [or, foreshadowing or in anticipation of] the sacrifice of Christ). (*Syst.* II, 943 sq. Baier III, 108.) The newer views on the sacrifices of the Old Testament are essentially based on the error that man himself must reconcile himself with God in a "religious-ethical" way. (Cf. Luhartdt, *Dogm.*, p. 243; H. Schmidt and v. Orelli in *RE.* 2 XVI, 363 ff. 410 ff.) Holtzmann (*Neutest. Theol.* II, 111 ff.) essentially takes the side of the old theologians in his view

To whom and for whom Christ made satisfaction.

The question about to whom Christ made satisfaction has already been sufficiently answered above, namely God, inasmuch as holiness and righteousness belong to God. Satisfaction was made to divine justice, as has been demonstrated above. And since the divine righteousness is not threefold [or, does not exist three times], but the one divine justice is due in number to the Father, the Son and the Holy Spirit, the old teachers are not wrong when they say that Christ also made satisfaction to himself. Baier: "Inasmuch as Christ made satisfaction, he is regarded as a mediator; inasmuch as he himself also demanded satisfaction, he is to be regarded as God, as the author and avenger of the law, who by

---

of the "concept of sacrifice"; otherwise Nitzsch-Stephan, p. 600 f. The interpretation of the individual parts of the Old Testament sacrificial ceremonial goes beyond the task of a dogmatic compendium. However, it should be remembered here that the substitutionary atonement made by Christ is clearly depicted in all its main ideas by the order of the Old Testament sacrifices. We have summarized above what Scripture teaches about Christ's substitutionary atonement in three main points: (1) God, according to his inviolable justice, demands that men fulfill his Law, and the transgressors of this Law have forfeited their lives. (2) Christ, taking the place of men, satisfies divine justice through his active and suffering obedience. (3) Through Christ's substitutionary action and suffering, God is now reconciled with man. All this is clearly shown in the Old Testament atonement sacrifices, especially in the ceremonial of the great Day of Atonement. (1) The inviolable holiness and righteousness of God is expressed in the fact that God demanded atoning sacrifices from the transgressors of his Law, who were killed and whose blood had to be brought before him (namely to the altar, on the great Day of Atonement in the Holy of Holies). (2) The fact that this was only a substitution, i.e. that it was actually the sinning man and not the sacrificial animal that was to die, was expressed by the fact that the person for whom the sacrifice was offered had to lay his hands on the sinless sacrificial animal, confess his sin, and thus transfer it to the sacrificial animal. 3. That God regarded the sacrifice offered as an atonement is evident from the fact that He calls the blood of the sacrificial animal the blood of atonement, Leviticus. 17:11: "For the life of the flesh is in the blood, and I have given it to you upon the altar to make atonement for your souls; for it is the blood that makes atonement for the soul." The reconciliation that was accomplished was also depicted in external events, for example, on the great Day of Atonement when the living goat, after the iniquity of the people had been confessed over him and laid upon his head, was led into the wilderness and there released.

his nature is absolutely righteous like the Father and the Holy Spirit." It is a scriptural thought that the one who makes satisfaction and the one who receives satisfaction are one and the same, 2 Corinthians 5:19: θεος ην ἐν Χριστw κόσμον καταλλάσσων ἑαυτῷ (God was in Christ reconciling the world to Himself). To be rejected[91] is the strange idea of Origen and others that Christ paid the ransom to the devil,[92] which smacks of dualism. In contrast, Quenstedt argues: The devil, through God's punishment, is only the jailer of men, not their lord and judge, to whom a ransom would have had to be paid. *Soli Deo, non diabolo,* λύτρον *persolvendum erat* (To God alone, not to the devil, ransom was to be paid).[93]

The answer to the question of for whom Christ made satisfaction is:

a. Not for himself, because the Scriptures consistently testify that Christ was without sin as to his own person; the αμαρτία which Christ bore (John 1:29) and atoned for (1 John 2:2; 4:10) was the sin of men transferred to Him [by a] *actu forensic* [judicial act] (2 Corinthians 5:21; John 1:29, etc.). That Christ also did not perform the *obedientia activa* for himself, but for men, has just been explained.

---

[91] *Kompendium* III, 120.

[92] Origen asks about Matthew 20:28 "τίνι δέ ἔδωκε τὴν ψυχήν αὐτοῦ λύτρον αντί πολλών"and answers:οὐ γαρ δή τῶ θεω. He asks furthermore: μή τι οὐν τw ponhrw and answers: οὐτος γάρ εκράτει ἡμῶν, ἑως δοQη τό ὑπέρ ἡμῶν αὐτw λύρον, ἡ τού Ιησού ψυχή κτλ. But that it is a great error to make this doctrine of Origen the actual doctrine of the church until Anselm is proved in "*Lehre und Wehre*" 1883, p. 308 ff. Even Origen does not merely speak of the ransoming of mankind by handing over the ransom to the devil, but also teaches a reconciliation of God, which took place through the fact that Christ, through the sacrifice of his body, made God gracious to man. About Romans 3:23. (Cf. Thomasius, *Dogmengesch.* I, 288.) The error of the church fathers, who are afflicted by these strange Origenist ideas, lies in the fact that they add a rationalist conclusion to the scriptural truth. From the scriptural truth that sinners are given over to the power of the devil by God's righteous judgment (1 Corinthians 5:5; Hebrews 2:14, etc.), they concluded that the devil had obtained a right over sinners for himself [or, in his own person] and therefore could demand a ransom.

[93] *Syst.* II, 648 sqq.

b. Not for the angels, neither for the good ones for the completion of their righteousness (as some Reformed theologians believe)[94] nor for the evil ones (as Origen and other representatives of *apokatastasis* believe)[95], but

c. for men, and indeed for all men. That the *vicaria satisfactio* applies to all men has already been discussed in detail in the *gratia unversalis*.[96]

What Scripture teaches about the perfection of satisfaction can be briefly summarized as follows: The satisfaction made by Christ is both intensively and extensively perfect. It is intensively perfect inasmuch as

---

[94] However, according to Colossians 1:20 and Ephesians 1:10, "the effect of Christ's atoning death also extended to the angels" (Nitzsch, p. 294), but through the reconciliation of men. According to Scripture, human beings and the angels who have remained in God's fellowship form a holy family. Therefore it is said of those who have believed in Christ that they have come (προσεληλύ'θατε) to the heavenly Jerusalem and to the myriads of angels (μυριάσιν αγγέλων πανηγυρει, Hebrews 12:22-23), and that the angels in heaven rejoice over every addition to the family in the form of a repentant sinner (Luke 15:10). When people became sinners, they fell out of the holy family. Because Christ reconciled sinners to God again, εἰρηνοποιήσας διά του αἵματός του οταυρου αντου, they are restored to the heavenly family. Meyer and others who reject any limitation of τά πάντα and want to refer it to everything "existing" overlook the fact that there is a limitation in the text itself on τά πάντα receives its closer definition and thus its limitation through the added είτε τά επί τής γης, είτε τά εν τοῖς ουρανοῖς, "be it that which is on earth, be it that which is in heaven." However, not all creatures are described in Scripture as inhabitants of heaven, but the heavenly *coetus* (company, host) is formed by the holy angels, the assembly of the firstborn, and the spirits of the righteous made perfect (Hebrew 12:22-23).

[95] What is meant by the ἀποχατάστασις πάντων (restoration of all things) (Acts 3:21) is explained by Christ when He says of John the Baptist's activity: ἀποχατάστασις πάντων. The ἀποκατάοτασις πάνταν is therefore accomplished through the testimony of Christ among Israel and in the Gentiles, and is actually accomplished in those who accept the testimony of Christ. By this means everything is established as God wants it to be in his kingdom, and as was also foretold by the prophets. Nitzsch-Stephan (p. 733) correctly states that Acts 3:19-21 does not speak at all of the final fate of the ungodly, but rather "restoration" signifies "the fulfillment of all the ancient divine prophecies."

[96] P. 21 ff.

God is completely reconcile with man through Christ's actions and therefore no more action or goodness of one's own is required on the part of man (rejection of the modern guarantee theory, "deepened" atonement theory), but only faith is required to be reconciled with God. It is also extensively perfect, inasmuch complete reconciliation extends equally to all men, not only to those who are actually saved (the elect), but also to those who are actually lost.

In discussing the sufficiency of the atonement made by Christ, the question has also been raised as to whether a drop of Christ's blood would have been sufficient ransom for the sins of the world. The Papists answered this question in the affirmative so that they could trade in the "surplus" [or, "excess"] merit of Christ.[97] Lutherans answered this question in the affirmative, inasmuch as the blood of Christ is the blood of the Son of God, and therefore has infinite value in every smallest part. It is not the quantity but the quality of the blood shed by Christ, as the blood of the Son of God, that gives it its infinite redemptive value. Having said that, however, since Christ shed his blood abundantly in accordance with the will and counsel of God,[98] we do not say that the abundance of his shedding was superfluous. In this whole discussion, Quenstedt appropriately reminds us of this principle: *Solus Deus optime novit, quantum ad plenam perfectamque pro peccatis nostris satisfactionem requiratur, et cur Filium suum unigenitum tot plagas, nec plures, nec pauciores, pati, nec minus sanguinis ac fuit effusum, effundi voluerit . . . Quantum iustitia Dei acceptare debuerit, non ex nostra phantasia, sed ex Dei verbo depromendum est* [God alone knows very well what is required for full and perfect satisfaction for our sins, and why he willed his only begotten Son to suffer so many plagues, neither more nor fewer, nor less blood than was shed, He wills to be

---

[97] Quenstedt II, 467-470. A wealth of dogmatic history material has been compiled here, some of which is reproduced from Philippi IV, 2, pp. 95-98.

[98] Luther IX, 995. B. Meisner bei Baier-Walther III, 121 sq. — Joh. Heermann's hymn "Where shall I flee to," *St. L. Hymnal*, No. 230, v. 9: "Thy blood, the noble juice," etc.

poured out . . . How much the justice of God ought to accept is not to be ascertained from our imagination, but from the word of God.]. In short, we hold all the doings and sufferings of Christ as described in Scripture to be the ransom by which divine justice has been satisfied. When we ascribe redemption to a part of the work of redemption, as also Scripture does (Rom. 5:10), this is not to be understood exclusively, but inclusive of the other parts.

According to the Old Testament type (Exodus 30:7-8; Leviticus 16:12, 13,[99] etc.), the high priestly office of Christ in the state of humiliation also includes the offering of intercession for people. Isaiah 53:12 mentions not only the *satisfactio* but also the *intercessio* in the description of the work of Christ: "He bore the sin of many, and made intercession for the transgressors." Christ intercedes a. for all men; example Luke 23:34 (*intercessio generalis*); and b. especially, as head of the church, for the believers; Example: John 17 (*intercessio specialis*). The purpose of intercession is to obtain forgiveness of sins and to preserve in it, as can be seen from the examples mentioned. The apparent contradiction between Luke 23:34 and John 17:9 is resolved in 1 Timothy 4:10.

The high priestly office in the state of exaltation.

The priesthood of Christ did not cease with the [the ceasing of] his state of humiliation. Scripture expressly ascribes the priesthood to Christ even in the state of exaltation. According to Hebrews 7:24, Christ has " because He continues forever, has an unchangeable priesthood" (ἀπαράβατον εχει την Ιερωσύνην) and from this it is concluded in v. 25: "Therefore He is also able to save to the uttermost (εἰς τό παντελές) [i.e., forever] those who come to God through Him."

But what does the high priestly activity of Christ in the state of exaltation consist of? Not in the repetition of the atoning sacrifice, which Scripture expressly rejects, Romans 6:9-10; Hebrews 9:12, 15;

---

[99] Philippi IV, 2, p. 340: "In Scripture, smoke [incense burning] is the symbol of prayer." Psalm 141:2, Revelation 5:8.

7:27 (*intercessio Christi in statu exaltationis non est satisfactoria* [the intercession of Christ in his state of exaltation is not for satisfaction), but in his intercession for the redeemed, to make them partakers of the salvation acquired once and for all (ἐφάπαξ) (*intercessio Christi in statu exaltationis est applicatoria* [the intercession of Christ in his state of exaltation is for application]). This is clearly taught in Hebrews 7:24, 25: ἐντυγχάνειν υπέρ αυτών, that is, for those who come to God through him; 1 John 2:1: παράκλητον εχομεν προς τον πατέρα, Ἰησουν Χριστόν (we have an Advocate with the Father, Jesus Christ); Romans 8:34: εντυγχάνει υπέρ ημών (makes intercession for us). Intercession therefore has to do with the gathering and preservation of the church. Baier wants to leave undefined[100] whether Christ's intercession for the redeemed is expressed in words and petitions — heavenly words and petitions, of course — (*intercessio verbalis*), or whether the intercession consists only in the fact that Christ, through his merit acquired in the state of humiliation, continually moves God to be gracious to us (*intercessio realis*). But here, as everywhere else, it is not advisable to depart from the wording of Scripture. According to the wording of Scripture, Christ himself speaks, not only his merit, Hebrews 7:25: "He lives forever and prays for them", πάντοτε ζών εἰς τό ἐντυγχάνειν υπερ αυτών; Romans 8:34: "who is also at the right hand of God, who also intercedes for us";[101] 1 John 2:1: "we have an Advocate (παράκλητον) with the Father, Jesus Christ." It goes without saying that this intercession is not "a plea on one's knees," etc., since it is the intercession of "the one who is at the right hand of God," Romans 8:34. It is diminishing Scriptures if we do not let Christ Himself speak, but only the merit of Christ. Quenstedt has the right argument against

---

[100] *Compendium* III, 126 sq., note d.

[101] The twice-repeated ος καί makes an emphatic distinction between intercession and sitting at the right hand of God, and presents the latter as a separate act.

the various forms of weakening the doctrine of Scripture.[102] As for the Socinians and their sympathizers, they deny completely Christ's high priestly office in the state of humiliation (the offering of an atonement by vicarious satisfaction). They transfer Christ's high priestly office to the state of exaltation, but understand by this only the help that Christ gives to men in the work of their self-salvation by keeping them from sinning through his word and example and by stimulating them to a pious life.[103] It goes without saying that all modern opponents of vicarious satisfaction also dismiss Christ's high priestly function in the state of exaltation in a Socinian way. According to Scripture, Christ's high priestly activity in the state of exaltation is based solely on the *satisfactio vicaria* achieved in the state of humiliation. The fact that, in case we sin, we παράκλητον ἔχομεν πρὸς τον πατέρα (we have an advocate with the Father) in the exalted Christ (1 John 2:1) is grounded in the fact that Jesus is δίκαιος and at the same time (καί αντός) ἱλασμός

---

[102] *Systema* II, 470 sq. Likewise Meyer against Düsterdieck: "Düsterdieck denies without exegetical justification that the intercession is *voealis et oralis* (voice or speech)" (on Romans 8:34).

[103] *Catechesis Racoviensis*, Question 476-479. Question 479 asks: *Qui* (in which way) *expiationem peccatorum nostrorum Iesus in coelis peragit? And the answer: Primum a peccatorum poenis nos liberat, dum virtute et potestate, quam a patre plenam et absolutam consecutus est, perpetuo nos tuetur et iram Dei interventu suo quodammodo a nobis arcet, quod Scriptura exprimit, dum ait, eum pro nobis interpellare. Deinde ab ipsorum peccatorum servitute nos liberat, dum eadem potestate ab omni flagitiorum genere nos retrahit et avocat: id vero in sua ipsius persona nobis ostendendo, quid consequatur is, qui a peccato desistit: vel etiam alia ratione nos hortando et monendo, nobis opem ferendo, ac interdum puniendo, a peccati iugo exsolvit.* (How (in which way) does Jesus in heaven perform the expiation of our sins? And the answer: First, He frees us from the punishments of sins, by constantly protecting us with the power and authority which He has obtained in full and absolute measure from the Father, and in a way, He wards off the wrath of God from us through his intervention, as Scripture expresses it, when it says, He intercedes for us. Then, He frees us from the slavery of sin, by the same power drawing us away from every kind of disgraceful behavior and calling us back: this He shows us in his own person, what follows for one who desists from sin; or by other means encouraging and warning us, offering us help, and sometimes by punishing us, He frees us from the yoke of sin.)

εστι περί των αμαρτιών ημών . . . καί περί ολου του κόσμου (the righteous and at the same time He himself is the propitiation for our sins and for the sins of the whole world). Romans 8:34 says the intercession of Christ εντυγχάνειν υπερ ημών (on our behalf, for us) is effective to put every accusation against us to shame: "It is Christ who died, and furthermore is also risen, who is even at the right hand of God, who also makes intercession for us." Meyer remarks on this: "These predicates present Christ's death as having propitiated us and his resurrection as 'our justification.'" Romans 4:25. The newer theologians, by inserting the "transformation of humanity" into Christ's work of reconciliation (through the modern "deepened" atonement theory, guarantee theory), the παράκλητος [advocate] is reduced to a "stimulator" of moral improvement in man. As Grotius interprets the atonement in 1 John 2:2: *Sensus est, (Christus) vires praestat, ne peccemus in posterum* (The meaning is, (Christ) provides strength, so that we do not sin in the future.) The Papists distort and falsify the doctrine of the high priestly office of Christ in the state of exaltation,

a. by the so-called "unbloody" repetition of Christ's sacrifice in the sacrifice of the Mass, whereby they deny the εφάπαξ (once for all) of Scripture (Hebrews 7:27; 9:12; Romans 6:10; Hebrews 10:14);

b. by allowing Mary and the saints to intercede for men with their merits[104] and thus setting them alongside Christ as intercessors.

The old Lutheran theologians also discussed the question of whether Christ would continue to pray for his own after the Last Day.[105] Feurborn answered the question in the negative, Calov in the affirmative. Quenstedt also shares Calov's opinion. But the scriptural passages that deal with Christ's intercession presuppose the conditions

---

[104] Bellarmine in Quenstedt II, 1444: *Sancti ex meritis praecedentibus impetrare possunt et sibi et aliis id, quod orando petunt.* (Based on their past merits, saints can obtain for themselves and for others what they ask in prayer.)

[105] Feurborn, Calov in *Baier-Walther III*, 127.

prevailing before the Last Day, namely, the gathering and preservation of the Church. Thus, there is no scriptural evidence for Calov's and Quenstedt's view. Referring to Hebrews 7:25 where Scripture says of Christ: "He is also able to save to the uttermost those who come to God through Him, since He always lives to make intercession for them," Gottfried Hoffman points out: "This [intercession], however, seems to be limited by the immediately preceding words about coming to God, that is, during the time when people are coming to God through repentance and faith."[106] One will have to agree with Hoffman.

---

[106] *Synopsis Theologiae*, p. 540.

Bibliography: Atonement

Anselm. *Cur Deus Homo.* trans. Sidney Norton Deane. Fort Worth: RDMc Publishing, 2005, 1903.

Aubert, Annette G. 2002. "Luther, Melanchthon, and Chemnitz: The Doctrine of the Atonement with Special Reference to Gustaf Aulen's Christus Victor." ThM Thesis. Westminster Theological Seminary.

Aulén, Gustaf, Christus Victor: An Historical Study of the Three Main Types of the Idea of the Atonement, trans. A. G. Hebert. New York: Macmillan Publishing Co., Inc., 1969.

Baier, Johann Wilhelm. *Atonement in Lutheran Orthodoxy: Baier-Walther,* ed. and annot. C. F. W. Walther, trans. Ted Mayes. Sidney, MT: Synoptic Text Information Services, Inc., 2023.

Calov, Abraham and Jack D. Kilcrease. *Atonement in Lutheran Orthodoxy: Abraham Calov.* trans. Matthew Carver. Sidney, Montana: Synoptic Text Information Services, Inc., 2024.

Chytraeus, David. *Chytraeus on Sacrifice: A Reformation Treatise in Biblical Theology,* trans. John Warwick Montgomery. St Louis: Concordia Publishing House, 1962.

Dau, William Herman Theodore. "Did God Have to be Reconciled by the Death of Christ?" *Theological Quarterly,* vol. XX, no. 1, January 1916, pp. 1-13.

Denny, James. The Death of Christ: Its Place and Interpretation in the New Testament, 5th ed. New York: A. C. Armstrong, 1907.

Dierks, Theodore. *Reconciliation and Justification.* St. Louis: Concordia Publishing House, 1938.

Eckardt, Burnell F. Jr. *Anselm and Luther on the Atonement: Was it Necessary?* San Francisco: Mellen Research University Press, 1992.

Edwards, Mark J., ed. *We Believe in the Crucified and Risen Lord* (Ancient Christian doctrine series; vol. 3). Downers Grove, IL: IVP Academic, 2009.

Evenson, George O. "A Critique of Aulén's *Christus Victor*," *Concordia Theological Monthly*, vol. XXVIII, no. 10, 1957, pp. 738-749.

Forde, Gerhard O. "Caught in the Act: Reflections on the Work of Christ," *World in World*, 3/1 1983, 22-31.

_____. "In Our Place," in *A More Radical Gospel: Essays on Eschatology, Authority, Atonement, and Ecumenism*, Mark C. Mattes and Steven D. Paulson, eds. (Minneapolis: Fortress Press, 2017), 101-113.

_____. *The Law-Gospel Debate*. Minneapolis: Fortress Press, 2007.

_____. "The Work of Christ" in Carl E. Braaten and Robert W. Jensen, eds., *Christian Dogmatics*. Philadelphia: Fortress Press, 1984, II.1-99.

_____. *Theology Is for Proclamation*. Minneapolis: Fortress Press, 1990.

Franzman, Martin H. "Reconciliation and Justification," *Concordia Theological Monthly*, vol. XXI, no. 2, 1950, pp. 81-93.

_____. An Explanation of the History of the Suffering and Death of Our Lord Jesus Christ, Elmer M. Hohle, trans. Malone, TX: Repristination Press, 1998.

_____. *On Justification through Faith*, Richard J. Dinda, trans. St. Louis: Concordia Publishing House, 2018, 52-109.

Gibbs, Jeffrey A. "The Son of God and the Father's Wrath: Atonement and Salvation in Matthew's Gospel," *Concordia Theological Quarterly*, vol. 72, no. 3, 2008, pp. 211-225.

Gieschen, Charles A. "Editorial." *Concordia Theological Quarterly*, vol. 72, no. 3, 2008, p. 194.

_____. "The Death of Jesus in the Gospel of John: Atonement for Sin?" *Concordia Theological Quarterly*, vol. 72, no. 3, 2008, pp. 243-61.

Grensted, Laurence William. *A Short History of the Doctrine of the Atonement*. London: University of Manchester Press, 1920.

_____. *The Atonement in History and Life*. London: Society for Promoting Christian Knowledge, 1929.

Hägglund, Bengt. "The Struggle Against Socinianism," in Bengt Hägglund, *History of Theology*, 4th rev. ed. St. Louis: Concordia Publishing House,

2007, 322-323.

Harnack, Theodosius. *Luthers Theologie mit besonderer Beziehung auf seine Versöhnungs und Erlösungslehre*. München, Chr. Kaiser Verlag 1927.

Halvorson, T. R. *Vicarious Satisfaction in Lutheran Catechisms, Confessions, and Hymns*. Sidney, Montana: Synoptic Text Information Services, 2023.

Hengel, Martin. *The Atonement: The Origins of the Doctrine in the New Testament*. Minneapolis: Fortress Press, 1981.

Jenson, Robert W. *Systematic Theology: The Triune God*. Oxford: Oxford University Press, 1997, I.165-206.

Johnson, Adam J., ed. *T&T Clark Companion to Atonement*. Oxford: T&T Clerk, 2017.

Judisch, Douglas. "Propitiation in the Language and Typology of the Old Testament," *Concordia Theological Quarterly*, vol. 48, nos. 2 & 3, 1984, pp. 221-243.

Just, Arthur A. Jr. "The Cross, the Atonement, and the Eucharist in Luke." *Concordia Theological Quarterly*, vol. 84, no. 3-4, 2020, pp. 227-244.

Kilcrease, Jack D. "Abraham Calov and the Struggle for the Christian Doctrine of the Atonement," in Abraham Calov and Jack D. Kilcrease, *Atonement in Lutheran Orthodoxy: Abraham Calov*. trans. Matthew Carver. Sidney, Montana: Synoptic Text Information Services, Inc., 2024, 1-44.

_____. "Gerhard Forde's Theology of Atonement and Justification: A Confessional Lutheran Response," *Concordia Theological Quarterly*, vol. 76, nos. 3-4. 2012, pp. 269-293.

_____. "*Heilsgeschicte* and Atonement in the Theology of Johannes Christian Konrad von Hofmann (1810-1877): An Exposition and Critique," *Logia: A Journal of Lutheran Theology* 22, no. 2 (2013), pp. 13-26.

_____. "Johann Gerhard, the Socinians, and Modern Rejections of Substitutionary Atonement," *Concordia Theological Quarterly*, vol. 83, nos. 1-2, 2018, pp. 19-44.

_____. *The Doctrine of Atonement: From Luther to Forde*. Eugene, OR: Wipf & Stock, 2018.

_____. The Work of Christ: Revisionist Doctrine and the Confessional Lutheran Response (Eugene, OR: Wipf & Stock, 2018).

Kleinig, John W. "Sacrificial Atonement by Jesus and God's Wrath in the Light of the Old Testament." *Concordia Theological Quarterly*, vol. 84, no. 3-4, 2020, pp. 195-208.

Long, Thomas E. The Viability of a Sacrificial Theology of Atonement: A Critique and Analysis of Traditional and Transformational Views. Minneapolis: Lutheran University Press, 2006.

Luther, Martin. *The 1529 Holy Week and Easter Sermons of Dr. Martin Luther.* Trans Irving L. Sandberg. St. Louis: Concordia Publishing House, 1998.

Maier, Walter A. III. "Penal Substitutionary Atonement?" *Concordia theological Quarterly*, vol. 84, no. 3-4, 2020, pp. 245-263.

Maxfield, John A. "Luther, Zwingli, and Calvin on the Significance of Christ's Death" *Concordia Theological Quarterly*, vol. 75, nos. 1-2, 2011, pp. 91-110.

Masaki, Noamichi. "Contemporary Views on Atonement in Light of the Lutheran Confessions," *Concordia Theological Quarterly*, vol. 72, no. 4, 2008, pp. 305-325.

Morris, Leon, *Glory in the Cross: A Study in Atonement.* Grand Rapids: Baker Book House, 1966.

_____. *The Apostolic Preaching of the Cross*, 3rd rev. ed. Grand Rapids: William B. Eerdmans Publishing Company, 1965.

_____. *The Atonement: Its Meaning and Significance.* Downers Grove: InterVarsity Press, 1983.

_____. *The Cross in the New Testament.* Grand Rapids: William B. Eerdmans Publishing Company, 1965.

Mozley, John Kenneth. *The Doctrine of the Atonement.* New York: Charles Scribner's Sons, 1916.

Peters, Albrecht. *Commentary on Luther's Catechisms: Creed.* trans. Thomas Trapp. St. Louis: Concordia Publishing House, 2011.

Pieper, Francis. *Christian Dogmatics*, St. Louis: Concordia Publishing

House, 1951, II.330-394

Preus, Robert D. "Justification as Taught by Post-Reformation Lutheran Theologians." March 26, 1982.

_____. "The Doctrine of Justification in the Theology of Classical Lutheran Orthodoxy," *The Springfielder*, vol. XXIX, no. 1, 1965, 24-39.

_____. "The Vicarious Atonement in John Quenstedt," *Concordia Theological Monthly*, vol. xxxii, no. 2, 1961, pp. 78-97.

Preus, Rolf D. "For Jesus' Sake: The Relationship between Atonement and Justification." Tromsø, Norway, July 4, 2015.

Quenstedt, Johannes Andreas and Robert D. Preus. *Atonement in Lutheran Orthodoxy: Johannes Quenstedt.* 2nd ed. trans. Matthew Carver. Sidney, Montana: Synoptic Text Information Services, Inc., 2024.

Remensnyder, Junius B., *The Atonement and Modern Thought,* Philadelphia: Lutheran Publication Society, 1905.

Scaer, David P. "Flights from the Atonement," *Concordia Theological Quarterly*, vol. 72, no. 3, 2008, pp. 195-210.

_____. "The Sacrificial Death of Christ," in *Christology*, (Confessional Lutheran Dogmatics, vol VI). Fort Wayne, IN: The International Foundation for Lutheran Confessional Research, 1989, pp. 66-82.

_____. *Without the Shedding of Blood.* Littleton, CO; Ad Crucem Books, 2024.

Scaer, Peter J. "Reckoned Among the Lawless," *Concordia theological Quarterly*, vol. 84, no. 3-4, 2020, pp. 209-225.

_____. "The Atonement in Mark's Sacramental Theology." *Concordia Theological Quarterly*, vol. 72, no. 3, 2008, pp. 227-242.

Schdmid, Heinrich. *Doctrinal Theology of the Evangelical Lutheran Church.* Minneapolis: Augsburg Publishing House, 1875, 1889, 342-370.

Thomasius, D. Gottfried. Das Bekenntniß der lutherischen Kirche von der Versöhnung und die Versöhnungslehre D. Chr. K. v. Hofmann's. Erlangen: Theodor Bläsing, 1857.

Wheaton, Benjamin. *Suffering, Not Power: Atonement in the Middle Ages.* Bellingham, WA: Lexham Academic, 2022.

Williams, George Hunston. *Anselm: Communion and Atonement*. St. Louis: Concordia Publishing House, 1960.

Bibliography: Pieper's Works[1]

Ji, Won Yong. *A Study Guide for Franz Pieper's Christian Dogmatics III*. St. Louis, Mo: Concordia Print Shop, 1991.

Mueller, John Theodore. *Doctrina Cristiana: manual de teología doctrinal para pastores, maestros y legos*. Edited by Dieter Joel Jagnow. Translated by Martinho Lutero Hasse. 4a edição, Revista e ampliada. Porto Alegre, RS: Editora Concórdia, 2018.

———. *Dogmática cristã: um manual sistemático dos ensinos bíblicos*. Edited by Dieter Joel Jagnow. Translated by Martinho Lutero Hasse. 4a edição, Revista e ampliada. Porto Alegre, RS: Editora Concórdia, 2018.

———. *Kristen dogmatik*. Translated by Tom G.A. Hardt. Uppsala: Bokförlaget Pro Veritate, 1985.

———. *Kristīgā dogmatika: doktrinālās teoloģijas rokasgrāmata mācītājiem, skolotājiem un lajiem*. Translated by Andris Smilgdrīvs. Rīga, Latvia: Luterisma mantojuma fonds, 1999.

———. *La doctrine chrétienne: manuel de théologie doctrinale pour pasteurs, instituteurs et fidèles*. Bruxelles: Editions des Missions Luthériennes, 1956.

———. *Христианская догматика: учебник по догматическому богословию для пасторов, учителей и мирян*. Edited by Алексей Комаров and Жанна Григорова. Translated by Константин Комаров. Macomb, MI: Lutheran Heritage Foundation, 2016.

Mueller, John Theodore, and Franz Pieper. *Christian Dogmatics: A Handbook of Doctrinal Theology for Pastors, Teachers, and Laymen*. St. Louis, Mo: Concordia Publishing House, 1934.

———. *Jidu jiao jiao yi xue*. Translated by Erhardt Riedel. 2nd ed. Hong

---

[1] Bibliography of the Works of Franz Pieper, First Edition, Compiled by Robert E. Smith. Supplemented and edited by T. R. Halvorson and Joel David. Used with permission.

Kong: Xianggang Lude hui wen zi bu, 1986.

Pieper, Franz. *A Brief Statement of the Doctrinal Position of the Missouri Synod*. St. Louis, Mo: Concordia publishing house, 1931.

———. "Adolf Harnack." *Concordia Theological Monthly* 1, no. 9 (1930): 651–59.

———. "Amadogmatics: ukufunda isifundiso sobuKristu kanye noFranz Pieper." Translated by Ernst Alfred Wilhelm Weber. *Fundisani ukugcina konke okuyalwa* 3 (2009).

———. *Christian Dogmatics*. Translated by Walter W.F. Albrecht. 4 vols. St. Louis, Mo: Concordia Publishing House, 1950.

———. *Christliche Dogmatik*. Edited by Ernest Eckhardt. 3 vols. St. Louis, Mo: Concordia Publishing House, 1917.

———. *Christliche dogmatik*. Edited by John Theodore Mueller. Louis, MO: Evangelisch-Lutherischen Synode von Missouri, Ohio und Anderen Staaten, 1946.

———. *Church Government*. Translated by George Schweikert. Okabena, Minnesota: G. Schweikert, 1956.

———. *Conversion and Election: A Plea for a United Lutheranism in America*. Translated by W.H.T. Dau. St. Louis, Mo: Concordia Publishing House, 1913.

———. *Das Fundament Des Christlichen Glaubens*. St. Louis, Mo: Concordia Publishing House, 1925.

———. *Das Grundbekenntniss Der Evangelischlutherischen Kirche*. St. Louis, Mo: Lutheran Concordia-Verlag, 1880.

———. *Das Grundbekenntniss der Evangelisch-lutherischen Kirche: Mit einer geschichtlichen Einleitung und kurzen erklärenden Anmerkungen versehen: Dem lutherischen Christenvolk zum 400jährigen Jubiläum der Augsburgischen Konfession dargeboten*. St. Louis, Mo: Concordia Publishing House, 1930.

———. *Das Sola Fide in der christl. Lehre von der Rechtfertigung: eine Reihe von Vorträgen*. St. Louis, Mo: N.P., 1900.

———. *Das Wesen des Christenthums: Vortrag, gehalten vor der zehnten*

Delegatensynode (1902) der Synode von Missouri, Ohio u. a. Staaten. St. Louis, Mo: Concordia Publishing House, 1903.

_____. "Der Eine Punkt." *Concordia Theological Monthly* 1, no. 3 (1930): 161–97.

_____. *Der Grosse Welt-Und Menschenbetrug Durch Das Päpstliche Jubeljahr.* Zwickau (Sachsen): Verlag von Johannes Herrmann, 1925.

_____. "Der Reichstag Zu Augsburg Der Reichstag Des Friedens Mit Gott Und Des Ewigen Friedens Im Himmel." *Concordia Theological Monthly* 1, no. 9 (1930): 643–51.

_____. *Die Gaben Der Christen.* St. Louis, Mo: Concordia Publishing House, XXXX.

_____. *Die Grosse Hauptsache, Um Die Es Sich Bei Der Reformation Der Kirche Handelte.* Zwickau: chriftenverein, 1918.

_____. *Die Grunddifferenz in der Lehre von der Bekehrung und Gnadenwahl: Vortrag, gehalten vor der "freien Conferenz" zu Watertown, Wis., am 29. April 1903.* St. Louis, Mo: Concordia Publishing House, 1903.

_____. *Die Kraft Des Evangeliums.* St. Louis, Mo: Concordia Publishing House, 1928.

_____. *Die Lehre von Christi Werk: de Officio Christi (Baier III, 100-133).* St. Louis, Mo, 1898.

_____. *Die lutherische Lehre von der Rechtfertigung: in Vortraegen dargelegt.* St. Louis, Mo: Seminary Press, 1916.

_____. *Die Rechte Weltanschauung Vortr.* St. Louis, Mo: Concordia Publishing House, 1928.

_____. "Die Wiederholung Einer Falschen Anklage Gegen Die Missourisynode." *Concordia Theological Monthly* 1, no. 7 (1930): 481–85.

_____. *Dr. C. F. W. Walther as Theologian.* Translated by Wallace H. McLaughlin. N.P: lulu.com, 2019.

_____. *Einige Beurteilungen der Schrift "Zur Einigung" etc. und der norwegischen Vereinigungsbewegung. Zur Einigung der amerikanisch-*

lutherischen Kirche in der Lehre von der Bekehrung und Gnadenwahl / Pieper, 1913 Anh. St. Louis, Mo: Concordia Publishing House, 1913.

_____. "Eröffnungsrede Zum Neuen Studienjahr 1930-1931." *Concordia Theological Monthly* 1, no. 12 (1930): 801–3.

_____. "Giving for the Kingdom of God." In *Der Lutheraner Potpourri*, translated by Erwin William Koehlinger. Fort Wayne, IN: Concordia Theological Seminary Press, 1993.

_____. *Ich glaube, darum rede ich": eine kurze Darlegung der Lehrstellung der Missouri-Synode.* St. Louis, Mo: Concordia Publishing House, 1897.

_____. "Luther's Doctrine of Inspiration." *The Presbyterian and Reformed Review* 4, no. 14 (April 1893): 249–66.

_____. Our Position in Doctrine and Practice: Lecture Delivered before the 1893 Synod of Delegates of the Synod of Missouri, Ohio and Other States. Translated by Kenneth E.F. Howes. Emmett, ID: Scholia.net, 2004.

_____. *Passionspredigten.* St. Louis, Mo: Concordia Publishing House, 1920.

_____. *The Church and Her Treasure: Lectures on Justification and the True Visible Church.* Translated by O. Marc Tangner. St. Louis, Mo: The Luther Academy, 2007.

_____. *The Difference between Orthodox and Heterodox Churches.* 2nd ed. Coos Bay, OR: St. Paul's Lutheran Church, 1981.

_____. *The Gifts of the Christians.* Translated by W.G. Polack. Fort Wayne, IN: Franklin Press, 1935.

_____. *The Lutheran Doctrine of Justification.* Fort Wayne, IN: Concordia Theological Seminary Press, 1998.

_____. "The Means of Grace." In *The New Life: Readings in Christian Theology*, edited by Millard J. Erickson, 115–25. Grand Rapids: Baker Book House, 1979.

_____. "The Synodical Conference." In The Distinctive Doctrines and Usages of the General Bodies of the Evangelical Lutheran Church in the United States, 119–66. Philadelphia, PA: Lutheran Publication Society, 1893.

_____. "Thesen, Die Dem 'theologischen Schlussexamen' Dienen Können."

Concordia Theological Monthly 1, no. 6 (1930): 401–6.

_____. *Theses on Unionism: An Essay Delivered at the 1924 Convention of the Washington-Oregon District.* Translated by L. L. White, 1980.

_____. "Unionism." *Concordia Journal* 11, no. 3 (May 1985): 94–100.

_____. *Unity of Faith: (Einigkeit Im Glauben): Essay given by Dr. Franz Pieper at the 12th Convention of the Ev. Lutheran Synodical Conference Held at Milwaukee, August 8-14, 1888.* Translated by Ewald J. Otto. Fort Wayne, IN: Concordia Theological Seminary Press, 1980.

_____. "Unsere Lehre Auf Dem Lutherischen Weltkonvent in Kopenhagen 1929." *Concordia Theological Monthly* 1, no. 5 (1930): 338–45.

_____. *Unsere Stellung in Lehre und Praxis. Vortrag gehalten vor der Delegatensynode 1893 der Synode von Missouri, Ohio und anderen Staaten.* St. Louis, Mo: Concordia Publishing House, 1896.

_____. "Vermischtes Und Zeitgeschichtliche Notizen." *Concordia Theological Monthly* 1, no. 6 (1930): 468–69.

_____. "Vicarious Satisfaction of Christ." Translated by Joseph Stump. *The Lutheran Church Review* 18 (1899): 444–55.

_____. "Vorträge Über Das Geistliche Leben Der Christen." St. Louis, Mo, 1893.

_____. Vorträge über die ev. luth. Kirche: die wahre, sichtbare Kirche Gottes auf Erden. 2. Aufl. St. Louis, Mo: Concordia Seminar Mimeograph Print. Co., 1895.

_____. *Vorträge über die Evangelisch Lutherische Kirche: die wahre sichtbare Kirche Gottes auf Erden.* St. Louis, Mo: Seminary Press, 1916.

_____. Vorträge über die Lehre von dem Unterschied zwischen Gesetz und Evangelium. St. Louis, Mo: Concordia Seminar, Mimeograph Print. Co, 1893.

_____. *Vorträge über die lutherische Lehre von der Rechtfertigung.* St. Louis, Mo: Concordia Seminar Mimeograph Print. Co, 1891.

_____. *Vorträge Über Die Lutherische Lehre von Der Rechtvertigung.* St. Louis, Mo: Concordia Seminary Mimeograph Printing Co, 1892.

_____. *What Is Christianity? And Other Essays.* Translated by John

Theodore Mueller. Decatur, IL: Repristination Press, 1997.

_____. *What Is Christianity? Faith & Morality Reconsidered.* Translated by Philip Bartelt. Irvine, CA: 1517 Publishing, 2023.

_____. *What the Synod of Missouri, Ohio, and Other States during the Seventy-Five Years of Its Existence Has Taught and Still Teaches.* St. Louis, Mo: Concordia Publishing House, 1922.

_____. "Wie Muss Gottes Wort Gepredigt Werden, Damit Glaube Entstehe in Den Herzen Der Zuhoerer?" *Concordia Theological Monthly* 4, no. 8 (1933): 577–89.

_____. "Wie Muss Gottes Wort Gepredigt Werden, Damit Glaube Entstehe in Den Herzen Der Zuhoerer?" *Concordia Theological Monthly* 4, no. 12 (1933): 898–908.

_____. *Wie Muss Gottes Wort Gepredigt-Werden: Damit Glaube Entstehe in Den Herzen Der Zuhörer?* St. Louis, Mo: Concordia Seminary, 1909.

_____. *Wie studiert man Theologie?: eine Reihe von Vorträgen, gehalten in den s.g Lutherstunden.* St. Louis, Mo: Concordia Seminary, 1899.

_____. *Zur Einigung der amerikanisch-lutherischen Kirche in der Lehre von der Bekehrung und Gnadenwahl: im Anschluss an die norwegischen Vereinigungssätze und deren Kritiken.* St. Louis, Mo: Concordia Publishing House, 1913.

Pieper, Franz August Otto. "Wie Muss Gottes Wort Gepredigt Werden, Damit Glaube Entstehe in Den Herzen Der Zuhoerer?" *Concordia Theological Monthly* 4, no. 9 (1933): 653–63.

Pieper, Franz, Augustus Lawrence Gräbner, H. G. Sauer, and August Crull. Reden, gehalten bei einer Versammlung der mit der Missouri-Synode verbundenen lutherischen Gemeinden Chicagos im Art Institute am 3. September 1893. St. Louis, Mo: Concordia Publishing House, 1893.

Pieper, Franz, and Walter A. Hansen. *The Gifts of Christians.* St. Louis, Mo: Lutheran Church–Missouri Synod, Dept. of Stewardship, Missionary Education, and Promotion., n.d.

Pieper, Franz, and Frederick R. Harm. *Pieper Speaks to the Church Year: A Manual of Theological Background Material Researched by Students in Systematic Theology.* St. Louis, Mo: Concordia Seminary, 1979.

Pieper, Franz, and John Theodore Mueller. "Theological Observer: Kirchlich-Zeitgeschichtliches." *Concordia Theological Monthly* 1, no. 9 (1930): 683–712.

Scaer, David P., and Franz Pieper. *A Latin Ecclesiastical Glossary for Francis Pieper's Christian Dogmatics.* Fort Wayne, IN: Concordia Theological Seminary, 1978.

Starck, Johann Friedrich. *Starck's Motherhood Prayers for All Occasions: From the German Ed. of Dr. F. Pieper.* Edited by Franz Pieper. Translated by William Herman Theodore Dau. St. Louis, Mo: Concordia Publishing House, 1921.

_____. *Starck's Prayer-Book for All Occasions: From the German Ed. of Dr. F. Pieper.* Edited by Franz Pieper. Translated by William Herman Theodore Dau. St. Louis, Mo: Concordia Publishing House, 1921.

_____. *Tägliches Handbuch in guten und bösen Tagen: nebst einem Anhang für Schwangere, Gebärende, Kind-betterinnen und Unfruchtbare.* Edited by Franz Pieper. St. Louis, Mo: Concordia Publishing House, 1900.

Starck, Johann Friedrich, and Franz Pieper. *Starck's Prayer-Book: From the German Ed. of Dr. F. Pieper.* Edited and translated by William Herman Theodore Dau. Concordia Heritage Series. St. Louis, Mo: Concordia Publishing House, 1981.

About Translator Susanne Russell

Susanne Russell, MA, MCIL, MITI, is a German British literary translator and editor who lives and works in Kent, UK. Her academic background is in German literature and Lutheran theology. Susanne studied Lutheran Theology at the Freie Universität in Berlin with Professor Friedrich Wilhelm Marquardt who himself was a student of Helmut Gollwitzer´s. Having spent 26 years teaching in British schools, Susanne is now happily dividing her time between translating and working as a visitors´ assistant at Dover Castle.

Printed in the USA
CPSIA information can be obtained
at www.ICGtesting.com
CBHW072352190724
11852CB00024B/580